The Refounding of the College Board, 1948-1963

An Informal Commentary and Selected Papers

Frank Bowles

College Entrance Examination Board, New York, 1967

Copies of this book may be obtained from the College Entrance Examination Board, Publications Order Office, Box 592, Princeton, New Jersey 08540. The price is $4.50 per copy.

Editorial inquiries concerning this book should be directed to Editorial Office, College Entrance Examination Board, 475 Riverside Drive, New York, New York 10027.

Library of Congress Catalog Card Number: 67–29470

Printed in the United States of America

To the memory of

William Carl Fels

1916–1964

Secretary of the College Entrance Examination Board 1948–1955

Associate Director 1952–1956

Foreword

The continuing contribution of education to American society has depended on adaptation to changing circumstances. Over the years there has been change in the schools, colleges, and universities as they have responded to the frontier, to the industrial revolution, to the explosion of knowledge and technology, and, overall, to what Gunnar Myrdal refers to as the American Creed.

Educational adaptations are often unplanned. The eventual contributions of the land-grant colleges, for example, were only faintly perceived a century ago, when these institutions were first established.

Sometimes the assessment and definition of purposes is a conscious effort on the part of an individual who directs an education institution. The papers appearing in this volume represent such an effort by Frank Bowles after he became the chief executive officer of an education association, the College Entrance Examination Board.

Mr. Bowles assumed executive responsibility for the Board in 1948, as the association was approaching its fiftieth year of service to its member colleges and universities. (There were 79 members in 1948.) This was also the time when the Board's chief raison d'être had just been transferred to the newly organized Educational Testing Service. The Board's traditional role between 1900 and 1948 had been the administration of college entrance examinations on behalf of its members. With the formation of ETS, there was good reason to believe that this function would be better performed by the new, broadly based, educational service agency. Why continue the College Board? And, if it should be continued, what should its new purposes be?

Hindsight tells us that in 1948 the Board stood on the threshold of a period of significant service and substantial growth. Its service was to include contributions in the following areas: identification and nurture of the intellectually able student, reduction of financial barriers to college attendance, curricular reforms in mathematics and English, improvement of college guidance in the schools, and improvement of admissions, placement, and financial aid administration in the colleges and universities. Its membership was to reach 707 higher education institutions, 231 secondary schools, and 46 education associations in the fall of 1966, a tenfold increase over 1948.

This potential for service and growth was by no means obvious in 1948. World War II had just ended, and the veterans, under the stimulus of the GI Bill, were seeking entry into the colleges and universities in unprecedented numbers. It was a time that forced preoccupation with the mechanics of college admissions: the testing and description of applicants and the selection or exclusion of would-be students. Further, the hiatus within education caused by the war gave postwar educators a long list of unfinished business dating from the 1930s. Neither the priorities nor the possibilities were clear. Altogether, it was a strenuous and confusing period, as education and the country adjusted to the promise and the peril of the postwar era.

Mr. Bowles's search for new purposes for the Board thus required considerable insight, as his papers in this volume make clear. He oriented his thinking to the long-term trend toward educational opportunity in the United States, one that had extended first to elementary, then to secondary, education—a trend that was beginning to reach higher education. His principal insight was a dynamic concept of "access to higher education." According to this concept, a student's chances of attending college are determined by social forces fully as much as by academic preparation, and the crucial decisions are usually made years before a formal application for admission is required. This idea, although it is implicit in most of the papers in this book, is most clearly formulated in a paper that appears near the end of the book, "Access to Education—A Global View," as well as in Mr. Bowles's *Access to Education*, published in Paris in 1963 by Unesco.

The concept of access to higher education led, in turn, to a way of thinking about purposes for the Board. Associational service ought to be directed toward supporting an open and expanding movement of young people through the schools and into the colleges and universities. It should aim at reducing barriers that interrupt or impede this movement. College admissions as an educational function, to this way of thinking, was an inclusive function, not an exclusive one. The success or failure of an admissions system was to be judged by how many young people were counted in, not by how many were selected out.

This way of thinking opened areas of service that had not previously been considered within the Board's purview. The identification of these areas and their relationship to the Board's potential membership among teaching institutions is the subject of the papers contained in this volume.

Many of these papers have not been published before. When Mr. Bowles resigned as president of the Board in 1963, the trustees believed that publication of the papers was necessary as a matter of record and was desirable as a tribute to Mr. Bowles for his intellectual leadership during this formative period. As the volume took shape, one further point became clear. It is not likely that any of Mr. Bowles's successors at the Board will duplicate the intensely personal contribution he made in writing these papers. Size and complexity alone will require group assessment of purposes, supported by increasingly sophisticated research inquiries. Like many other educational ventures, the Board has now become an institution—in large part because of the perceptive insights contained in these papers.

Richard Pearson
President of the College Entrance Examination Board
May 1967

Preface

In the fall of 1963, after 15 years and 5 months as its chief executive officer, I resigned from the staff of the College Entrance Examination Board to accept a position as director of the Education Program of The Ford Foundation.

Not long after my resignation became effective, the trustees informed me, through Acting President Richard Pearson, that they wished to publish a selection from the papers—speeches and reports—that I had written during my tenure of office. The offer was generous and flattering, and I accepted the task of making the selection.

In working on the papers, I found that the problem of selecting was more complicated than I had anticipated. They did not fit together in any neat pattern. Some of the best of them, considered as exposition, were addressed to points and problems and causes that had receded into history—or worse, into oblivion. Others seemed merely to pick at issues that later took on major importance. The number that fit immediately into a clear pattern was, on first reading, alarmingly small.

I finally realized that the papers fell into two broad groupings. One group was a collection of source material for a history of the College Entrance Examination Board from 1948 to 1963—a period of important change in purpose and organizational expansion. The other was an assortment of topical papers produced as part of the job of chief officer of the Board, but not as part of the administration of the Board.

It has seemed to me that it is particularly important to establish the record of the Board's expansion in function and purpose since 1948, and I have therefore concentrated on that task, using speeches and sections of reports to establish the line of development. I have also used certain of the topical papers when they fitted into the narrative, or, as in the case of the ones entitled "The Three Great Callings" and "Patterns of Dominance and Choice," when there were a number of requests that they be reprinted.

I have arranged the papers in a rough chronological order and have prefaced each of them with an account of how it came to be written and why.

As a history, it is of course incomplete. In the first place, it leaves out most of the day-to-day and routine matters that give continuity to a history. In the second place, centered as it is on one man, it leaves out the contributions of other members of the staff, of our colleagues at Educational Testing Service, and of our elected trustees and their chairman and vice chairman. All these individuals played a part in writing the Board's history, and any full record should show that part. I hope that this volume will be supplemented by a professionally prepared history of the Board.

I must note particularly that this record does not trace the contributions that William Carl Fels made to the Board during the eight years—1948 to 1956—that he served as its secretary and later its associate director. Many of these contributions are concealed in the papers reprinted in this volume: suggestions of new ideas, criticisms of the papers as they were being prepared (including even the courageous one that a paper I had worked on for a week was still worthless), or support in the presentation of a program that would be certain to outrage at least half of the Board's membership.

In fact, William Fels did not leave a large quantity of written material in the Board's archives, perhaps because so many of his important contributions were made in small meetings, where the resolution of an issue or the phrasing of a motion would clarify a stubborn problem. His quick mastery of informal presentation made him the most valuable of colleagues but did not add bulk to the record. But the record should include the facts that he was responsible for the Board's present publication program; that he was the chief architect of the College Scholarship Service; and that he was the individual who patiently put together bits and pieces of separate programs into what became the Advanced Placement Program and who capped the construction by suggesting the appointment of Charles R. Keller as its first director.

A number of talks and papers have been omitted from this collection. Also, for lack of documents, some important events have been left out. Some of these omissions deserve comment.

The struggles over the problem of testing facility in writing, which began in the late 1940s, have a documentation of endless committee meetings and reports. They would make a fine doctoral thesis, but it is almost impossible to compress them into such a volume as this. Thus, the progression from the General Composition Test and the Writing Sample to the Commission on English and the revival of a written section of the English Composition Achievement Test is not a part of this record.

The Board had a true financial crisis in 1955–56. It had taken on a good many new ventures, particularly the Advanced Placement Program, the cost of which had been badly underestimated. The cost per candidate, as charged to the Board by Educational Testing Service for the first year of operation, was in fact shocking. It came to something more than $90 per candidate against an income of $10 per candidate, and for this and other reasons we had substantial deficits to meet. In addition, ETS, in the process of expanding, was badly in need of capital, and there were looming demands for new programs still to be dealt with. Finally, we raised fees, readjusted the Advanced Placement Program, and compromised on a solution for the ETS capital needs. These actions took care of immediate problems and also taught us that there are no easy solutions to the day-to-day problems of financing and organizing an operation.

Nor have I discussed the problem of the Board's organization. By the mid-1950s we had completely outgrown our town meeting structure and were searching hard for new ways to maintain contact with our growing membership and with the secondary schools. Finally, we hit on a scheme for incorporation that provided for an elected Board of Trustees, but that also reserved to the Board's full membership the right to final vote on any issue, and the right to initiate any action by vote. I was strongly concerned on this point, for I felt then and still feel that the Board could never run the risk of becoming a monopoly in the hands of a small group. The risk has not materialized, I am glad to note.

The question of renewal of our tax exemption, which came up after we had changed to an incorporated status, came to be something of a problem. The Internal Revenue Service in the latter days of the Eisenhower administration did not appear to favor tax exempt institutions that engaged in business that might compete with taxable private enterprise, and they held up the issuance of a new tax exemption certificate for the Board for several years. Finally it came, without comment or explanation.

Another item of interest, otherwise undocumented, was an exploration in 1954 and 1955 of the possibilities of founding a national scholarship program under the direction of the College Board. The idea was being broached at this time, and The Ford Foundation was rumored to be working on a program. Eventually, Roy Larsen, of *Time* magazine, precipitated the matter by giving to the College Board, in December of 1953, a $25,000 check to start such an enterprise. With this in hand we returned in earnest to the discussion and had reached a staff and committee agreement to take the idea to the next meeting of the Board, when our deliberations were cut short by the announcement that The Ford Foundation had established the National Merit Scholarship Corporation to operate a program of scholarships to which business firms were to be encouraged to contribute. So, instead of starting a program, the College Board had the honor of being the first cash contributor to the National Merit Program, transmitting the $25,-000 from Time, Incorporated.

I do not draw any powerful conclusions from the 15 years that these papers cover, except that it was a period of extraordinary challenge and change in American education, and the Board played a role, sometimes important, in the events that came out of this conflict of past and present.

On balance I would say that it was our efforts in the area of guidance that were most successful. Here we had great opportunity for innovation. The Demonstration Guidance Project, which would not have been planned, organized, or financed without the active participation of Board staff and the approval of the Board's membership of a grant of $60,000, was the most conspicuously successful and the most heartwarming in its achievement. But the broader problem of guidance, of getting needed information to college candidates, of opening the veil of secrecy that surrounded college admissions, was in fact far more difficult. The action of the Board in developing *The College Handbook* into a true guide for the perplexed candidate and in publishing the later *Manual of Freshman Class Profiles*, containing class characteristics invaluable for counseling purposes (the two books to be used together), was a major achievement. The further encouragement a candidate received from having access to his own preliminary test scores and ultimately to his admissions test scores carried effective guidance a good deal further. If these steps had not been taken, the problem of entrance to American colleges would be far more difficult and mysterious than it is today.

Even so, there is ample room for dissatisfaction. The profession of guidance has moved slowly in accepting responsibility for college advisement and literature. For that matter schools and colleges and regional associations have done little in the way of joint effort to keep the paths open to college. But in saying this it must also be said that it is perhaps an impatient remark—that there are signs now of movement and assumption of responsibility, belated, perhaps, but welcome.

The publications program was successfully built around the idea that the Board could never afford the size of field organization necessary to communicate with the schools and colleges that were the real users of the Board's tests, hence that publications could be made to do the job. In the process of proving the theory, the intelligent application of design, fine printing, and exacting editorial standards had a measurable effect on the quality of American academic publications.

I felt most keenly the failure to make any genuinely new approach to test planning but realized too late that all of the efforts we did make were circumscribed by the boundaries of applied psychology. I am now convinced that new approaches to testing depend on getting outside those boundaries or, alternatively, moving them.

I also felt profoundly disappointed by the inability, despite repeated efforts, to establish any agreed-upon plan of cooperation between institutions to cut down on the uncertainties of candidates or colleges at the time of admission. There are any number of ways this can be done, but I have no memory of ever knowing any group of admissions officers who addressed themselves seriously to the problem of choosing a way to tackle the problem.

Despite these disappointments a warm optimism remains. The College Board is a unique organization with a diverse membership, controlled and governed by its members, managing its own finances, dealing with an eternally important phase of education. With its resources, its flexibility, and its freedom from external controls, it enjoys infinite possibilities for growth in the achievement of its one permanent goal—service to American education.

Frank Bowles
The Ford Foundation
Advisor on international education
August 1967

Contents

1. Partition and Reorganization: 1946-1948

For those who do not understand the distinction between the College Entrance Examination Board and Educational Testing Service—and there seem to be many—it will be useful to review some history.

The history begins, of course, with the fact that it was the operating part—that is to say, the test development and administration part—of the College Board that became the core of Educational Testing Service. Other testing activities were joined to it, but ETS, in the form it took in 1948, could not have come into existence without the action taken by the Board in divesting itself of its operations and a substantial part of its assets.

But the history also goes further back in time—almost 50 years.

The College Board was founded at the turn of the century to establish common entrance standards for American colleges. In approaching its task, it used certain definitions and standards that had already been set up by professional bodies such as the Conference on Uniform Entrance Requirements in English and the Committee of Seven of the American Historical Association. Later the Board developed its own system for the definition of requirements by appointing commissions to review and revise definitions.

Once the definitions were established, it followed that a course syllabus could be developed which the college could accept as a fair test of mastery of the given subject. When these steps had been taken, it remained only to develop methods for ensuring that the definitions of requirements were kept up to date, and that the examinations were pitched, from year to year, at the same level of difficulty and marked on the same standard.

All of these steps were, in time, accomplished. By 1915 the Board had an established community of schools and colleges that it served, in the sense that its definitions of requirements were indisputably accepted as the curricular controls for the college entrance program and its marking standards were the quality controls. This was a community consisting of some 30 to 40 independent colleges, located with a few exceptions in the northeastern United States, and some hundreds of private and public secondary schools that supplied their students, also located for the most part in the Northeast.

It was a close-knit community, bound together by several factors.

First, there was the classical university entrance curriculum, based on Latin and often Greek, inherited from Europe, and hardly maintained in both public and private secondary schools. It offered minimal mathematics and science and traditional courses in history. Modern languages, encouraged as a gentleman's skill, were often surprisingly well taught.

Second, there was the tremendous communalizing effect of the College Board program itself. The program necessarily involved hundreds of teachers, from both schools and colleges, in the work of reading the examinations. These reading sessions provided a wonderful forum on the state of school and college education, which convened annually and lasted about 10 days. The time was devoted to appraising intensively the results of education for college entrance during the preceding year. Gathering to read the examinations was sociable, financially rewarding, intellectually profitable, and a grand climax to the school year. It bound together, in acquaintance-ship and friendship, hundreds and in the end thousands of teachers within the community. Probably there has never been anything else quite like it in the world of education in any country.

This specific community lasted for 40 years. The Board's first examinations were given in 1901, and its last examinations of that type in 1941. The span was a long one. It covered one-fourth of the history of education in the American republic—the fourth that had seen most of the changes that had taken place up to the start of World War II. Nevertheless, there were men active in the Board in 1941 who had been present to see the drama of its establishment—described so well in the opening chapter of Claude Fuess's book *The College Board: Its First Fifty Years.*

These 40 years were a success, but a limited one. A standard was established, but it was, in reality, a regional standard. It had never dealt with the great and growing mass of American public education in the Midwest and on the Pacific coast, nor the dogma-dominated church colleges—Protestant in the South and Midwest, and Catholic in the North—nor the burgeoning service institutions in the cities. In point of fact, the Board's standards were too high for these colleges. It was never considered polite to say so, but this was the fact.

The majority of the "membership" of the Board—which included in this sense the examiners and readers—probably never had any real awareness of the existence of this educational mass. The students who came from other parts of the country to the great independent colleges of the Northeast, came through the approved channels of the private boarding schools or, exceptionally, from public high schools in Denver, St. Louis, Minneapolis, Cincinnati, and the suburbs of Cleveland and Chicago, which operated on Northeastern standards. There was a considerable flow of students from other regions into the graduate and professional schools of the Northeast, but this was beyond the ken of the Board. The Board's educational world was compact, elegant, and self-sufficient.

But this was not at all a true description of the composite of public high schools and public and private colleges that existed outside the Board's world. These institutions were keenly aware of the formal standards and the reputation of the schools and colleges that made up the Board. They considered that these standards imposed controls on their own methods and programs, and to a considerable extent they resented these impositions.

Particularly in the early 1930s, the remarkable democratization of the American public high schools encountered Board definitions of requirements as a barrier to the kind of curriculum making that the times called for. Equally, they found the Board's testing concepts to be unsuited to the mass education that was the necessity of the times.

These conditions were a foundation for real hostility to the Board, a hostility that in time became a part of the professional dogma of teacher education—the dogma that it was the Board that was responsible for the 16-entrance-unit curriculum, the definitions of requirements, and for the undemocratic idea of selective admission to college.

Another part of the historical background of the formation of Educational Testing Service has to do with the evolution of testing itself.

The College Board for many years represented the best and most careful testing in the traditional sense. However, by the close of World War I another concept of testing had begun to emerge, which in time took form as objective testing. The new kind of testing rested, as all testing must, on a sampling technique. More important, it provided an opportunity for a broad sampling of information and, as the techniques developed, of intellectual skills. It had one advantage in speed of marking, and another, discovered in time, in the possibility of evaluating the individual questions in terms of their contribution to the merit of the test as a whole.

The new concept had tremendous values for the public schools, which were already entering the process of democratization, and it was widely adopted. A number of agencies, supported in several cases by The Carnegie Foundation and by the Carnegie Corporation, came into being to support the new idea and service the growing demand.

The Cooperative Test Service and the allied Educational Records Bureau serviced the secondary schools and made valiant efforts to extend their activities into colleges. The Graduate Record Examination was developed to evaluate fitness for admission to graduate study, and in time the National Teacher Examination was developed to test qualifications for teaching. Other efforts developed from these institutions. The Pennsylvania Study presented a startling documentation of student performance in schools and colleges that were equal before the law but terribly unequal in their learning productivity. The Eight-Year Study, also related to this movement, came along to establish that formal subject-matter requirements were far less significant in college performance than the ability of the student—a conclusion that would have seemed obvious enough at any time but that, in fact, had never been seriously explored.

While these movements challenging established requirements and traditional tests were gaining momentum, there came another problem that had a particular effect on the Board and its membership. This was the problem of maintaining enrollments in the face of a continuing financial recession, which by the mid-1930s was having serious effects on the private schools of the Northeast and on the private colleges, which had relatively high costs.

The response of the Board member colleges to the enrollment problem was twofold. On the one hand, they began to develop scholarship programs, work opportunities, and other financial aids to students. Doing so, they found a need for earlier decisions on scholarship awards, and in consequence the Board established a program of objective subject-matter tests, administered along with the Scholastic Aptitude Test in April, well in advance of the usual June testing period.

On the other hand, they yielded as gracefully as possible to the ideas of the progressives by restating their entrance requirements in terms of intellectual readiness for college rather than in terms of a fixed unit requirement. This change made possible a broadening of recruiting activities to include students from schools that had not formerly sent students to Board member colleges. For these students the new tests were perfect. In fact, the new testing program proved to be magnificently timed, and it grew rapidly. Its growth brought a new staffing pattern to the Board, requiring for the first time a staff trained in test construction and measurement.

This, in brief, was the condition of the Board at the time war broke out. The first thing that happened as a result of the coming of the war was the discontinuance of the written examinations. It was done, sensibly, in view of certain limitations on travel and planned changes in college calendars. And there were also some who held the belief that, under any circumstances, it would have happened sooner or later.

The second thing that happened was that the Board, with great energy, entered into contract work with the government. This was a natural development, for the fact was that the Board was the largest professionally staffed, nonprofit, testing operation in the country. There was, furthermore, the fact that it was accustomed to testing for the same type of skills —reading, computation, comprehension—in which the armed services were interested.

In any event, the Board became a major contractor in test development and later in other training activities for the armed services, particularly the Navy. By the end of the war, it was a large, well-staffed, and well-equipped testing organization in an excellent financial position. It was probably better equipped to develop a postwar testing program than any other agency in America.

Before the close of the war, John M. Stalnaker, who had been executive secretary and the chief organizer of Board activities during the war, had foreseen the rush of veterans to college and had had the prescience to develop a test especially for use in admitting veterans. The idea was a new one and, as it proved, tremendously important. Colleges and universities all over the nation, some of which had never before received more than five scores from the Board in a year, turned to the new test as a guide in their perplexity over the admission of the strangely assorted and often strangely prepared veterans.

It was at this point that in 1946 The Carnegie Foundation for the Advancement of Teaching asked a committee under the chairmanship of James Bryant Conant, president of Harvard, to examine national testing operations as then conducted by nonprofit agencies. These agencies included the

College Entrance Examination Board, the Educational Records Bureau, the Cooperative Test Service and National Committee on Teacher Examinations of the American Council on Education, and the Graduate Record Office of The Carnegie Foundation. The College Board was financially self-supporting; the other four agencies depended in part on foundation subvention. All five agencies were constructing and administering their own testing programs and conducting their own research.

The committee, reviewing operations and potentials, reported that none of the agencies was strong enough or well-to-do enough to support the development of testing as it should be developed. It reaffirmed what was already known—that there was little basic research being done that was relevant to testing and that development of new testing programs was very nearly at a standstill. It pointed out the importance of test development and of research and recommended that these functions should be assumed by a new testing agency, to be created under the name of the Cooperative Educational Testing Commission, which would take over all operations of the Educational Records Bureau,[1] the Cooperative Test Service, and the Graduate Record Office, and the operating functions of the College Board, and would be placed under the general suzerainty of the American Council on Education.

The basic idea of combining the several independent testing activities that were then functioning into one agency was well accepted. The suggestion that it be placed under the American Council, which carried a clear implication of subordinate rather than independent existence, was not, and the organizational arrangements for the proposed agency became a matter for negotiations prolonged over a period of some months. Eventually a plan was put forward and subsequently was formalized as an agreement of merger between the several agencies involved.

Under the plan, the new organization to be formed would be named Educational Testing Service. It would take over all the research, test development, test construction, publication, and administration activities of the programs mentioned above. It was to have a broad charge to continue and extend their work by supporting and conducting basic and applied research and developing and administering tests at all levels of education. It

---

1. Early in the negotiations, the Educational Records Bureau withdrew.

was to be an independent body, not, as originally suggested, a part of the American Council. It was to have, as its initial capital, a large portion of the assets of its founding organizations. In addition, The Carnegie Foundation was to make a grant of $750,000 to carry Educational Testing Service through the period of deficit operation that was foreseen during the necessary consolidation of the existing staffs and programs and the formation of a single enterprise.

The point stressed throughout the negotiations bringing Educational Testing Service into being was the role of the new organization in research and development. These activities, admittedly costly, were to be financed in part from the economies to be realized through consolidation, in part from income from reserves serving as endowment, and in part through a research surcharge on all contract operations. It was assumed that the new organization would make tests so acceptable, and ultimately so popular, that the operation would soon come to be self-supporting.

The technical and service aspects of the new organization were essentially taken for granted, for there was little discussion of them. It was assumed that there would be a large question bank and that the new organization would work on the development and construction of a wide variety of tests.

The Board, no longer to be responsible for test administration, was to continue as an association, maintain its committee structure, establish the testing program and test dates, and, by appointing examiners for the tests, control standards and requirements. The provision in the merger agreement that it was to retain $300,000 of its assets was essentially a method of providing interim support until a new basis of operation could be established. However, the question of how and when to develop a new program and financial base seemed at the time to be quite academic, as the plan seemed to leave the Board without any real function and in fact to make it probable that the Board would become a paper organization within Educational Testing Service, administered by a functionary, retaining its separate identity only as a legal fiction, for the sake of convenience, and possibly only temporarily.

The plan went through its ratification formalities without comment or discussion. The absence of formal opposition puzzled some Board members at the time, but the fact is that only a few individuals had any real concern as to the fate or future of the Board and that even this concern was more sentimental than practical.

The Board, which had set the standards for two full generations of students in the great colleges of the land, had owed much of its influence to the great annual ritual of examination reading. But the written examinations had ended at the beginning of the war, and so had the times and the whole way of academic life that supported them. The Board itself was no longer the "old" Board. Its real business was a program of objective tests made by experts (with the help of committees of examiners), managed by professional administrators, and scored by machines. There remained a committee structure manned by a faithful nucleus of perpetual members, but its function of stating Board policy had been eroded by the very tests that made up the program, for in fact there was no longer any policy to state. The "old" Board could define subject-matter requirements and establish marking standards including the critical 60 percent mark, which was commonly accepted as passing, and the carefully protected 100 percent, which was the symbol of perfect achievement. But the new objective tests forbade both forms of definition. They needed no requirements, for they could sample across the whole face of a subject-matter field; they needed no passing mark or perfect mark, because they could report in terms of means and percentiles, which would permit the user to pick his own passing mark in terms of the caliber of the total group of his candidates.

The Board thus really did not have a powerful membership, united behind a policy and determined to create a new program to replace the old. In truth, it did not even have a unified membership, for the "new" people who came to the postwar meetings seemed often to feel themselves outsiders and had little to bring to a discussion of future activities.

In addition to its internal problems, there was the fact that within the community of professional educators, detestation of the Board and its works was an article of faith—a part of the required course of learning in every teachers' college in the land. This attitude was supported by the most influential education editor of the time, who took every opportunity to attack the Board in his daily and weekly columns. The Board, in a word, was no longer in a position of power. Hence actions that might reduce the scope of its activities attracted little attention and no significant opposition.

Events moved rapidly after the report was submitted, and Educational Testing Service came into being on January 1, 1948. According to plan, the Board's director, Henry Chauncey; the associate director, Richard Sullivan; and the secretary, William Turnbull, became respectively, its president, vice president, and secretary, retaining their College Board titles and responsibilities as additional duty but without receiving additional compensation.

However, the arrangement of dual roles for the ETS-Board officers proved less workable and less valuable than had been hoped. At the regular spring meeting of the Board in 1948, its three officers submitted their resignations, leaving the Board, to all intents and purposes, without either staff or program.

To many, perhaps to most, of those attending that meeting, the resignation of its officers seemed to be merely one more step, perhaps the penultimate, in the closing of the Board's affairs. However, the chairman of the Executive Committee, George W. Mullins,[2] was one of those who felt that the Board's usefulness was not ended. He acted on his feeling by appointing an ad hoc committee to examine and report on possible future activities. Professor Mullins asked me to serve as chairman of that committee.

This committee examined the possibility, suggested by a number of Board members, that the Board should appoint a secretary, essentially attached to Educational Testing Service, who would appoint committees, convene meetings, and otherwise act as a caretaker for the organization. The idea was rejected on the grounds that the Board should take the opportunity given by its quite substantial assets—approximately $350,000—to examine needs in the testing field and develop its own program without concern for the routine administration now being taken over by ETS. The

---

2. George Walker Mullins, 1881–1956, professor of mathematics, Barnard College, served the Board as reader, as director of reading, and, on the retirement in 1936 of Thomas Scott Fiske, as secretary. He gave strong support to Carl C. Brigham, research secretary, supported a research program against considerable opposition, and saw to it that research results were applied to the Board's program. With John Stalnaker as his associate secretary, and in fact executive director, he engaged the Board in a wide variety of activities during World War II. He retired as secretary in 1946 and was succeeded by Henry Chauncey, whose title was changed to director. He personally opposed the recommendations of The Carnegie Foundation's committee, but he believed that his retirement dictated silence on the matter. He continued active in Board affairs until his death.

report of the committee did not go beyond this to discuss program; it rested on the point that the next step to be taken was to get a director and a new staff.

A special meeting of the Executive Committee adopted the report as a guide and authorized a search for a new director. While the search was in progress, the affairs of the Board were conducted by an Interim Administrative Committee, consisting of Dorothy B. Osborne, headmistress of the Spence School, Samuel T. Arnold, provost of Brown University, and myself.

The search for a new director lasted longer than anyone had foreseen. All the experienced Board administrators were now with Educational Testing Service and already well established in Princeton, since the Board's main offices had been there for some years. There were few young men, among those who worked with the Board as representatives from schools and colleges, who were interested in it as a career, and the veteran representatives were either deeply rooted in their own institutions or fearful of the Board's early demise.

I had occasion to examine all of these problems when the committee cannibalized itself by asking me to accept the post. I weighed the opportunity and the uncertainties offered by the Board against the relationships built up at Columbia over 25 years as student and faculty member and made the decision to move in the belief that the Board had a very important task to perform and was inherently a stronger organization than it then appeared to be. Specifically I believed that the postwar rush to college was not an isolated phenomenon, but was rather the first sign of a major increase in college attendance. Part of this belief rested on a wartime observation that enlisted men in the Navy, without college experience and, indeed, often not high school graduates, could master concepts and problems that were actually pitched at the college level. The observation indicated that there was a tremendous reservoir of potential college students within the population which would be tapped if ever a change in the intellectual atmosphere should turn them toward the idea of college. Another part of the belief, even more important at the time, rested on the certainty in my own mind that the college opportunities opened by the liberalizations of the GI Bill of Rights would never close again. The future, it seemed to me, would be marked by a long series of continuing pressures for college entrance.

Hence, in my view, an agency connected with the problem of college admissions had a future, provided the correct methods of organization and administration could be found to direct it. The years that followed offered ample opportunity to apply this view.

The report of the Committee on Testing, reprinted with the permission of The Carnegie Foundation for the Advancement of Teaching, is really the document basic to the modern history of the College Board. It is worth noting, by the way, that this is a preliminary report. No final document was ever submitted. I think that no one felt the need for further inquiry, hence the disposition of the matter was pushed immediately. Two other notes should also be added.

First, the president of the American Council on Education, George F. Zook, was greatly disappointed when the Board's membership refused to accept the idea of transferring the Board to the control of the American Council, as recommended by the Commission on Testing. When, further, the National Teacher Examination, with its sizable operating funds, was withdrawn from the control of the council, he began actively to oppose the entire series of actions and continued his opposition during the remaining years of his service with the council. He never explained his opposition as far as I know, and certainly never in my hearing, but I believe he felt that the council should have been supported by the presidents of the major universities and by Carnegie as the central agency in American testing and in American college entrance.

Second, I point out that the Committee on Testing was really dealing with two concerns. One was the organization of testing. This problem was recognized, and a solution to it was offered. The entire emphasis of the preliminary report is on the development of testing as a profession and particularly on the indispensable first step of creating a professional testing agency. The second concern should have been the support of the movement of students between the various levels of education, particularly between school and college. But this went unrecognized. There is scant mention of who is to be tested and why, and no discussion of the role of testing in American education. There is only a suggestion that an agency be formed to meet needs that are essentially stated in professional and technical terms.

It may well be that all these matters would have been dealt with in the final report of the committee. However, as has been remarked, there was no final report, and the rapid implementation of the plans that came out of the preliminary document effectively closed off discussion of educational purposes and goals. As a consequence it was necessary to work these out without guidelines, by trial and error, over a period of years—with a good many strains and problems attendant on the process.

Preliminary Report of the Committee on Testing, to Oliver C. Carmichael, president of The Carnegie Foundation for the Advancement of Teaching, dated October 4, 1946. James B. Conant, chairman of the Committee on Testing.

Dear Mr. Carmichael:

In your letter of May 15, 1946, to the members of this committee, you wrote "The Carnegie Foundation is interested in seeing the program of testing in our schools and colleges improved and strengthened." You have asked us to examine the nonprofit testing agencies now operating on a national basis, with particular reference to the problem of overlapping in their programs and functions and the possible strengthening of their efforts by coordination or consolidation.

After a large amount of preliminary material had been gathered and circulated among the membership of the committee, meetings were held in New York on September 20 and 21. Representatives of four agencies, the College Entrance Examination Board, the Educational Records Bureau, the Committee on Measurement and Guidance of the American Council on Education, and the Graduate Record Office of The Carnegie Foundation, discussed matters with members of the committee and expressed their views.

It was clear on the basis of the studies and discussions that the functions of the agencies, even when most strictly defined, are overlapping and that their programs tend to expand beyond those precise definitions to meet real and occasionally urgent problems. It became increasingly obvious that the overlapping is already serious and that, as the programs developed and matured, the overlapping would become wasteful and likely to impede the scientific development of testing. There was unanimous agreement on the part of all consulted that research and development were prime necessities and that none of the agencies as now constituted could furnish proper leadership over the broad field or had funds enough to support an adequate research program.

The committee came to the unanimous conclusion that the interests of American education could best be served by the creation of a single cooperative testing agency, within which the functions now being carried on by the existing nonprofit agencies would be continued and expanded on a unified basis. The committee further concluded that an independent organization could not maintain the most fruitful contact with the whole scope of American education without being affiliated with an agency which represented all the participants in the testing programs for schools and colleges. The committee believed that the American Council on Education was the only agency so representative.

The following recommendations of the committee are unanimous.

1. That there be established the Cooperative Educational Testing Commission affiliated with the American Council on Education.

2. That the present nonprofit testing organizations which are operating on a national basis join in the creation of this commission, and that these include the following organizations: the College Entrance Examination Board, the Educational Records Bureau, the Cooperative Test Service and National Committee on Teacher Examinations of the American Council on Education, the Graduate Record Office of The Carnegie Foundation for the Advancement of Teaching, and any other organizations active in the field.

3. That the functions of the commission shall include the services now being rendered by such organizations:

a. The school testing and advisory service of the Educational Records Bureau;

b. The examination service for college entrance as provided by the College Entrance Examination Board;

c. General examination service at all educational levels for schools, colleges, universities, professional schools, the government, industry, and professional societies as at present provided by the College Entrance Examination Board, the Cooperative Test Service, the Graduate Record Office (including the Measurement and Guidance Project in Engineering Education), and by the American Council on Education's

National Teacher Examination, Psychological Examination, and Primary Mental Abilities Test.

4. That the commission shall consist of 15 members, equal numbers to serve initially for terms of seven, six, five, four, and three years, as determined by lot among the members.

5. That the original members of the commission shall be appointed as follows:

a. Five by the College Entrance Examination Board;
b. Three by the Executive Committee of the American Council on Education;
c. Two by the trustees of the Educational Records Bureau;
d. Five selected by the 10 members appointed as above.

6. That, as vacancies occur, successors be appointed for five-year terms by a method to be determined in agreement between the commission and the Executive Committee of the American Council on Education.

7. That the commission shall exercise complete policy control and administrative direction over its affairs, and appoint a director responsible for their conduct, with such staff as may be required.

8. That 80 percent of the assets contributed by the constituent agencies to the organization shall be earmarked as a fund for research and development in the field of educational measurement, not more than 10 percent of this fund to be spent in any one year; and that this limited fund shall be used for the support of research by the organization and, through grants, for the support of research of other agencies and individuals.

9. That as an addition to this fund, not less than $750,000 be provided by foundation grants, to be largely for research purposes.

10. That the American Council on Education shall be the fiscal agent for the commission.

11. That the Cooperative Educational Testing Commission, thus established, shall have the following functions:

a. To promote the understanding of scientific educational measurement and appraisal.
b. To exercise leadership in individual education by furthering the use of testing at all levels and by encouraging ever high standards in testing.

c. To conduct research and to stimulate and support research by independent groups.

d. To construct and develop better examinations.

e. To select from among tests published by other agencies (including commercial publishers) and make available, as required, tests suitable to the particular purposes of primary and secondary schools, colleges and universities, vocational and professional schools, government agencies, industries, and individual students; and to provide administrative, scoring, and computing services for these tests together with reporting and cumulative record service as desired.

f. To counsel test users on the techniques of measurement, on the interpretation of test results, and on the uses of a systematic testing program.

The committee has been led to make the following recommendations as a result of certain basic considerations.

A. That sound basic research in educational measurement and human abilities on a scale necessary for continued advance in this field is dependent on a concentration of resources which can only be accomplished by the establishment of a cooperative testing commission.

B. That the commission should be continuously responsive to the developing needs of schools, colleges, and universities and representative of the whole field of American education.

C. That the continuity of the educational process and the common purposes of testing agencies can be served with maximum effectiveness through cooperation.

D. That the organization should be so constituted as to preserve the essential services of the present nonprofit groups; and to provide, by more comprehensive activities on a national scale at all levels, the additional services required.

E. That a unified testing organization should be a cooperative enterprise, sensitive to new ideas, encouraging and not competing with regional, state, and local testing; and that its activities, both in research and service, should so far as possible be decentralized in nature.

It is a firm belief of the committee that no solution short of the complete integration of the present nonprofit testing agencies in such a commission can provide the quality of research and service required. Furthermore, we believe that only an agency which takes in all those mentioned in the recommendations above can eliminate the present duplication of effort and prospective overlapping of programs, which hamper fullest development of educational testing.

The committee was impressed by the fact that there are now and will continue to be many regional, state, city, and individual school programs operating in the testing field, and that very many commercial agencies are producing tests. Thirty-eight states, for instance, have regular programs, and it is estimated that four-fifths of all tests used in the United States are sold by the commercial publishers. These facts guarantee that no monopolistic evils will follow the union of these nonprofit agencies. Indeed, the agencies which would be combined in this commission, while adequate to support a sound program of research and development and service, would still constitute only a portion of such activity. Without engendering a monopoly, the commission would supply leadership, which would be a powerful influence for the improvement of standards of testing.

In this committee's view, it is not the object of such a commission to take upon itself projects which might be better done elsewhere. It would carry on research primarily in areas in which effective work is not being done; it would develop tests in areas where new tests are badly needed; it would provide a type of advisory service which has hitherto been unavailable except to limited groups; and, finally, it would stimulate and encourage research everywhere and help educators needing greater guidance in the selection, use, and interpretation of tests.

The committee is convinced that in the period of expansion certain to follow the war, the functions exercised by the separate agencies will best be discharged by the cooperation of all under the commission.

The committee does not feel that it has finally discharged the responsibility assigned it. The plan outlined above is framed solely from the viewpoint of the best interests of American education. In this first phase of the committee's work, no attention is given to the practical problems (including the continuation of appropriate separate activities) of the several organizations whose cooperation is necessary to the plan's accomplishment. While the committee is firm in its belief in the principles involved, it presents its report in this preliminary form in order to stimulate the fullest possible discussion of the practical means of arriving at the objective. The committee, or a subcommittee, plans to reconvene two months hence, at which time it will again seek the advice and counsel of the representatives of all the organizations involved, in the hope that a final plan may be developed.

Committee on Testing

James B. Conant, president, Harvard University (*chairman*)

Edmund E. Day, president, Cornell University

Walter S. Hunter, Brown University (*adviser*)

James L. Morrill, president, University of Minnesota

William W. Pierson, dean, Graduate School, University of North Carolina at Chapel Hill

Francis T. Spaulding, The State Education Department, University of the State of New York

Robert G. Sproul, president, University of California at Berkeley

Stephen H. Stackpole, The Carnegie Foundation for the Advancement of Teaching (*secretary*)

Alexander J. Stoddard, superintendent of schools, The Board of Public Education, Philadelphia, Pennsylvania

Raymond Walters, president, University of Cincinnati

Henry M. Wriston, president, Brown University

T*he actual action of the Board in supporting the formation of Educational Testing Service is of interest and is here reprinted as an excerpt from the minutes of the annual meeting.*

For those who may wish to go more deeply into the documentation, it may be noted that the text of the agreement is available as Appendix B to those minutes.

Excerpt from the minutes of the annual meeting of October 29, 1947, pp. 15-18.

The chairman of the Board then opened for discussion the proposal to merge into a single testing organization the testing offices of the College Entrance Examination Board, the American Council on Education, and The Carnegie Foundation for the Advancement of Teaching. The latest revision of the proposed Agreement (dated October 8, 1947) was before the Board representatives as an attachment to the agenda. This revision is reproduced in these minutes as Appendix B.

The chairman reported that the special committee appointed to consider the matter had held a great many meetings by itself, with representatives of the other agencies, and with the Executive Committee; and that within the last month the Executive Committee had held a special meeting to discuss the question. The matter was again considered at a meeting of the Executive Committee on October 28, and as a result of that meeting the following resolutions (which were before the representatives as an attachment to the agenda) were brought to the Board with the unanimous recommendation of the Executive Committee:

Resolved:

1. That the Agreement (dated October 8, 1947) between American Council on Education, College Entrance Examination Board, The Carnegie Foundation for the Advancement of Teaching and Carnegie Corporation of New York (a copy of which has been submitted to this meeting), *amended* in Article 4 to provide:

    1. that the initial Board of Trustees shall remain in office for five years, and
    2. that the successor to a term trustee who shall vacate his office shall be selected in the same manner as was that term trustee, and
    3. that the Board of Trustees shall prepare a plan for the selection of future trustees and shall present it to the parties to this Agreement for approval before the end of the fourth year,

    and the plan of merger of the testing functions of the College Entrance Examination Board, of American Council on Education and of The Carnegie Foundation for the Advancement of Teaching as therein set forth be and they hereby are authorized and approved;

2. That the chairman of the College Entrance Examination Board, with the approval of the Executive Committee, is authorized to make any changes in said Agreement or in the plan of merger set forth in said Agreement, which he shall deem necessary or desirable and which shall not, in his opinion, materially adversely affect the interests of the College Entrance Examination Board;

3. That the proper officers of the Board be and they hereby are authorized and directed to execute and deliver said Agreement substantially in the form submitted to this meeting with any such changes as may be made by the chairman, with the approval of the Executive Committee, as provided in the foregoing resolution; and

4. That the proper officers in this Board and the custodians of this Board be and they hereby are authorized and directed to make such payments, to transfer and convey such assets, to enter into such agreements, to execute and deliver such other documents and to take any and all such other action as they may deem necessary or desirable to carry out said Agreement and the plan of merger as therein set forth, with any such changes as may be made as provided in the foregoing resolutions.

In response to a question, the chairman explained that the provision whereby the initial Board of Trustees would remain in office for five years and would prepare a plan for the selection of future trustees was inserted because the manner of selection of their successors had not been determined to the satisfaction of all parties to the proposed Agreement. The committees of the College Board had, in general, favored a representative Board of Trustees elected by the constituent agencies, whereas the draft of the Agreement called for a self-perpetuating Board. In order not to postpone action longer but at the same time to enable a satisfactory plan to be worked out, the Executive Committee had recommended the amendment in question.

A further question was raised as to whether or not there was real enthusiasm on the part of the officers of the Board for the merger. In reply, the chairman stated that it would be too much to expect enthusiasm, since the outcome was of course not a certainty and since dangers as well as opportunities could be foreseen. He stated, however, that in presenting their unanimous recommendation the members of the Executive Committee clearly believed that the interests of the College Board were sufficiently safeguarded by the Agreement and that the chances for success of the Educational Testing Service were excellent.

The chairman asked Mr. Chauncey to reply to a question concerning the advantages of the merger. Mr. Chauncey said that the fundamental questions now at issue were two: If the merger is consummated, is it probable that the resultant organization will better serve American education than the separate agencies continuing along their separate lines of development? Are the Board's interests adequately safeguarded?

Mr. Chauncey said that the answer to the second question seemed clear: the Board was fully protected and would continue to exercise all of its present prerogatives, but instead of being responsible directly for the operating office would contract with a new agency for the administration of its testing program.

The advantages to be listed in answer to the first question—Will American education stand to gain?—include the fact that the merger would make good tests more widely available, Mr. Chauncey explained. The care with which the Board's tests are constructed would be applied with profit to a wide range of examinations. Moreover, coordination of the several testing programs would establish relationships among the tests that would increase their usefulness and give them greater meaning. The combining of research workers would provide a group that could well become a focal point for testing research throughout the country and would be capable of tackling important areas of investigation that could not be studied adequately by small groups. The centralized research department should, he pointed out, eliminate the duplication of effort and the gaps that now characterize much of the work done. The facilities of the new agency would permit more extensive advisory services and wider dissemination of information about testing.

Mr. Chauncey then cited some of the dangers that have been foreseen and his reasons for believing that they can be avoided. The fear that bigness brings mediocrity is answered by the steady improvement in the Board's own program as the size of its office has increased. Likewise, the possibility that in a large organization research becomes subordinate to operations is at variance with the Board's development, since a separate research department did not exist until the Board reached substantial proportions, and the amount of research done has increased with the Board's growth since that time. The danger that originality and healthy disagreements may be stifled in a large unit is undoubtedly a possible one, but again such has not been the Board's experience. The professional staff now includes individuals of the most diverse training and interests—a diversity that would be impossible in a smaller group. It is only by bringing together such a variety of viewpoints that one can hope for rapid progress. The possibility that the organization would dominate education and curriculums is best answered by the fact that the policy of the Board, which would form such a large part of the new agency, has tended increasingly in the opposite direction, so that a marked reversal of trend (for which no cause is apparent) would be required if this danger were to be realized. The possibility that antagonism would be felt toward the group by state and local testing units would have to be avoided by the ordinary exercise of judgment and tact and by work of a quality that would win respect for the organization. The danger that a large organization would lack responsiveness is overcome by the fact that the source of responsiveness is the relationship between the educational organizations such as the College Board and the groups they serve. If the College Board remains responsive, the testing agency that works on contract for the Board must necessarily reflect that responsiveness.

There are two general points, Mr. Chauncey remarked, on which a person might tend to base his decision pro or con. The first is a personal philosophy as to the effectiveness of large organizations. While it is true that there is a danger of bureaucracy in a large agency, the proposed organization would be infinitesimal beside big business corporations or government agencies and would simply be closer to the size at which a testing agency could operate most effectively. The second general point is the fear that the other organizations would be a drain on the College Board. This outcome seems unlikely. The Cooperative Test Service and Graduate Record Examination, both of which have been conducted on a philanthropic rather than on a business basis, serve important areas for testing, and there is every prospect that they could be run in a profitable fashion.

Mr. Chauncey concluded by stating his belief that the prestige of the new organization would foster the increased use of the Board's examinations—a result that would be of mutual advantage and that would be a large factor in assuring a successful future for Educational Testing Service.

Dean Heermance stated that, while there were differences of opinion as to whether or not the merger would benefit American education, the belief that it would be beneficial was supported by enough of those who had investigated the problem to reassure him on that score. His chief reason for favoring the proposal, he stated, was his belief that the merger would allow the Board to divest itself of the responsibility of "big business," to turn over to a testing agency the important but extraneous measurement programs it is now carrying for the government and other agencies and which brought about its million-dollar budget, and to return to the consideration of educational problems within its own province—questions in which school and college men are primarily interested.

After the foregoing discussion the chairman put the question, and the resolutions recommended by the Executive Committee were approved by the unanimous vote of the Board. The chairman expressed his faith in the successful outcome of the merger and congratulated the Board on an act of generosity unparalleled in the history of education.

2. The First Two Years: 1948-1950

I became the Board's director in August 1948. William C. Fels, whom I had admitted to Columbia College 15 years earlier and who had been a colleague at Columbia for several years as assistant to the general secretary of the university, joined me in September with the title of secretary.

The first two years were slow moving. The Board's membership enlarged slowly, and the number of candidates grew, also slowly. The increased income meant that we were under no great pressure to push or develop a new program. Nevertheless, Mr. Fels and I agreed that if the Board were to be as useful as we felt it should be, it would have to grow. To find out what would have to be done, we took on the task of visiting schools and colleges, trying to learn what we were doing right (or wrong). He concentrated on schools, hoping to encourage more use of Board tests. I concentrated on colleges, hoping to encourage more members and firmer requirements for use of tests.

As we worked, the evidence for the need for such work accumulated. Mr. Fels found himself trying to convey the most rudimentary principles of guidance and college application—when, indeed, he could get any opportunity for a reasonable conversation with school principals or guidance officers. His problem was to make progress against a built-in hostility from the majority of the public secondary school administrators whom he met. We finally analyzed this hostility as having three sources.

First, outside the Northeast there was a generalized resentment directed against the Board as agent and symbol of the so-called exclusive private colleges. Second, the Board's tests and the admissions procedures based on them were taken as clear infringements on free communication between schools and colleges. Third, one of the major national professional organizations for school administrators was strongly and directly opposed to expansion of the Board's influence.

The hostility expressed itself in a variety of ways. There was a great deal of opposition to use of Board tests, and this meant that a number of schools directed candidates away from colleges that required them. (This opposition was not really dissipated until the advent of the National Merit Scholarship and General Motors Scholarship programs established Board tests as a national standard for the testing of excellence.) We also experienced, fairly regularly, direct denunciation of the Board as an educational oligarchy from the floor of public meetings held by the Board for the purpose of discussing admissions problems. (This was a recurrent event in the Midwest.) As another problem, which we also considered a symptom of hostility, we had great difficulty in getting public school personnel to participate in Board affairs. It was several years before we could invite school principals and guidance officers to participate in committees and programs with any confidence that the invitation would be accepted.

For my part in dealing with colleges, I often found myself discussing steps in the handling of college admissions with a registrar who saw tests of any kind as only a procedure imposed between him and a school principal whom he had known for years, or with a college president who could see tests only as threatening to reduce the number of students from whom tuition could be collected.

Nevertheless, and despite all problems, we made progress, and above all we sensed a gathering need for help and services to deal with a swelling tide of candidates. Curiously enough, many school and college people denied that there was any present or foreseeable increase in the number of high school candidates for college; perhaps because the increased enrollments caused by veterans continued to engage their attention and tended to obscure the slightly increasing enrollments of students coming directly from high school. By the early 1950s, however, it was generally accepted that the percentage of high school graduates seeking college entrance was increasing.

---

*T*he first expression of the possibility that the Board might grow and face new problems appeared in the Annual Report of the Director covering the year that closed in June 1948. This document, actually written in the fall of 1948, made some very general comments on the prospects of change and, significantly, mentioned the possibility of entering the field of college-level testing.

As it turned out, the Board did construct and add to its program a test for transfer students, which began with rosy prophecies of success and closed, sev-

eral years later, with a net loss to the Board of about $100,000 and the implacable hostility of every junior college in the land. It was during this process that the Board staff was forced to learn that the junior college of the time, viewed as an institution, was nonselective by instinct and that external tests such as those of the Board, either for admission or for transfer after the completion of courses, were anathema.

"The Future of the Board"

48th Annual Report of the Director. New York: College Entrance Examination Board, 1948, 112 pp., pp. 59–62.

In any consideration of the Board and its activities, past, present, and future, three facts stand out.

First, the Board exists by and for colleges that follow selective admissions practices.

Second, in order to meet the needs of those colleges which follow selective admissions practices, the Board supplies a complete testing service, including test construction, test administration, test scoring and score reporting, all conducted with optimum security and accuracy.

Third, the Board has existed and can continue to exist only as it responds to the needs of those who use its examinations. As a static organization resting on its present program and operations, the Board would surely become archaic and outmoded with the first major change in either college or secondary school curriculums. Indeed, there is evidence that in the past the Board on at least one occasion came perilously close to outliving its usefulness by reason of such changes.

The following comments on the future are made in terms of the foregoing three statements.

Organization and membership

It is reasonable to expect wider use of Board examinations in the future. This does not necessarily mean that more candidates will take more examinations, but it does mean that more secondary schools will send candidates to the Board and that more colleges will make use of the results.

With more participation in the Board program on the part of schools and colleges, there will be a tendency for Board membership to increase. Such an increase, if freely permitted, would bring in its train some organizational problems.

The Board was planned, and until recently has existed, as a small organization made up of institutions and associations working with a common purpose on problems of college admissions. It has functioned in such a way that all have had an opportunity to be heard and to participate in discussions and decisions. Its form of administration and its philosophy of operation have been related to its small size. It is possible, even probable, that the Board's success in its field has been due to its singleness of purpose and the active support of its small, coherent membership.

If membership becomes large rather than small, it will become so by bringing in institutions that have interests and philosophies divergent from those of the original membership, with the result that centrifugal rather than centripetal forces will begin to operate on matters of policy. This will mean that Board operations will come to represent compromises of the diverging interests of a number of institutions rather than a single policy arrived at by the full consent of a few institutions.

Looked at from this viewpoint the question that the Board must deal with in the not-too-distant future appears as one of philosophy of membership. The question might be stated as follows: "Is the Board to adhere to policies and practices appropriate to the limited objectives of a group of institutions that are on the whole similar, or is it to broaden its purposes and alter its practices to accommodate the varied objectives of a larger number of institutions?"

The question is one that may require an early answer. The present organization was planned for a small membership. It is an organization based on policy recommendations by appointed committees, voted by the full Board in open meeting, and carried out by elected and appointed officers, with details of planning and performance the responsibility of the director and the secretary, its appointed officers. As membership increases, the organization tends to slow its operations or, as an alternative, to concentrate power in the hands of committees and officers. At present these are only tendencies. Before they become fact the Board must face its future and plan wisely.

The philosophy of the Board

Since the abandonment of essay examinations in 1942, the Board has announced and adhered to a philosophy of test construction that can be summed up as "maximum subject-matter coverage for minimum interference with curriculums." This position, representing complete abandonment of the practice of defining requirements in each subject as a frame of reference for both teacher and examiner, was widely approved at the time of announcement. Many secondary school officials felt that the removal of the definition of requirements was a figurative breaking of shackles to free secondary school teachers from hampering restrictions.

It is interesting to report that the Board's action in moving away from definitions of subject-matter fields is now being questioned both at secondary school and college levels and that hope is now expressed by critics of the present procedure that the Board will return to offering the guidance that the definition of requirements supplied in the past.

The questions center on the belief that college curriculums must be built on known preparation and that without the definition of requirements it is not now possible to know what preparation is being offered. From that point it follows, according to the critics, that the lack of definition has weakened the value of the criterion that Board tests have supplied for the judgment of preparation. And from that it would follow that preparation and, in turn, college instruction will be weakened by thinning out content in order to provide wider coverage, a tendency that it must be admitted already exists on both secondary and higher levels. The raising of these questions is reported to the Board, not as a basis for recommendation for action, but as an indication that the Board's role in setting formal requirements has not been settled for all time.

Other forms of college entrance tests

From time to time the Board has offered testing programs related to college entrance that were distinct from its regular offerings. Recent examples are the so-called scholarship tests instituted in the thirties, which were expanded into the present Board examinations and the more recent Special Aptitude Test for Veterans.

At this writing there is indication that the Board has reason to consider still another college entrance field, that of students wishing to enter senior colleges or professional programs after completing junior colleges. The junior college in America, like the automobile and the telephone, appears to have come to stay. It is therefore high time to ease the problem of transfer of students and credits between them and their sister institutions. To date, the effort has been to deal with the problem through the accrediting agencies, but it has been only partially successful, owing largely to the fact that the growth of junior colleges has outstripped the capacity of accrediting agencies to evaluate them. Examinations based on the curricular pattern of junior colleges and standardized on both junior college and senior college fourteenth-grade student groups offer a much more promising and immediately useful answer. The Board, with its experience in college entrance testing, appears to be the logical body to develop such examinations. It is hoped that it can move to do so.

The fact that more than 10,000 candidates take Board examinations each year as preliminary candidates is evidence that there is room for consideration of their needs as a group. It may well be that the present program is ideally suited for their needs, or, on the other hand, it is possible that modifications as to content or services might be desirable. At any rate the group is large enough to warrant consideration of its problems by a special committee.

These questions on organization, philosophy, and possible new activities are mentioned here not because they are the only questions for the future but because they happen to have been the first to confront a new administration. In a time of flux the only thing certain is that there will be more questions in the years ahead.

It would be both unjust and ungracious to close this report without grateful acknowledgment of the help freely accorded to your officers by their predecessors, Messrs. Chauncey, Sullivan, and Turnbull. The Board is fortunate to have had them as its officers. It is doubly fortunate to have them as advisers and friends and, in time of need, ever helpful counselors on the myriad small problems that beset an administration.

The excerpt from the 1949 report that follows makes curious reading in 1967. At the time it represented acceptance of a pattern of development that seemed unalterable. The high schools had accepted the concept of general education as part of the whole life-adjustment philosophy, and all the colleges could do was to take the students who came out of that matrix. I do not recall that any one questioned this assumption in 1949. The direction of this report was therefore to urge acceptance of the status quo and to develop tests to measure what the students had accomplished in terms of the accepted curriculums.

The tests suggested were, in fact, finally constructed as the Tests of Developed Ability, after an expenditure of several years of time and several hundred thousand dollars of Board funds. They failed of adoption at the very last moment (in 1955), because of what I considered to be essentially captious objections from Board committees relating to the need for scores in specific subject fields such as physics and mathematics. I have always felt that it was a mistake to stop the tests in committee, after all development work had been done, for reasons that, however valid, were present from the time the idea was first broached. I would have preferred to see them tried as an experimental program within the regular administrations, and allowed to stand or fall on their merits as tests. The particular feature that appealed to me was the breadth of field covered in each test, which permitted the introduction of cross-disciplinary problem-solving questions. In the long run they would have evolved into better aptitude measures than the Scholastic Aptitude Test, or so I have always thought. However, there were a good many who disagreed with me, and they prevailed.

"The Future of the Board"
49th Annual Report of the Director. New York: College Entrance Examination Board, 1949, 83 pp., pp. 49–52.

As of the date of this writing, more than two years after the Board contributed more than two-thirds of its resources, all its staff and facilities concerned with testing, and all its testing activities save those related to college entrance, as its share in the bold experiment that took final form as Educational Testing Service, it seems safe to say that from the Board's point of view the experiment has worked. At any rate, the Board is now serving more institutions and more candidates than it did two years ago and, in spite of increased expenses resulting in part from having added two full-time officers for Board work alone, and in part from ETS organizational costs, is living within its income.

As the pages of this and the previous report show, the passage of the two years has not been without its troubles and its problems, but these can be characterized as settlement of details of organization or procedure.

With the settlement of these details it is time for the Board to consider its future in terms of probable developments in secondary and higher education. Here there are very real judgments to be made and plans to be worked out, for there are now operating in education important forces for change, forces that will have both direct and indirect effects on the Board and its activities.

The most important present force for change is the concept of general education. The phrase itself means many things to many people. It has been invoked with equal facility in eloquent defense of established programs and in rosy forecast of the benefits of programs yet to be tried; but the concept, expressing urgent belief that education must be specifically planned to offer both breadth and depth of knowledge, is today a compelling one in educational planning. The word "today" is used advisedly, for there have been other concepts and other standards. "German thought, method, honesty, and even taste," to quote from Henry Adams' description of Harvard College in his undergraduate years, was such a concept a hundred years ago, and before that the same institution had lived by another concept, described by Van Wyck Brooks in *The Flowering of New England*:[1] "The object of study was to form the mind, but this was to form the character; and Massachusetts knew what its character was and took a certain satisfaction in it. . . . A clear, distinct mentality, a strong distaste for nonsense, steady composure, a calm and gentle demeanour, stability, good principles, intelligence, a habit of under-statement, a slow and cautious way of reasoning, contempt for extravagance, vanity and affectation, kindness of heart, purity, decorum, profound affections, filial and paternal. . . . This was the type, and almost the only type, the curriculum of Harvard contemplated. Whatever studies favoured its formation, whatever were the best ways to form it, these were the ways and the studies that Harvard knew."

These are concepts that have yielded to their successors with changes in

---

1. New York: E. P. Dutton & Company, 1936, 550 pp., pp. 34–35.

intellectual climate until the present ascendancy of general education has brought about a reshaping of methods of presentation of the materials that are now the basis of the college curriculum. These materials, for many years labeled English, history, economics, foreign language, philosophy, psychology, science, and mathematics and presented by instructional task forces known as departments, are today being broken down into new groupings called by such titles as humanities, communications, social sciences, physical sciences, natural sciences, and life sciences and presented by teachers drawn from several departments in a kind of academic "combined operation." Parenthetically, it may be noted that some of these combined operations have been harried by interdepartmental difficulties in the same manner that military combined operations are often plagued by interservice feuds.

The general education concept, having taken hold in the higher institutions, has, be it noted, continued its progress into the secondary schools. Although it has not yet happened, it is reasonably certain that on a day in the not-too-distant future an applicant will present to a startled admissions officer a record showing communications (in place of part of what is now taught as English); humanities (in place of the rest of English and foreign language); "tools of learning" (in place of mathematics and laboratory experience); "science in our culture" (in place of physics and chemistry); and, of course, social studies (in place of history).

It is to be understood, of course, that acceptance of the general education concept cannot be measured by changes in course titles. It is change in method that is the controlling factor, and it is change in method that will affect the future of the Board. Where general education has taken hold firmly, subject-matter entrance requirements and subject tests are bowing out.

This is an obvious development, since subject requirements including subject-matter tests were established to measure readiness to continue, in college, work that had begun in secondary school. In other words, requirements and tests were the cement that bound together the college and the secondary school. Aptitude tests, when they came into use, came as supplements to requirements and subject-matter tests because they were found to measure readiness by extrapolation. However, when the concept of general education is applied to college entrance procedures, the questions asked of the entering student are directed to his aptitudes and interests, since these, rather than his specific preparation, will control his ability to carry his college work. In this situation, therefore, it is the aptitude tests that give the needed information and the subject-matter tests that contribute only to the extent that they measure aptitude by extrapolation.

In making the prediction that, given a continuance of present trends in education, aptitude tests will become progressively more important and subject tests progressively less important, there is no intention to advocate or even indicate an eventual abandonment of subject tests. What is more likely to happen is a change in form that will see what are now subject tests becoming, in effect, tests of developed aptitudes. This statement is made on the postulate that any subject-matter test today measures the sum of three factors: first, basic aptitude for understanding and study of the subject; second, the extent of the development of that basic aptitude, or, in other words, acquired skill in the use of the aptitude; and, finally, specific results of the training in terms of knowledge of the subject. It follows, then, that the transmutation of existing subject-matter tests will be largely a matter of increasing emphasis on measurement of depth of understanding and ability to apply knowledge of principles to solutions of problems, and of decreasing emphasis on measurement of knowledge of specific details.

Another important development in higher education is widespread acceptance of the concept that all must have a chance to continue schooling beyond the secondary level. This concept has already had its very important effects in the founding in recent years of junior colleges, technical institutes, specialized programs attached to existing institutions, and, more recently, the newly popular but still undefined community colleges—all offering instruction above the secondary level, but many offering forms of instruction new to our colleges.

With acceptance of this concept has come acceptance of its alternative statement—to each a higher education in accordance with his abilities— and, with acceptance of this, there must come acceptance of appropriate entrance procedures. The form that these entrance procedures will take ultimately is not to be determined from the present admissions practices of these institutions, for they, like most institutions in their early stages of development, have few entrance requirements and are generous in their enforcement of those they have. However, since most of these emerging institutions aim to develop skills and motivations, it seems safe to venture a prediction that their entrance requirements will eventually be couched in terms of aptitudes and interests. Here again, clearly, is a call for the development of tests of specific, defined aptitudes and tests of the extent to which the aptitudes have been developed. Also, be it noted, there is an apparent need for tests to deal with motivations and interests, a form of testing that presents all the usual test-construction problems, plus a group of problems all its own.

As a third (and, for this report, final) development in secondary and higher education, it is necessary to mention the renascence of interest in guidance. The term "renascence" is used advisedly because much current interest has been stimulated by the discovery, stemming directly from the performance of GI students, of the tremendous effect that motivation and interest have on college success. This discovery has been parent to the conviction that a large percentage of college failures today could have been avoided had the student's interests and motivations been correctly determined before his assignment to a program. Here, clearly, is a problem that calls for the construction of a form of test distinct from any now regularly employed in college testing—a form already known to be difficult to construct and to yield results that to date are only moderately satisfactory with respect to validity, reliability, and broad usefulness.

This discussion of the future of the Board has, in effect, said that this future rests on the Board's ability to supplement its present aptitude tests with additional tests yielding reliable measures of ability to work in specific fields, and to develop generally usable tests of interest and motivation. This may, to some, seem a sudden conjuring up of a large and not particularly attractive stage setting, but the assurance must be accepted that here is no magic, used or intended. Instead, here is the presentation of a problem. The problem is an old one for the Board—whether to face toward the past and to throw its considerable weight into the maintenance of traditional requirements or to adjust its plans to changes and developments as it sees them in the future.

The following excerpt from the 1950 Annual Report of the Director is hardly exciting, but it does include the first mention, to a Board audience, of the possibility of changing the composition of the college-bound group through precollege guidance carried down to the eighth or ninth grade. This is commonplace today and is even considered impossibly late in communities where admission to nursery schools is weighed in terms of ultimate significance for college entrance. But in 1950 precollege guidance was by and large a novel idea. Out of the idea, with Board stimulus and direct financial support, came the Demonstration Guidance Project in New York City's Junior High School 43, which was the parent of the Higher Horizons idea. And out of it came too a whole series of inquiries into problems of motivation and direction in their influence on achievement.

The report also suggests that tax-supported institutions would in time go to selective admissions procedures, a wild idea in 1950 but commonplace 10 years later, in 1960.

"The Future of the Board"
50th Annual Report of the Director. New York: College Entrance Examination Board, 1950, 83 pp., pp. 48–51.

In the consideration of an organization, its policies, and its activities, it is sometimes desirable to change the frame of reference and to approach the subject from an entirely new viewpoint.

Such a change of viewpoint in the case of the College Entrance Examination Board can be achieved by considering it, for the moment, in commercial terms. So considered, the Board has, throughout its 50-year history, enjoyed the advantage of supplying a needed service for a continuing market. The service has been supplying basic data for the evaluation of individuals in terms of their probable success in college. The market has been primarily colleges themselves, and secondary schools have formed an important related outlet or market for its services.

To continue the commercial analogy, it can be said that the Board has enjoyed something of the same advantage that a manufacturer of ball bearings might enjoy. So long as there are wheels that must turn, such a manufacturer has a market; and so long as he operates within requirements of quality and cost combined with an awareness of current needs, he may have his share of that market. He may even, by discovering new uses for his products, expand his share and develop new markets. Similarly, so long as there are colleges that can use the services the Board supplies and so long as those services are satisfactory, the existence and the future of the Board are, in a purely commercial sense, assured.

Within the past two years, two distinct and in large measure unrelated phenomena have resulted in conditions that call into question the future of the Board's market for its services. On the one hand, the independent colleges and universities, which make up about 80 percent of the Board's market, have suffered through inflation a relative loss in capital assets. In other words, these colleges are today relatively less able to support themselves than they have been at any time during the past 30 years. And, on the other hand, these same colleges and universities are under the heaviest imaginable pressures to broaden their services and increase their facilities. Indeed, they can be assured that unless they do so, they will lose stature and eventually the drawing power that has made it possible for them to maintain high standards of instruction and scholarship.

In planning its future services to its present member colleges, the Board has certain facts to consider.

1. One factor controlling the quality of colleges is the quality of their students, which in turn is controlled by the quality of the candidate group. (This statement represents an amendment to the classical accrediting agency approach, which, in evaluating quality, emphasizes instruction, curriculums, and facilities. The amendment is merely a statement that the ultimate quality of an institution is determined by the results of these factors operating in relation to a student body.)

2. The group of candidates for college admission can, without diminution in quality, be increased by 25 percent by applying guidance and testing to develop motivation for college in the sizable group of able students who do not now consider college entrance. (This statement constitutes a change of emphasis in the current saying that large numbers of able students are restrained from college attendance by reason of finances. The change is made because study of current data does not support a figure larger than 25 percent and because lack of motivation appears to be a more important factor in college nonattendance than lack of finances.)

3. The appalling attrition in American colleges (only half of entering

students graduate) is today diverting 20 percent or more of the money disbursed by higher institutions on undergraduate education into the education of students who, by reason of failure or dropout, will not complete the course. In other words, each college must deal with the fact that the students who fail to meet the college's own criterion of success, which is graduation, and who amount to from 10 to 60 percent of each entering class, are responsible for increasing its total financial outlay by 20 percent or more. (This statement does not undertake to argue the incidental benefits to those students who drop out before completion, nor does it argue the highly dubious possibility that such students may not constitute an extra burden. It merely points out a result of a firmly established policy that controls admission to American colleges.)

In terms of the foregoing statements, it seems reasonable to comment that the future of the colleges that constitute the Board's present membership depends on their ability to maintain the quality and increase the size of their candidate group, and simultaneously to reduce per capita instructional costs by better and earlier elimination of those who, once admitted, require but do not profit from instruction.

These steps, when so stated, seem in no wise to differ from the present activities of those colleges. Almost without exception, they are active in trying to increase the number and quality of their candidates and conscientious in their attempt to select those students who will profit from instruction. Yet in their present efforts, there are two large areas so far not covered.

The first area relates to the size and quality of candidate groups. Most of the effort made today to attract able candidates is concentrated on twelfth-grade students, which is another way of saying that it is concentrated on students who have already decided on college and are undecided only about which college. For any one college such efforts can obviously have only limited success, measured perhaps in terms of a 10 or 15 percent increase in applications. They cannot reach students of comparable ability who have not taken a college preparatory course, nor those who have dropped out, nor, except in rare instances, those who have long since decided not to go to college.

Students who cannot be reached in the later grades can clearly be reached only in the earlier grades—and then only by a careful and strenuous process of early identification of ability, careful guidance, and, in most cases, the participation of the parents in career planning. These steps constitute for most individual higher institutions an almost impossible program, but for an organization such as the Board, made up of representatives from both higher and secondary education, they represent a logical activity. Certainly it would be in no sense impossible for the Board to enter upon a controlled experiment, extending over a period of several years, which would include the testing of eighth-, ninth-, and tenth-grade students, the identification of potential college candidates, and the building of an appropriate guidance program directed at both students and parents. The tests and the programs exist already, and both the manpower and the support can, on an experimental basis, be made available through the Board as a legitimate investment in its future and the future of its supporting members.

The second area—that of reducing expenditures on inadequate students—is in some ways more difficult than the first. Many colleges have spent a good deal of thought and time on the problem and still find themselves unable to explain why candidates of comparable promise perform differently under the stress of college work. It seems clear that in this area the Board is approaching the limitations of its present tests and that any genuine advances must come from using new techniques and perhaps from using new instruments.

Here again is an area in which the Board should be able, through its membership, to undertake studies in the prediction of college success and of college failure, studies that could employ not only the conventional approach via measurements and estimates of aptitude and ability derived from tests, performance records, recommendations, and interviews, but also the largely unexplored approaches—at least for education—through the domains of the clinical psychologist and the psychiatrist. This suggestion is made with full understanding of the reluctance of colleges to pry or seem to appear to pry into the private lives and the behavior patterns of their students. Nevertheless, these lives and patterns are determinants for success or failure in or out of school and college, and if there is any path to even partial understanding of them it should be explored. To put it negatively, nothing can be lost and possibly much can be gained. Certainly, if through the medium of such studies colleges are enabled to admit students with reasonable assurance that they will profit by instruction and will graduate, some of the present problems of college instruction, including the heavy loading of the first two years as compared with the light loading of the last two years and the constant necessity for differentiating between the fit and the unfit, will be, if not eliminated, at any rate diminished. Such diminution will in turn lower the cost of instruction and thereby provide some cushion against the ever present worries of finance and facilities.

In the Board's future there are bound to be other problems and developments. There are, for example, real possibilities that tax-supported institutions will shortly move toward a larger measure of selective admissions. Indeed, it is hard to see how they can avoid doing so unless greatly increased tax funds can be found to finance major increases in plant and facilities. If such moves develop, the Board can make a very real contribution to them and must stand ready to do so.

The Board's concern has always been with the problems of the transit of individuals from secondary to higher education, and it must conceive of its future as a projection and a broadening of that concern. Only in such terms can it justify and continue its existence as a worthwhile institution in American education.

C*rystal Balls and College Admissions," which follows, was not the first speech I made after I became director of the Board, but it was the first one I care to remember. It reflects very clearly the problems of the time. In 1950 the secondary schools had not yet accommodated themselves to the change in the pattern of college admissions. Most schoolmen assumed that there would be a return to the "normal" pattern, in which 20 percent (or fewer) of high school graduates went to college from most high schools. Hence they were making no real effort to adapt to college demands for specific preparation.*

This speech assumed that the resolution of the conflict between the secondary school "life-adjustment" philosophy and the specific subject demands of the colleges would be in the form of a carefully planned general education program for all secondary school students.

The assumption, of course, has proved wrong. No one at that time foresaw that colleges would be able to reassert themselves and regain control of their en-

trance requirements. However they did so within five years of the date of this speech, and the idea of general education in the secondary schools vanished (for the time).

Whether or not general education in secondary schools would have satisfied the college requirements of the fifties I do not know. I am fairly certain that the programs, if established, could not have met the rising subject-matter requirements of the sixties. But I believe that the idea will be given a new hearing in the 1970s as a consequence of the current political action, which is accomplishing the general democratization of grades 11 through 14.

I make these observations because educational ideas seem to go in cycles, and I suspect that another cycle stressing general education is in the making.

The idea of aptitude measures that would yield scores on several differentiated aptitudes was not new in 1951. It continues to appear now and then in 1966, but the chances that it will be applied to test development are not good so long as the present empirically developed aptitude tests continue to work.

"Crystal Balls and College Admissions"
A report of the fifteenth Educational Conference, New York, October 26 and 27, 1950, held under the auspices of the Educational Records Bureau and the American Council on Education. Conference subject: Measurement and Evaluation in the Improvement of Education. Published in *American Council on Education Studies*, Series I, Reports of Committees and Conferences, Vol. XV, No. 46, April 1951. Edited by Arthur E. Traxler. 145 pp., pp. 8–16.

I should not want you to misunderstand the title of my talk this morning, "Crystal Balls and College Admissions." I did not mean to imply that admissions officers—that is, that all admissions officers—select their students by gazing into crystal balls. Some use more, some less, scientific methods. I merely wished to say that I would myself gaze into the clouded spheres and try to tell you what seemed to me to be the problems most likely to face admissions officers in the future.

Consider a not-too-hypothetical applicant for admission to college in

1955. He comes from a well-known and respected secondary school and applies to a college whose entrance standards are high. He presents impeccable recommendations as to character, leadership, and promise of growth. He has an excellent score on a standard scholastic aptitude test. And he presents to a startled admissions officer a record of high achievement in four years of secondary school work in the following subjects: communications (written and oral), four years; humanities, four years; tools of learning, three years; science in our culture, two years; social studies, four years; community welfare, one year.

After the admissions officer examines the record, he finds that communications and humanities are, when considered together, essentially a history of cultural stimuli and their passage between peoples. There is full use of translations of appropriate masterpieces originally written in a language other than English, but there is only a fragment of foreign language instruction as "enrichment."

"Tools of learning" turns out to be the elements of algebra, geometry, and statistics, plus instruction in the scientific method and its application in laboratory and in field work. Here again "enrichment" has been provided by trips to large laboratories, preferably, if security permits, to major enterprises in physical or biological research.

"Science in our culture" is a capsule history of science, plus instruction in elements of physical and natural science, with the instruction related to parallel work in the subject labeled "tools of learning." Time has been devoted to study of cultural changes resulting from scientific developments, and progress in pure and applied sciences resulting from social pressures, including those of both war and peace.

Social studies as a descriptive title is already familiar to us. In this case it stands for a carefully planned course in world history with appropriate attention to economic and social, as well as to political, history.

Community welfare is the most deceptively titled of the subjects. It is a seminar course for twelfth-grade pupils. It undertakes to supply method and motivation for a synthesis of the entire program of secondary school studies. The aim of this course is to relate studies to the social unit.

Now I am not suggesting this curriculum as a straw man to be knocked down and kicked about. As a matter of fact, I see admirable things in it. I find it a little hard to get used to the disappearance of foreign language, but

I realize that I might as well get accustomed to the idea, for it is surely disappearing as a required study in school and college. Laying aside the lament for language, I believe that such a program, well planned and well taught, should offer to the student at least as much opportunity to acquire the beginning of an education as does a good present-day college preparatory program. It could even be an improvement on some programs.

Now consider another hypothetical candidate for admission in 1955. This candidate, like the other one, has the highest possible recommendations as to citizenship, leadership, and promise of maturity. His score on a scholastic aptitude test is high above the national mean. His school record places him in the top 10 percent of his class. He is, in short, a first-rate candidate for college. He presents a record showing the following subjects: two years of English; one year of journalism, creative writing, French, German, Spanish, algebra, geometry, applied mathematics, biology, sociology, world history, plastic and graphic arts, auto driving and safety education, social dynamics, and nucleonics; and one-half year each of puppeteering and play production.

The record I have just read—I cannot call it a program because the word "program" implies a plan, and this agglomeration of subjects is certainly unsullied by any planning—is more extensive than the first one. It calls, as you will note, for 4½ courses a year as against the other's requirement of 4 a year. And, may I add, this record, or, if you prefer, pseudoprogram, is not a forecast for five years hence. We have prototypes—and plenty of them—today.

Except for the courses in social dynamics and nucleonics, all these subjects are today offered in secondary school. Their contents are known and accepted, and students, even good students, have been allowed to build up programs as diffuse as this one. I am not able to tell you what is taught under the titles social dynamics and nucleonics, though I presume that the tutelary deity knows and will in time reveal this knowledge to us, possibly through some modern Isaiah of education.

I think we would all agree that these two programs I have presented have little in common. One is planned, the other unplanned. The one points toward a goal, the other nowhere. But they do have in common the fact that there is almost no continuity of subject-matter presentation between them and college programs as we know them.

And now comes the question: "What of it?"

Before undertaking to answer that question, I had better stop to defend myself on the point of possible occurrence of programs like these. Here is my defense.

The first program, the one with the new course titles, is a secondary school version of what in the colleges is called general education, a topic you may recall as having been under discussion from time to time in recent years. I think it is safe to say that no two discussions of general education lead the listener or the reader to exactly the same conclusion, but the gist of them seems to me to be something like this: (1) education, particularly in the thirteenth and fourteenth school years, should, through the humanities, the social studies, and the sciences, make available to students the facts and the intellectual experiences that are by general consent important for comprehension of society and culture; (2) the instruction must stress the interrelations of the several disciplines and draw interpretive material from areas where two or more disciplines meet; (3) these two precepts must be made effective by rethinking the curriculum and rearranging the presentation into groupings that disregard traditional subject boundaries. The effort is always to supply the broadest possible base of facts and to offer them in the most teachable and most digestible way.

The carrying-out of the precepts of general education is therefore usually marked by abandonment of old course titles and the establishment of new courses that cut across departmental lines. And, if this is sound doctrine and practice in colleges, then it is sound for secondary schools. Such, at any rate, will be the reasoning of secondary school administrators—and the reasoning seems valid. I believe we can expect this reasoning to be widely accepted in the near future, particularly by those schools that seek an acceptable substitute for the defined and prescribed programs of an earlier day. General education as a concept does not offer a substitute for a classical preparation or even for the college entrance program of today. Instead, it offers a distinctive opportunity and challenge all its own. It may well be that the opportunity and the challenge will be accepted by schools that we think of as conservative. If that be the criterion, then the program I offered first will perhaps prove to be the conservative one of the future.

The other program—the one with standard titles and fancy additions—does not come out of any philosophy as closely reasoned as general education, but it does come out of a philosophy. That philosophy is currently titled "education for living." The general position of this philosophy is that it is the responsibility of formal education to provide, within its framework, every type of experience that can be duplicated in a school or school-related situation, and that the greater the number of situations sampled by students the better the preparation for living. Admittedly, the proponents of this philosophy are not advocating it as a cure-all for college preparation, but, nevertheless, in schools where the philosophy prevails, college preparation will have a strong tendency to follow the pattern of breadth at any cost. This pattern, as I have suggested, has its philosophers and its defenders, but mostly it just has practitioners. My belief, I regret to say, is that the practitioners will increase and that the number of students passed through this undirected kind of program on their way to college will increase.

Now to turn to the question of what is to be done about evaluating these new patterns of secondary school subjects.

Subject-matter requirements were established to measure readiness to continue in college the work begun in secondary school. It was the assumption and indeed the demonstrated fact that there was a relationship between secondary school achievement and college achievement, a relationship that arose in part from the continuity between secondary school subjects and college subjects. This relationship can be and has been translated into co-efficients whose delightful decimal and digit appearance of exactness makes them a favorite tool and justification of admissions officers. This, despite the fact, obvious to anyone who considers their origin, that these coefficients are the end products of so many variables that they are in fact only the roughest kind of approximation. However that may be, in present-day college entrance procedures (or at least in any procedures more complicated than lassoing and hog-tying the candidate) this exact statement of an approximation is the main reliance of admissions officers. This is as it should be, for so long as there is subject continuity between school and college, as, generally, there is today, any statement predicting relationship between school and college achievement is bound to be the best single guide to good admission. Sometimes this prediction of relationship can be improved by administering subject-matter tests. Still another aid in the prediction of relationship between school and college achievement is the result of a scholastic aptitude test. Such tests have the advantage of throwing some light on the candidate's abilities and aptitudes or, more simply, on his readiness for further academic work. Thereby they supply another criterion to be used in conjunction with scholastic attainment.

Parenthetically, let me say that I decided, in the interests of brevity for this paper, not to quibble over the fact that the aptitude or readiness criterion is not in fact a fully separable and discrete one. The student's aptitude has already figured largely in the school grades and will figure largely in the college grades. That is a point for the technicians to argue and refine. Actually, the items we are dealing with are used as separate criteria and are so treated in this paper.

Although the criterion of aptitude has the recommendations that it is cheap and easy to use and that it has been proved to have a thoroughly satisfactory validity of its own, we have not come to the point of full reliance on it. By this I mean that I do not know of any college that routinely uses an aptitude test as its sole criterion for admission. This is entirely understandable. A college using the best available single criterion, proved achievement, should not consider discarding it completely in favor of another criterion—in this case, aptitude test scores—even though such scores can, as has been proved repeatedly, predict college success without the aid of any other data. But the fact that this has not been done to date does not indicate that it cannot be done. As a matter of fact, the military services have, for better or for worse, used aptitude tests for some years as their controlling criterion for admission to training programs of almost all types. It should be said that they have employed other, and sometimes hidden, criteria and that their selection procedures are in a sense wasteful as far as manpower is concerned. Nevertheless, the fact that these services can use tests in this manner indicates that colleges can.

I have already recorded my belief that the pattern of college preparation will change and that the present-day variety of continuity from school to college will dwindle. That means, of course, that the familiar relationship between scholastic achievement in secondary school subject matter and scholastic achievement in college subject matter will tend to disappear and that what I referred to above as the best single available criterion for prediction of achievement, namely proved achievement in related subjects, will not be available because the related subjects will not be available. If that happens, and I am sure it will, we must perforce turn to aptitude tests —and you will note that I said tests, not test—if only because we will not have any other criterion for determining who is to continue in college, unless, of course, we wish to turn entirely away from scholastic criteria and search instead for personality measures as the answer to our problems. Again parenthetically, such measures will probably have their day, but that day is not in the foreseeable future. Therefore, if we must place our emphasis on measurement of scholastic aptitude, we must go further in measurement of that aptitude than we have gone to date.

At present our aptitude measurements rely largely on verbal and numerical facility. In its simplest form this is a measurement of extent of vocabulary and ability to manipulate simple number combinations. In more complex forms we have gone into ability to distinguish shades of meaning, into reading ability, into reading comprehension, and into capacity for inductive and for quantitative reasoning. In these areas we have usable and statistically reliable tests. It should be mentioned that some tests that specifically avoid verbal materials have been developed. There are interesting tests in the area of spatial relations that measure aptitude for three-dimensional visualization, and there is a nonverbal general ability test relying on graphic materials.

On the other hand, aptitude testing has not been carried successfully to the point where we can distinguish pure mathematical aptitude, nor pure aptitude for comprehension of science, nor pure aptitude for the learning of languages, nor pure mechanical aptitude. This is not to say that experiments in measurement in these areas have failed utterly, but merely to say that we have been unable to separate the effects of training or lack of it, and the effects of verbal facility or lack of it, from that factor, lurking somewhere in the middle of the results, which some would like to label "pure aptitude." I doubt that we shall ever get to measures of pure aptitude, regardless of expenditure of brains, money, and time. We should in fact look with suspicion on anyone who claims to have devised such a measure, for it is hard to see how any measures can be devised that are not in the last analysis achievement measures.

I feel that fortunately the evidence is clear that we can go beyond our efforts to date. By this I mean that we can move from the rough measure of scholastic aptitude that we now obtain from measurement of verbal ability and numerical facility, to sharper measures of aptitudes or readiness for families of subjects—as, for example, mathematics and the exact sciences in one family; the descriptive sciences in another family; the social studies and certain humanistic studies in another; the foreign languages in still another; and so on into perhaps six or eight separable ability areas.

Furthermore, there is no real reason why tests—aptitude tests—when so developed as to supply for families of subjects a measurement of a student's abilities, cannot be combined for ease of administration and use, into a single test package. Aptitude tests are now available that yield two or three scores, measuring or purporting to measure two or more distinct sets of abilities, usually verbal and mathematical. There is every reason—except the present lack of tests to do the measuring—why they can and should be made available in a form that will yield three, or four, or even more separate scores, each score conveying a definite and usable bit of information to the user of the scores. Of course combination packages like these require time to administer and time to use. Such a package cannot be administered during a class period or a visit to a college campus, nor used after one glance at a single score. Indeed, in its final form the test will be an all-day affair. And when the time comes I think the effort will be worth it, for, in my judgment at any rate, this is the only kind of testing program that can cope with the problem of allotting college admission to products of what we can call generically the "new education." In fact, I can go further and say that it represents the basis of the only kind of admissions program that seems to me to be rational in the kind of future I have suggested.

Let me sum up now what I have been saying about aptitude tests. Aptitude tests can be used by themselves to predict college success, and they will predict it, regardless of the pattern of subjects studied or to be studied. Aptitude tests can be improved, and prediction can be improved. And as tests and prediction are improved, use of aptitude tests as the controlling criterion for college entrance will increase. This increase will be accelerated by the need for an admissions criterion to take the place of the vanishing continuity between school and college programs.

Now let me pose and answer several practical questions: How can students with college entrance equipment differing from standard offerings enter (a) technical and scientific schools, (b) colleges with conventional curriculums, and (c) colleges operating within the general education framework? These questions revolve around specific relationships in subject matter between school and college. These relationships established a continuity, historically present and now vanishing. This continuity will not, I believe, be reestablished in the foreseeable future.

Procedures will have to change. These changes can take two forms. The first form can be to change entrance requirements; the second form, to change the administration of entrance requirements. I believe that both changes will take place. Entrance requirements will change to accommodate the increasing breadth of freshman programs. There will be fewer subjects required. This will mean that those college programs which require specific preparation will have either to abandon their requirement or change their course in such a way as to supply the preparation themselves. Of course, we all realize that this will mean ultimately a change in college curriculums. The administration of entrance requirements must, then, change too. I think I have already made clear my belief that this change will be, in fact must be, toward increasing reliance on aptitude measurement.

There are many who will feel that such changes as those I have discussed will result in irreparable loss in the quality of education. Within their frame of reference, I am sure they are right. Yet it is possible to accept such a loss, if we must, to establish a new continuity, a continuity of understanding of the individual. When we have done that, we will begin to achieve an understanding of the complex of reasons for success or failure in college. By this I mean that, since predictions of scholastic success or failure based on refined measures of aptitude will be sharper than predictions based on our present crude measures, we shall, in this brave future, be able better to separate the modifying factors of personality, of motivation, and of circumstance from the academic pattern. I wish I could take time to stress the fact that the study of these modifying factors is in the long run our most important task in college admissions, but, since today I am dealing essentially with a coming problem and the techniques necessary to deal immediately with it, I shall leave this problem for some other minor prophet.

Such separation will make possible the weighing and balancing of each factor. It will not lessen the burden on human judgments, for the judgments must continue to be made, but it may make accuracy easier, just as the development of each new medical laboratory test has made it easier for the physician to make an accurate diagnosis.

For whatever value it may have, I have offered my view of the future. I said at the outset that my crystal ball was clouded, a fate that forever pursues admissions officers, even when they reform—for an admissions officer, like an umpire, must always rule in favor of one side or the other and is therefore always wrong in someone's opinion. Therefore the decision about your acceptance or rejection of this future that I present is yours and not mine. I happily leave it so, for I know it is in good hands.

3. The Statement of a Program: 1951-1953

It is fair to say that by the close of 1950 the Board had been reestablished. It had a new staff that had learned to search for its tasks by working directly with schools and colleges. Its supporters had gathered again after the dismal year of 1948, when fewer than 100 representatives of the member colleges came to meetings. Its business, measured by numbers of candidates and colleges applying for membership, was picking up.

Its next task was to establish a program. This took place substantially during the next two years. It became evident that college-going would continue to increase and that there would have to be changes in preparation, in standards, in admissions procedure, and in tests.

All these needs were laid out in talks or reports during the next two years, and eventually something was done about all of them except testing. Here there was a block—one that still exists. The Board's officers and some of its committees thought there should be changes in tests, but, as it turned out and was to turn out repeatedly over the next 10 years, the bulk of the membership—both school and college and, with few exceptions, the testing professionals—opposed change and imposed its will on the program. Fortunately the tests in the program, although they have changed very little in conception, are empirically based, are honest, are skillfully made, are well administered, and work well (which is why change has always been successfully opposed). But it is too bad that test development cannot break out of empiricism to draw on work in developmental psychology, physiological psychology, psychiatry, and cultural anthropology to explore alternative paths to knowledge.

The discussion and formulation of a program was assisted greatly by two developments coming from outside the Board.

In the first of these developments John D. Millet, professor at Columbia University (now Chancellor and Director of the Ohio Board of Regents), conducting a study on financing higher education, persuaded the Board to examine the question of who might go to college if the conditions of college going were redefined in terms of talent, thus upsetting the classical economic controls on college attendance. The Board engaged Byron S. Hollinshead, former president of Scranton-Keystone Junior College and

Coe College, to direct the study. Mr. Hollinshead, in effect, joined the Board's staff for two years, bringing to it an interest in large-scale student movement that was to have a profound effect on our activities and that is reflected in many of the papers in this section and later sections of this book.

In the second of these developments, the National Science Foundation, alarmed by the small numbers of scientists and engineers emerging from higher education each year, began consideration of ways of influencing students to enter those fields and turned to the Board to undertake a study of the problem. This new obligation opened up the entire subject of the identification and nurture of talent, paving the way directly for the Advanced Placement Program and indirectly for uncounted changes and ideas that are still unfolding.

The papers that follow indicate the extent to which the Board's activities opened up during this period and the nature of the program statements as they emerged.

The 14 paragraphs that make up the first item were the product of observation of the haphazard methods of schools and colleges in handling candidates for admission around 1951. These remarks were a trial balloon to find out whether the membership would support active work by the Board on the problem.

It turned out that they would. In fact the suggestion that the Board should accept responsibility for study, for identification of procedures, for adoption of improved methods, and for speeding interchange of information proved to be the turning point in the Board's history. Until that time it had been a small organization, examining a few candidates, holding small meetings to discuss small problems. But, after the October 1951 meeting, when the membership began serious examination of the needs for services, the new interest in the Board and its capabilities brought new members, more candidates, more income, more staff, and of course more demands for services.

"Old Methods and New Problems"
Excerpt from the report of the director, at the annual meeting of the College Board, October 31, 1951. From the minutes of the meeting of October 31, 1951, pp. 12–15.

. . . At this point I end my detailed report on the state of the Board. I debated with myself a good bit over whether or not to use the next pages I prepared. They are not as specific as I wish they were, and some, at least, of the things I will say are truisms.

Yet, I am going to accept the risk of being justifiably accused of easy generalizations because I am convinced that in the Board's field of college entrance, the status quo, defined as "the mess we is in," is not good and will get worse before it gets better. I think troubles are piling up because we are attempting to deal with new problems in terms of old methods and techniques, and I think they will get worse until we analyze our new problems and devise techniques to deal with them. My plan, then, is for new evaluations, new methods, and new techniques.

In our work, in our travels, and in the conduct of the study[1] for the Commission on Financing Higher Education, Mr. Fels and I have become increasingly aware that there are three major unsolved problems at the college-entrance level: (1) the early identification and stimulation of potential college material, (2) the simplification of the machinery of admissions, and (3) the articulation of school and college programs.

The college population potential
The first problem has been brought sharply into focus by Byron Hollinshead's forthcoming study, "Who Should Go to College in America."[2] There are in America about 525,000 out of each age group who have an IQ of 110 or better and who are, therefore, to be adjudged capable of doing adequate or superior college work. Of this 525,000, as far as can be determined, only 210,000 get to college. The remaining 315,000 apparently fail to enter college because of lack of money or lack of motivation, or because

---

1. See the excerpt from the *51st Annual Report of the Director*, on page 59.
2. *College Board Review* No. 16, February 1952, pp. 248–253. Mr. Hollinshead's book of the same name was published in 1952 by Columbia University Press.

of overriding and, to them, more attractive other plans. It is obvious that with proper attention to guidance, planning, motivation, aim, and finances a number of these students can be moved to college. Under optimum conditions, we might move half of this group each year into college.

It requires very little arithmetic to make clear that such a move would increase the size of every freshman class in the land by 25 percent, or that, alternatively, it would hold freshman classes at the same size and eliminate most of the students who now catch the D's, Incompletes, and F's, and who account for the genuinely disgraceful attrition rate of American colleges, more than 50 percent from entrance to graduation. There is no simple solution for the remotivation or for the activation of this group as a potential group of college entrants, but it is apparent that little can be done if the attempt is delayed until they have reached the twelfth grade. The job must be done before then, probably in the tenth grade, possibly even earlier.

Simplifying admissions

The second problem with which we deal is that of the mechanics of admission. By mechanics I mean such things as catalogs, application forms, dates of application, requirements for admission, notifications, acceptances, deposit fees, and so forth. I do not need to point out to you that no two colleges employ, except by accident, the same catalog statement of their requirements (although let me say that most college entrance requirements are the same, or at least one comes to think so when they are read in large numbers, as they were for *The College Handbook*[3]), nor the same wording of application forms, nor the same dates of application, nor the same admissions procedures and correspondence operations.

It may seem a small thing to two college admissions officers to find that they have different admissions procedures, but to the candidate this may be a matter of great importance. Very few college applicants are sophisticated about business correspondence. Some of our candidates enjoy the protection and advice of schools magnificently equipped to assist them in the details of college admissions. Many do not. The actual mechanics of admissions can be far more bewildering and discouraging to a candidate from a small country high school in the Midwest than to an applicant graduating

---

3. The first edition of *The College Handbook*, edited by William C. Fels, was published in 1951. The introduction to the following paper explains the genesis of the *Handbook*.

from one of the northeastern preparatory schools, even though both may be applying to the same university.

It seems to me entirely justifiable to call upon the members of the College Board in the strongest possible appeal to resolve this problem—to act decisively to clear away many of these barriers to admission. We have already, in an amazingly short time and with very little hardship, cleared away much of the problem of the Uniform Acceptance Date.[4] It is now high time that we looked to our member colleges and asked them to consider other steps for the simplification of the mechanics of admission. Very few of you realize the actual number of students being lost to colleges that take care of admission by the direct approach—having the admissions officer approach the candidate, help him fill out the application blank, take his signature and fee, and go away. This is a low level of recruiting, but some fairly strong colleges are employing it. There is no reason why the Board member colleges need move to such a form of recruiting, but there is also no reason why, by their insistence upon individuality at the clerical level, they should make it possible for such recruiting to exist and to succeed.

School and college—hiatus or harmony?

The third problem is that of articulation of schools and colleges. The Board was founded originally to solve a recognized problem in the relationship between the instruction in secondary schools and the instruction in colleges. It was felt necessary at that time to appoint a committee of ten to consider the problem and to bring in a report. On this report the foundation of the Board was ultimately based. If a committee of ten was needed in the 1890s to consider the matter, I submit that today a committee of a thousand would be insufficient.

In the nineties, the lack of articulation between a school and a college was a lack of articulation in detail. One institution would require certain orations of Cicero; another would require certain others. Today our lack of articulation is not a matter of detail; it is a matter of complete difference

---

4. The Uniform Acceptance Date, originated in 1948 by eight Board member colleges and since 1953 called Candidates Reply Date, allows an applicant maximum opportunity to receive and consider all acceptances before choosing a college. A candidate who has been admitted to a college need not notify the college until a certain date, set by the College Board each year (now usually May 1), of his decision to attend it or to accept financial aid from it.

in philosophy and in understanding of the approach to education. I submit that it needs a thoroughgoing, broad study in an attempt to resolve the differences and to find out why it is that our public education system is going in a direction which is different from that of the independent secondary schools, different in another way from the direction in which the independent higher institutions are going, and different in still another way from the direction in which our tax-supported higher institutions are going.

I believe that the problems of college entrance which are particularized here in the Board meeting in terms of preparation in English composition and in mathematics, science, and the social studies are in reality not these problems. They are only the symptoms of the deeper problem: that secondary education in this country has, at least in its tax-supported aspects, one set of purposes and higher education has another, and that there has been no real attempt to reconcile them. There has not even been real recognition that they have drawn apart, but in fact they *have* drawn apart. This, I think, is clear enough from two simple statistics. In 1900, three-fourths of the graduates of high school went to college. In 1950, fewer than one-third of the graduates of high school went to college.

Toward a solution

In the final analysis, these three problems boil down to one—that the relationship between school and college in America is failing at the critical point of mutual understanding. In order to get about our business of education, we must restore this understanding.

If we choose to face up to this problem squarely, I should like to have your encouragement to make these topics the programs of our regional conferences and to move them from these conferences to our October 1952 meeting as the topic for our morning symposium. From there I should hope we could take the next step of appointing and supporting a commission which could begin, as did the Board's founding fathers, with the understanding that no conceivable combination of little solutions would suffice for a massive problem.

This is no program for the dismayed, nor bait for the timid. If it is true that fools rush in where angels fear to tread, then I can say only that here is an area where no angels have trod. If it is foolishness to dare to approach it, then I can only remind you that the founders of this Board committed us long ago to a tradition of such foolishness, and that we as a Board have a reputation of reverence for tradition.

---

*T*he following two excerpts from the 1951 annual report deal with undertakings that had a very important long-term effect on the Board. The first one is mainly noteworthy for its mention of the need for a program of training admissions officers. The proposal lay dormant for several years until it was picked up by Mr. Fels, who engaged Columbia's Arden House as a meeting place and plunged ahead to make a program. The Colloquium on College Admissions, as it was called, enjoyed a useful 10-year life, from 1954 to 1963, and was then discontinued only because it became nearly impossible to find a comfortable meeting place that was not a hotel and could accommodate 100 participants.

It will be noted also that the report refers to the revision of The College Handbook. This undertaking was, although indirectly, probably more responsible for the expansion of the Board than any other single Board activity, a result totally unanticipated at the time.

In point of fact, the "revision" was not a revision at all, but the development of an entirely new publication titled The College Handbook, for in fact there was no such publication in existence. What did exist was a publication entitled Terms of Admission to the Member Colleges, merely a compendium of formal statements of entrance requirements, totally uninformative as to the features, the programs, or the environment of the colleges listed, presented with all the refulgence and poetic sweep of catalog prose—in short, incredibly dull and forbidding.

The Board's own staff came to full realization of the problem in trying to use the publication in some informal student advising and decided to attempt a revision. The assistance of Eugene S. Wilson of Amherst College and Mary E. Chase of Wellesley College was enlisted, and they were asked to write two-page statements about their colleges, presenting, in any form or order desired, the requirements, costs, attractive features, makeup of freshman classes, scholarship and admissions procedures, and any other information they wished to include, always having regard to the space limitation. The excellent papers that resulted from this exercise were accepted as evidence that a useful revision of the volume *could be achieved, and all the member institutions were asked to assist in the task. The Amherst-Wellesley papers were used as models and circulated. The assembled papers, carefully edited (which in some cases meant substantial rewriting by Board staff), with pertinent College Board information added and an introduction in the form of a general discussion of college choice and college entrance, were put in an attractive format and sold at a modest price set to cover costs.*

The actual result was the appearance of a new medium of communication between colleges, schools, and students. A good many colleges that did not have access to the medium hastened to obtain it by joining the Board. The result was a marked increase in the rate of growth in membership. In time the size of the membership was to become a major issue, but in the early stages of growth the increase was a pleasant sign that days of uncertainty were ended.

The second excerpt deals with the production of a book that, seen from the standpoint of college entrance, may well have been the most influential book of the decade—Byron Hollinshead's Who Should Go to College.[5] *Its importance lay in the fact that it showed the possibility of a tremendous increase in college enrollments. It is fair to say that at this time no one, and this included Mr. Hollinshead, foresaw the extent of the enrollment increase, but at the time it was so well hidden that such prescience was probably beyond any reasonable expectation.*

"Looking Ahead"
51st Annual Report of the Director. New York: College Entrance Examination Board, 1951, 80 pp., pp. 20–22.

In each of the last three reports of the director, the final paragraphs have, under the heading "The Future of the Board," discussed certain of the Board's problems and obligations. These discussions have made three main points.

1. That the Board as a testing organization must in the operation of its programs always meet and always seek to anticipate the needs of its users. This it must do in the knowledge that a policy of pushing research projects into new areas and of venturing into experimental forms of testing is the only possible policy for accomplishing these objectives, even though it may

---

5. New York: Columbia University Press, 1952, 190 pp.

sometimes seem costly by reason of inevitable percentage of negative results inherent in experimentation and willingness to try out new ideas.

2. That the Board must be alert to encourage broader use of its tests and services in the interests of making easier the transition from school to college, and of better matching of candidates and colleges. This, too, must be done in the knowledge that such encouragement will sometimes conflict with institutional policies or with sacred concepts in the field of testing, with consequent anguish and unhappiness to some of the Board's loyal supporters.

3. That the Board must maintain its position as a forum where questions of school and college relationships can be presented, discussed, clarified, and sometimes resolved—in brief, that it must be a main channel of communication between schools and colleges on matters of interest to both types of institutions.

With these points made and amplified, the heading "The Future of the Board" has now served its present usefulness and can be displaced temporarily by discussion of the specifics of work done and to be done.

It should be clear from the earlier pages of this report that a substantial part of the work of the past year, in the form of research projects and test development activities, has been directed toward meeting the first point, while another substantial part of the year's work, the revision of *The College Handbook* and the publication of the *College Board Review*, has been directed toward the second point.

As to the third point, which deals with the Board's role as a channel of communication between schools and colleges, it is necessary to say that while the need for such a channel is great, and while much of the Board's membership is aware of the need and wishes to meet it, the results in terms of actual fulfillment are considerably short of success.

So far, the attempts to meet the communication problem have turned upon the semiannual meetings, which have been considerably rearranged to provide more time for presentation and discussion of problems, but which are necessarily limited in effectiveness. Regional meetings have made their contribution, by no means negligible, but have also made it clear that no plan of meetings can of itself solve the problem.

The problem is itself elusive and undefined. Essentially, it begins with the fact that school–college relationships tend to focus on the individual passing from school to college. The result of this focus is the creation of a number of small overlapping communities of interest and understanding, consisting of (a) the colleges with which a given school may have good working relationships and (b) the schools with which a given college may have good working relationships. Viewed broadly, these communities of interest work very well in terms of their purpose of dealing with individual students, but since they are essentially ad hoc, subject to change, and ordinarily related to administrative rather than educational matters, they fall far short of constituting a scheme for joint study of such problems as subject-matter articulation, the choice of a college, and the rationale and operation of the admissions procedures. In fact, by their existence, they tend to inhibit the development of such a scheme, since satisfactory relationships within one of these small communities of interest obscure the absence of understanding between groups of colleges and groups of schools.

The solution of the problem depends on the understanding, knowledge, and ability of a relatively small number of college admissions officers and school guidance officers. The Board can make a direct contribution to it by organizing and supporting a series of seminars on problems, policies, and techniques in guidance and admissions. Specifically, it can enlist the aid of its member colleges to furnish classroom space and living facilities, can draw upon school and college administrators for the specialists to conduct concentrated courses in such important areas as the administration of admissions, the design and use of publications in admissions, the use of test scores in guidance and admissions, the guidance functions of the admissions officers, the training of admissions and guidance officers, and a host of other topics which almost instantly suggest themselves.

Such a series would recognize that admissions officers usually come to their work without benefit of any previous training in its intricacies, details, or relationships; that there is no existing manual or textbook on the subject which they can regard as authoritative; and that they must perforce learn their jobs by trial and error. The same statements are, in lesser degree, true of those secondary school teachers who take on college guidance assignments, though they do have a substantial literature to fall back on and can take courses in the general principles of guidance if not in their specific applications.

The question of the Board's willingness to expend its funds in the support of a series of such workshops has not been explored. However, there is every reason to believe that the support would be forthcoming were any member institution to come forward with an offer of facilities and an expression of interest in developing a plan for what would certainly be a most interesting experiment.

"Study for Commission on Financing Higher Education"
51st Annual Report of the Director. New York: College Entrance Examination Board, 1951, 80 pp., pp. 10–11.

During the year under review, the Board undertook, at the request and with the financial support of the Commission on Financing Higher Education, to study college attendance as an aspect of the utilization of human resources. Essentially, this study undertook to answer two questions: Who does go to college in America? Who should go to college in America?

Since a study of this magnitude indicated clearly implied demands on staff time which could not be met by the Board's officers, it was necessary to add to the staff an individual who would offer a combination of understanding of the organization and operation of both secondary and higher education with capacity for analysis and insight and a well-developed competence in expression. The Board was fortunate in finding such a person in Byron S. Hollinshead, president of Coe College, who joined the Board's staff in November 1950 and continued thereon until July 1951, when he transferred his activities to the Commission.

Mr. Hollinshead's analysis of the problem (which is to be published in 1952) is already familiar to Board members to whom he has reported both verbally and in writing, but the point he makes is so important to all who are responsible for the direction of education that it not only bears but virtually requires repetition in condensed form.

Briefly, Mr. Hollinshead points out that (a) our college population is drawn to a large extent from an intellectually superior group, and to a lesser extent from a group that can best be described as on the borderline between superior and average in ability; (b) these two groups now utilize substantially all of the facilities for higher education in America, and most of the scholarship funds available to help needy students; (c) in addition to the superior students now going to college, there is an equally large group of students of comparable ability not now going to college; (d) it is customary to assume that able students who do not go to college fail to do so by reason of lack of finances, from which usually follows the assumption that a large increase in the amount of scholarship help available is the only possible solution for utilization of college abilities; (e) studies of reasons for noncollege attendance by able students indicate lack of motivation as the primary reason for not entering college, with lack of opportunity (which includes lack of finance) as a secondary reason.

From his findings Mr. Hollinshead concludes that while the commonly prescribed panacea of increased scholarship funds would increase college attendance, it would do it in a haphazard way and without significant increase in the number of superior-ability students attending college unless the administration of the funds were combined with changes in our approach to the problem of identification of ability and motivation for college. In short, Mr. Hollinshead points out that the problem is guidance, not money, a problem with which the Board is already working, although much of our work in this field has been secondary to our main effort of testing for college admissions. Mr. Hollinshead's finding is, in effect, a suggestion that this secondary effort is as important as our present main effort, a suggestion which is surely the most important educational idea to come before the Board in recent years.

---

*T*he *1951 Report of the Director included, as an appendix, a report on three weeks spent in Great Britain in February 1951, visiting English and Scottish schools and universities in a frantic round of travel. It was a difficult time—austerity was heavy on the land, food was still rationed, and heat was even scarcer than usual. The value of the trip lay, I think, in the realization that tight control of all standards by universities might result in admirable standards, but would also produce and perpetuate a closed system.*

As one outcome of the trip we tried an interchange of examinations with one of the English examining boards. It proved, in the upshot, very little except that English examinations required highly specific preparation. In a longer-term outcome, it established a relationship with the English examining system, which has been a most pleasant one over a good many years and has certainly played some part in the development in English university entrance procedures since 1960.

"Visit to England"

51st Annual Report of the Director. New York: College Entrance Examination Board, 1951, 80 pp., pp. 23–30.

The purpose of my trip to England was to compare the university entrance examination system of England (and Scotland) with our College Board examinations. This, I found, was perfectly possible but amounted to oversimplifying the matter. In my desire to establish firm bases for comparison, I kept broadening my inquiries and activities until I ended up by trying to compare examining and university entrance procedures in England with examining and college entrance procedures in this country. This, of course, was a much larger job than could possibly be accomplished in three weeks, so there are necessarily gaps in the report.

The widest gap is in my information on the operation and attitude of secondary schools. Much of my information on these points is secondhand, albeit from excellent sources. The rest of my information as used here is the result of my questioning, reading, or observations.

British and American higher education

Although it is hard to see how a comparison of English and American higher education can be brief, it is equally hard to imagine a discussion of examinations which was not prefaced by such a comparison. Hence it must be attempted.

The important contrast between British and American higher education is as to percentages of population. The British, according to some figures compiled by Sir Godfrey Thomson, offer higher education to about 3.75 percent of the population. We offer it to about 15 percent. The British accept national obligation to identify all of this upper group and educate them and, at need, supply the funds to a striking amount—60 percent of all university-supported funds, plus an even larger percentage of students receiving scholarships. Probably as much as 80 percent of the money involved in higher education in England comes from the government, counting both direct and student subsidy.

Naturally, the identification of ability is more rigorous than ours. Certainly the results, which show that very few English students fail to finish once they have entered university, are in striking contrast to our 50 percent attrition, taking the country as a whole. Obviously, this means that doubtful candidates are eliminated, no matter how small the doubt.

The purpose of English higher education is different rather than narrower or broader than ours. They seem to be educating scholars who will make their living as teachers or civil servants, with a sprinkling of other occupations. They also are training men for the established professions of law and medicine, as well as the developing profession of scientist. We, of course, are doing some of these things and many more besides, but we have not, until recently, thought of our liberal arts colleges as training grounds for civil servants, and have not for many years thought of them as having the training of teachers as a major task, though we have talked a lot about this latter function. On the other hand, we have gone farther in professional training, have carried nontechnical and nonspecialized education (our standard A.B.) farther than have the English, and have founded many specialized institutions to meet needs that in the British system are met below the university level.

The final important comparison is between our secondary schools. The British channel their able students in grammar schools on the basis of an examination given at age 11½–12. Students not passing these examinations are sorted into other types of schools not offering university preparation. We, of course, except for a relatively small number of private school students, carry all students through a common secondary school program which makes a university preparatory course available to all, regardless of ability. Of course not all can take it with profit, but we offer it widely; the British do not.

Once in grammar school, the British students follow a fairly traditional and rigorous program culminating in a series of examinations at age 16. These mark the end of all schooling for some, and of general schooling for all, in the grammar school line. Those trying for university then go on to two years of specialized study in their grammar school—the sixth form—after which they may take advanced examinations as the last preliminary to trying for university entrance. This is, of course, a feature that doesn't exist in our system and that is often misleading in attempts to compare credentials. This—to us—heavy and even odd specialization emphasizes the close tie between schools and universities.

The mean of standards for students in the university line seemed to me to be higher than our American mean as I know it. Their mean is, in general, about that maintained by the top one-third of our student population, which is, of course, about the right figure—since we are dealing with about 15 percent of an age group while they deal with about 5 percent. The matter of standards is complicated by the difference in method of presentation. They teach more narrowly, in terms of the academic spectrum, than do we, but more intensively. This has a masking effect, sometimes confused with standards, since their students at almost any point in their education know more about some one area than do ours at the same point. Nevertheless, I believe that our students *of equal ability* are as well taught as theirs and as well supplied with the materials and equipment of education. Here, of course, I must draw a kindly veil over quite a lot of our colleges that do not attract, and are not equipped to deal with, students of superior ability.

The examinations

I consider that the one outstanding thing I learned in England was that another system of entrance examinations, completely different from ours— and indeed from anything ours has been within recent memory—could exist and operate to the apparent satisfaction of all concerned. This was interesting, even surprising, because on all points which we consider to be proper criteria for examination construction, their examinations differ from ours. They are constructed on different concepts of validity and reliability, their construction methods and their reading methods are looser than ours, there are fewer safeguards for the individual student in terms of care of accuracy of marks, the quantity of examinations is much greater than we administer to any student, and the student's choice among questions is much greater than anything we employ. Finally, the examinations are more or less under university control, which means that they are instruments for the university supervision of the secondary curriculum.

Detailed discussion of these points of difference follows.

A. Validity and reliability. We define validity as an expression of degree of relationship between results on an examination and results of later examination in the same field. In other words, if the test is a predictor, how good a predictor is it? We define reliability as an expression of the degree to which we can rely on the test as a consistent measure.

In their test construction and analysis, the English do, of course, concern themselves with both accuracy and consistency of measurement, but this concern expresses itself differently. For example, their tests all have high face validity, that is to say, they are closely related to the subject being tested. They do not employ narrow or restricted tests which have been proved empirically to be good predictors.

For their reliability, which, considering all the variables in essay testing, must be fantastically low, they rely upon serried batteries of tests, going on the theory that a number of tests, however low their individual reliabilities and validities, are bound en masse to present a reasonably fair picture of a candidate. And that, be it emphasized, is all they are looking for.

B. Examination construction. Examination construction is usually in the hands of two-man committees, one from the school and one from the university, with a third man of experience and wisdom acting as reviewing agent and moderator. Examiners are trained, if at all, by apprenticeship. Examinations are not pretested. Efforts are made to equalize item difficulty and to avoid all the more obvious pitfalls of essay-type construction. An inspection of the tests and talks with the examiners lead to the conclusion that the tests are good ones of their kind.

C. Reading. Reading of English examinations—scripts, as they are called— is under the general supervision of the men who constructed the examinations. They engage, directly or indirectly, a number of assistant examiners who will be responsible for the actual reading. The examiners work with these men in the setting of a standard and then turn over to them the finishing of the job. This is usually, as I understand, done by the men in their own homes or offices, which is of course a contrast to our method of having all reading done in one place and under constant supervision. As reading is completed, the scripts are returned to a central office. So far as I could determine, there was no procedure for the kind of check reading that the Board used to do—that is, reading of all marginal and all superior papers, continuous sampling, and so forth.

On the other hand, the English spend a good deal more time than we do in making adjustments of entire groups and in rechecking the performance of selected individuals. The group adjustments are of two kinds: first, adjustment of the passing grade to bring the percentage of passes into conformity with the percentages adhered to (a) in the past, and (b) in other examinations in the current series. (This is not to say that at all times a fixed percentage of pass or fail is assured, but merely to point out that these percentages are kept fairly consistent.) The second form of group adjustment is with respect to schools. The assumption is made that performances of pupils of individual schools should remain fairly consistent. Therefore, when a group from a given school deviates from the established record of the school, the papers for the entire group are reread before the new record is accepted.

The rechecking of individual performances is done for several quite distinct reasons. First, as indicated, papers may be reread by school groups, as a check on school performance; second, individual papers may be reread when the candidate's performance on one examination is markedly different from his achievement on others; third, the schools may initiate requests for rereading on candidates who have failed to live up to expectations; and fourth, papers may be reexamined when awards or certificates based on an individual's total performance may be affected by a higher grade.

It is worth noting that reading is apparently done rapidly and that reader unreliability, halo effect, and other ills are, like the tobacco tax, accepted as inevitable evils.

D. *Protection for students.* The point has been sufficiently made that by our standards the individual examinations are deficient as to reliability and validity, that they are read in such a fashion as to accentuate these deficiencies, and that the saving grace for the individual is, in theory, that a number of tests, whatever their individual deficiencies, will en masse present a reasonably fair picture of a candidate. The question is then as to whether this saving grace exists. Essentially, the answer is that it probably does. While we are much concerned with the abstractions of reliability, validity, reader reliability, accuracy of computation, and so forth, the English are able, by reason of smallness of groups, to concern themselves with individuals. Thus, as indicated in the previous section, an individual's total record is scanned, and the reason for any inconsistency is reviewed. Similarly, if he is on the border of any important group, that is, a pass for the entire series, or qualification for a government scholarship, he is assured of special and individual consideration. Basically, then, the protection for the individual student is not in the procedures, but in the knowledge of him as an individual. For some this is the best of all protections; for others, probably, woefully inadequate.

E. Quantity of examinations. The total number of examinations taken by a student who completes all requirements for admission to the university of his choice is impressive. These examinations divide themselves into three groups:

1. Grammar school entrance. This is a short series of examinations taken by children between the ages of 11 and 12. It consists ordinarily (there is no fixed pattern) of (a) an intelligence test, (b) an arithmetic test, (c) an English vocabulary test. Ordinarily, all tests are objective. Students are screened for grammar school admission on the basis of test scores plus some other criteria (which vary from place to place) such as age and academic promise. Ordinarily this series is the only path for grammar school entry, but there are two others. The first is entry into one of the independent schools which will admit on a lower standard than the tax-supported schools. (Not all independent schools will do this.) The second is by taking advantage of a provision for later crossover into the grammar schools. A few, usually exceptional cases, are permitted so to do.

2. University entrance. After 1952, university entrance will require a minimum of five examinations: English, a language other than English, mathematics or science, and two subjects at an advanced level.

3. Advanced examinations. Over and above the minimum entrance requirements, a number of universities require either of all candidates, or of candidates in certain departments, or of candidates for individual colleges, or of candidates for scholarships or bursaries, one or more examinations taken at either the advanced level or at the higher scholarship level. Such examinations uniformly come at the end of the sixth form, as contrasted with the examinations for minimum university entrance, most of which come at the end of the fifth form.

The place of the examinations in the university system

In my original notes, my heading for this section was the phrase "Reasons why the system works," and this is still its theme, although the wording has been recast to keep it in line with the other headings.

The main thing that struck me about grammar school and university education—and it must be recognized that my views were colored by the fact that many of the people I talked with were professional administrators, that all the teachers I met were at least part-time administrators, and that I met no students—was that it was controlled by an interest in scholarship for its own sake. Emphasis, I felt, was always upon ability as a scholar— no doubt this includes much of the personality judgment that we tend to make separately—and the development of this ability was an end in itself. As I have indicated, I think I may have been, by those I met, unintentionally led a little too far into this conclusion, but after 17 years of inspecting colleges for accreditation, I don't think I could have been completely fooled, even intentionally, as to the trend of their program. Therefore, I set this interest down as a prevailing and, I think, controlling characteristic of the English higher education line (in which I include the grammar schools).

Given this interest, I think the entire system with its array of examinations works, despite its defects by our standards, because it is a closed system. Everyone in it—teacher, headmaster, school inspector, fellow, tutor, master, lecturer, examiner, registrar, and vice chancellor—is a product of the system. They live within it and they perpetuate it. Their standards are about the same, and they know what will be expected of those whom they produce and send on up to the next echelon.

Here, it struck me, is one of the most profound differences between the two national programs of higher education. In our program I have, for my own amusement, identified at least seven different types of higher institutions granting the A.B. degree, each having arrived at this degree through its own development and for its own purposes. They are:

1. The large independent universities whose entire program is built around the concept of a liberal arts degree with a minimum of professional studies.

2. The older state universities following much the same philosophy as the independent universities.

3. The land grant colleges and the newer state universities, building their curriculums around the useful arts, the quasi-professions, and the professions, offering an A.B. out of the surplusage of courses not required in professions.

4. The church-related smaller colleges operating as local institutions,

offering a modified or attenuated A.B. of the type offered by the large independent universities.

5. The Catholic colleges, offering an A.B. degree derived from the *Ratio Studiorum* with heavy religious overtones.

6. The teachers' colleges recently arrived at collegiate status, offering a degree heavily laden with professional education.

7. Municipal colleges, state colleges, grown-up junior colleges, and other tax-supported institutions with a local clientele, offering A.B. degrees with a strong vocational tinge.

This system pretty obviously is different from a system that was molded essentially by the Cambridge-Oxford pattern and is still dominated by that pattern, even though the dominance is not as marked (so I gather) as it once was.

In our country we have only barely arrived at a common understanding of what an A.B. represents in terms of entrance requirements, graduation requirements, and resources that must underlie the offering. In England this understanding has existed for a long time and pretty much without change.

It is not only the fact that the contrast between the two systems is so striking, but the further fact that any one of the seven types of institutions mentioned in our program, and some not mentioned, may place graduates on any rung of our teaching or administrative hierarchy. For example, our tax-supported secondary schools are in some parts of our country staffed by teachers who have no personal experience of the type of college work for which they are preparing their pupils. In such a situtation, there is simply not the community of understanding that prevails in English education. Perhaps there will be in another 25 years, but that is another story.

As a result of the English community of understanding, a program of examinations that would in our country set off a chain of teachers' strikes is accepted in their country as regular and ordinary. The teachers passed through it themselves. So can their pupils. This is another way of saying that English examinations are accepted as part of the normal pattern of instruction.

I can sum up my comments on English examinations by saying that they served, by my finding, three purposes. First, they serve as checkpoints to insure university control over university preparatory instruction. Second, they serve as selective devices to parcel out those who *may not* come up to university standards. Third, they are instructional devices. There is no pretense that they are "taken in stride" as the Board says that its examinations should be, but in fact they are, since all students are routinely prepared for them.

By way of postscript, I must add that I hope the Board will see fit to authorize more travel of this sort for more of its officers and committee chairmen. It is logical that the Board should acquire information on other systems of university entrance, and in such acquisition three weeks of visiting outvalues a dozen books. Specifically, I think English secondary schools should be visited, something I was unable to accomplish, and at least one continental system should be viewed at first hand.

Note: It will be of particular interest to those who fostered the General Composition Test to learn that the English professional examiners are aware of the experiment and are following it with interest.[6]

---

6. The reference in the last paragraph to the General Composition Test touches on an attempt to develop an essay examination that would be a genuine test of ability in English composition. The Board began its efforts in 1949 and put the examination into its program in 1951. It was dropped in 1956. The idea did not exactly fail, but it made slow headway. Part of the difficulty was due to the implacable hostility toward the idea shown by the members of the staff of Educational Testing Service who had to administer it, part to the total lack of interest (with a half dozen exceptions) the colleges showed in the examinations. It is ironical that within two years after its discontinuance, a hue and cry from member colleges, led by several college and university presidents who could profitably have taken time to learn better, forced on the Board, over the strong protests of the professional staff, an intellectually indefensible monstrosity called the "Writing Sample." This continues to plague candidates and schools as of this writing.—*F.B.*

The following paper was an accident. It resulted from the fact that Dael Lee Wolfle, who had written America's Resources of Specialized Talent,[7] was unable to go to a meeting and, for reasons never satisfactorily explained to me, suggested that I be invited to submit the memorandum that he had been asked to prepare. (He showed good judgment. The memorandum took two weeks out of my vacation.) The purpose of the meeting was to explore the need for a national scholarship program to attract students into science.

My memorandum[8] was an attempt to estimate what would happen if our educational system continued at its present pace and with its present program. I was genuinely surprised when it attracted attention, for I considered myself a rank amateur in the field.

The meeting itself was exploratory, and I do not recall that any findings, decisions, or recommendations came out of it. However, it is interesting to note that the individuals who were at the meeting and the organizations represented there were all sooner or later involved in a series of actions that did affect the future supply of scientists.

A partial listing of these actions follows.

1. John Stalnaker, who had been serving as a consultant to The Ford Foundation, became president of the National Merit Scholarship Corporation, established by The Ford Foundation.

2. The National Science Foundation made substantial contributions to the improvement of facilities for science teaching.

3. The National Science Foundation contracted with the College Board to study the question of whether or not scholarship programs would affect the career choices of secondary school students. The question was not answered with a clear yes or no and can never be. On the whole, the probability is that out of career choices made by a random sample of 100 students, about half will be random—that is, determined essentially by trivialities and accidents. About half will be influenced to a greater or lesser degree by parents, schools, and the general press of the public evaluation of careers. Whatever influence scholarship

7. *America's Resources of Specialized Talent: A Current Appraisal and a Look Ahead.* The report of the Commission on Human Resources and Advanced Training. New York: Harper & Brothers, 1954, 318 pp.

8. This memorandum appeared in several versions. The one given here is a revision of the original draft.

programs may have will be exerted on this half of the group, which means that they have less influence than some would choose to believe.

4. The contract with the College Board produced a book published by the Board in 1956 by Charles C. Cole Jr. (now dean of Lafayette College), entitled Encouraging Scientific Talent. *As part of the preparation of that book, the Board contracted with Educational Testing Service for a series of studies on talent utilization, which provided the first actual quantification of what was shortly popularized as "talent wastage," or "talent loss," referring to the individuals with college-level ability who did not enter college.*

5. The College Board within less than two years established its Commission on Mathematics, which pointed out the need for major revisions in the secondary curriculum in mathematics and put forward the recommendations on the basis of which revisions were eventually initiated.

"The Future Supply of Scientists"

This paper is the amplification of a memorandum entitled "The Future Supply of Scientists," prepared in August 1953 for presentation at a conference called by the National Science Foundation to discuss the need for a broad program of undergraduate scholarships for prospective science students. Published in *The Educational Record*, Vol. 35, April 1954, pp. 108–113.

In order to discuss the future supply of scientists properly, it is first necessary to define the terms "scientist" and "future."

A "scientist," for the purposes of this paper, is defined in accordance with the reasoning used by R. H. Knapp and H. B. Goodrich in *Origins of American Scientists*[9] as one qualified to practice as a professional scientist by virtue of the possession of a Ph.D. degree in one of seven fields: physics, chemistry, biology, mathematics, geology, astronomy, psychology. This criterion is also suggested in the recently published book *A Policy for Scientific and Professional Manpower* by the National Manpower Council.[10]

9. Chicago: University of Chicago Press, 1952, 450 pp.

10. New York: Columbia University Press, 1953, 263 pp.

It should be noted that this definition will exclude a number of individuals who will practice as professional scientists—that is, who will teach, carry on research, or administer scientific programs even though they do not hold the Ph.D. But the number excluded by this definition will probably just about balance the number of Ph.D. holders in science who will not practice as scientists, so the criterion remains a reasonable one, at least until proven otherwise by studies based on careful samplings.

The "future" we can define as the next 20 years. Within this span we can be fairly confident that present trends and present or projected facilities will control the production of scientists. We also know the size of the population with which we deal, for all of it is now on earth. Beyond 20 years—that is, after 1973—we have no facts on which we can base judgments.

Having established these definitions, we come to the first question: What is the size of the supply of human resources from which scientists will be drawn?

The basic figure here is the size of the age group. Some confusion may arise from the fact that references to college entrants and college graduates are based on the 18-year-old age group while references to graduate students and doctoral candidates are based on the 22-year-old age group. If these facts are kept in mind, the statistics are not too formidable.

In 1951–52 the 18-year-old age group numbered 2,114,000. Of this number 1,186,000, or 56.1 percent, graduated from high school. Of this number 436,000, or 34.7 percent, entered college, representing 19.5 percent of the age group. We can expect that 265,000, or 64 percent, of this entering group will graduate from college, constituting 12.6 percent of the 22-year-old age group. The number of this group receiving doctor's degrees can be estimated at from 5,300 to 6,000—not less than 2 percent, nor more than 2.3 percent, of college graduates.

For the group who will be 18 in 1969–70 the figures are different. There will be 3,364,000 in this age group, of whom 2,583,000, or 70.5 percent, will graduate from high school, and 912,000 will enter college. This number is 35.3 percent of all high school graduates—not a great increase over the percentage figure cited for 1951–52, but constituting, because of the increase in number of high school graduates, 24.9 percent of the age group. We can expect 656,000 college graduates from this group, and about 16,000

Ph.D.s, a figure which will represent not less than 2.4 percent of the college graduates.

Although the tendency is to focus upon the great increase in the size of the age group as the determining factor in the increase in the number of Ph.D.s, the fact is that it is the percentage increases in high school graduation, college attendance, college graduation, and graduate school attendance which can be expected to make the big difference. Proof of this can be found by applying the 1951 percentages to the 1969 age group. It will be found that the maximum Ph.D. output in 1975 using this combination of figures and percentages would be 9,600, as compared with the minimum of 16,000 predicted for 1975 on the basis of a projection of present trends.

Out of this welter of statistics we emerge with two facts that are significant to us—that in 1957 we can expect a production of 6,000 Ph.D.s, and in 1975 we can expect 16,000. Note that this sizable increase in the group is the product of a series of small percentage increases acting upon an age group which will have increased slightly more than 50 percent.

Our next question is: How many of these will be scientists? Here we have one gloriously firm statistic. In 1952, 7,683 doctoral degrees, exclusive of M.D.s and other professional doctorates, were granted, of which approximately 4,200 were in scientific fields. In other words, about 55 percent of all doctor's degrees are in one of the science fields. If we apply this figure to our 16,000 projected for 20 years hence, we come out with 8,800.

This is, of course, a series of assumptions based on trends as now identified. Is there any possibility that these assumptions will need to be modified? Yes, a good deal. In order to examine this possibility, we need to consider several factors.

First, we now draw on 490 colleges, universities, and technical schools for our scientists. Most of the doctoral training is now done in 60 institutions. Much of what has been forecast depends upon (a) the ability of these 490 institutions to handle the additional load of students, or (b) our ability to foster institutional mitosis and develop new undergraduate institutions (every new institution is built out of parts of existing institutions), and (c) the ability of graduate schools to take more students. None of these abilities has yet been certified to. The problem of undergraduates is more nearly solvable than the problem of graduate work. Basic structures now exist for development of 100 or more colleges, which, if developed, would be capable of producing graduates who would be potential doctoral candidates.

To put it another way, these institutions have either already been established in some form or will be established, either by separation from existing institutions or developing entirely new institutions in new population centers, as, for example, the almost unavoidable certainty that the concentration of scientific talent at Los Alamos, Hanford, and Oak Ridge will bring about the development of degree-granting institutions serving these communities. Whether they have been established or will be established, they can be expected to develop into undergraduate institutions granting bachelor's degrees in science fields.

On the other hand, there are no signs that any substantial development of new graduate schools is to be expected. There will be some institutions which will move into master's-level work, and a few more which are now on the master's level and are offering a few doctor's degrees that may expand their present programs, but with three or four exceptions none of these now appears to have the resources, the faculty, or the leadership to move into full-scale doctoral work with, for example, the potential that Duke University offered 25 years ago. At the most, 10 of the institutions now doing good graduate work on a small scale may be able to move up to the level of large-scale graduate work. Significantly, there are no tax-supported institutions that appear to fall into this category, perhaps because this expansion has been channeled into development of professional schools and other activities of a technical or even a technological nature, rather than into strengthening the arts and sciences.

Parenthetically, it may be noted that the present concern over increasing scholarship funds and bringing more able students into college has pretty well avoided the question of providing instructional facilities. In other words, we have not figured out what to do if our present plans work. If they do work, we may find ourselves in the position of the congregation that gathered one day to pray for rain, but did not bring umbrellas.

Second, there is a marked tendency for the scientific profession to increase at the expense of two professional groups: the teachers and an oddly assorted combination that Eli Ginzberg calls "arts, letters, and entertainment."[11] Should this trend continue, two things will happen: there will be fewer teachers for our pupils, and possibly a larger proportion of pupils in science. Any hope that this trend may cut down the number of television entertainers is probably illusory.

Third, we may find some way to tap our reserve and make a still further increase in the number of college graduates and hence of potential doctoral candidates. It is very doubtful that we will be successful in doing this as a result of conscious effort. We are dealing here largely with motivation. Motivation based on social status, or on family obligation, or on immediate opportunity is likely to be very difficult to change. Motivation which is determined by lack of financial resources can, of course, be changed. But any real change in college attendance which would affect either the numbers or the quality of the student group must and will come as a result of parent attitude, which so far has not been touched as a result of any direct efforts. However, it is obvious that such a change is now taking place even as we worry about the fact that it is not. A recent remark by an experienced school visitor that the number of able students who get to college despite school guidance efforts and college recruiting efforts is surprisingly large, may have a wry sound, but it reflects the fact that it is the home, not the school, which sends people to college. The change is the result of social and economic events, not educational planning, and it is slow moving. It is also cumulative. By 1970 it will have had a good deal of effect. As a result of this change, the percentage of the age group attending high school is increasing steadily, the percentage of high school graduates entering college is increasing, though very slowly, the percentage of college entrants who graduate is increasing markedly (.3 percent a year), and the percentage of college graduates who go on to doctor's degrees is increasing. Each of these increases will take place concomitantly with population growth. In total, then, they amount to normal population trends multipled by an unexpected coefficient representing additional academic success of the age group. From these increases it may be concluded that there is a trend toward a net increase in the number of able students going to college. Since this can only be the result of a changing attitude toward education on the part of parents, we may expect further

___

11. National Manpower Council, *A Policy for Scientific and Professional Manpower.* New York: Columbia University Press, 1953, 263 pp.

increases over and above the figures quoted. These expectations have not been and cannot be quantified, but if realized they will result in groups larger than those estimated upon the basis of the percentages cited earlier. In other words, what we want to see done is taking place, and more of our better students go to college. Of course, we should also like to see the less able students dissuaded from entering college. This is not being done, and our ability to do it is questionable. But this side of the problem does not at the moment affect our central question.

Fourth, the necessary growth in institutional size may affect the number of scientifically oriented college graduates. Studies indicate that the best results in motivating students to follow science as a career come from liberal arts colleges drawing on semiagrarian areas in the Midwest and South. Population growth, industrialization, and college growth may change these areas and these colleges.

If we accept the proposition that the results to date are related to the types of institutions or the economy of the regions, it would be logical to assume that industrialization might actually reduce the number of prospective doctoral candidates. However, this proposition and the assumption based on it do not really make sense. It is far more sensible to rely on the quality of the students in those regions and to assume that if their opportunities are increased, their numbers will increase, and that the number of scientifically oriented college graduates will increase rather than decrease.

Fifth, the demands of the engineering profession may—since engineering and science training draw individuals with the same types of ability—reduce the number of potential doctoral candidates. The evidence to date is that there is little overlap between these areas. Interestingly, they also show that technological institutions as a group produce fewer potential scientists than arts colleges.

Sixth, recognizing that motivation for a career in science usually develops before college entrance, we may increase our group as an indirect result of changes in college curriculum. At present there is a considerable loss of potential science students who change direction after they enter college. Much of this change is healthy, but some of it is unquestionably a loss. At present, only one-fifth of those who possess doctoral ability actually go on to doctor's degrees (including medicine). This means that the colleges themselves are failing to provide stimulus for graduate study. Here, however, a caution must be observed. We cannot channel all of our able youth into graduate study. They are needed everywhere in our economy, and we must not tinker too much with their distribution. Allowing for this caution, it does seem probable that better undergraduate instruction would provide more scientists. However, note that a substantial number of this group are women, and that opportunities for employment of women scientists and the attractiveness of science as a career vis-à-vis marriage would both have to increase to bring about a marked change.

Seventh, military service may have an effect on science specialization. If we assume, as we must, that all physically fit male youth of $18\frac{1}{2}$ years of age or over will be called into military service during the period described at the outset as "the future," we must try to assess the results of this upon college. There are three factors to consider here.

A. The obligation—often called the threat—of military service affects the total college attendance by distracting some potential students from college attendance. We will grant that any student who can be so distracted is not strongly motivated. Nevertheless, there are some known and many unknown cases of minimally motivated individuals who have found their goals in or even after college and eventually performed well. All such individuals may not be irretrievably lost to higher education because they are called into service, but the chances are that most of them will be.

B. The operation of ROTC programs militates against science concentration. This has nothing to do with the fact that the ROTC is criticized, and sometimes justifiably so, on the grounds of academic nonrespectability and in many institutions does not attract the abler students. It is simply a matter of time distribution. The usual science major in college takes from three-fifths to three-fourths of his work in science fields and from one-fourth to two-fifths of his work in nonscience fields. But a full ROTC program requires from one-fifth to one-fourth of curricular time. This can only be taken at the expense of regular science or nonscience courses or both. In either case, the student emerges with a substandard preparation for graduate work in science. Furthermore, the ROTC orientation is toward military service. An extreme case in point is the Air Force, which of all our military services should be the most science-oriented, and yet has recently taken a stand which in effect states that the only orientation it will accept is toward pilot training. It may be argued that this stand will not inhibit the dedicated prospective scientist, but the argument is not a persuasive one despite the fact that the Air Force actually has a very liberal policy on education of its personnel. This policy unfortunately cannot affect those who did not elect to go into the Air Force.

C. The fact that military service must be done after the end of the college course if it is not done before unquestionably interrupts many graduate careers. The extent of this interruption can certainly be affected by the manner of the enforcement of the law, but administrative procedures cannot affect the standing fact of the obligation to serve and—considering the size of our age groups and the nature of the machinery for dealing with them—can probably never be flexible enough to deal satisfactorily with the problem. The only satisfactory solution lies in an approach to the problem which will recognize advanced study in specified fields as a form of national service comparable to military service, and this is, of course, an alternative which opens up a whole series of very serious problems which are not within the scope of these comments.

No one of the variables that have been mentioned is subject to statistical analysis. However, the fact that most of them, if they operate, will tend to increase the supply of scientists leads to the suggestion that the supply will in fact increase more rapidly than present projections indicate—if we can supply the facilities. And here it must be noted again that facilities are not markedly on the increase. As was commented earlier, there is reason to expect that there will be some expansion in the number of undergraduate institutions. But the expansion present or projected does not begin to keep pace with the growth of either primary or secondary school population, and, so far, there has been almost no expansion in the facilities of the independent colleges and universities that have made the heaviest contributions to the present supply of scientists. And, as pointed out, there has been no significant expansion on the graduate level.

It is worth commenting that the immediate result of failing to provide facilities for instruction in science will be a failure to provide teachers in science. This failure is already being felt in the secondary schools and is reflected in the fact that the science preparation of college freshmen is not, by general report, as good as it was 20 years ago. This shortage of science teachers was, of course, felt by the colleges during and immediately after the war. At present the condition is one of uneasy balance, but, as college student bodies expand, the balance will tip downward, unless it can be restored through measures not now in prospect. There is, of course, still another drain on the teaching profession in the form of governmental and private research agencies which tend to draw off research and administrative talent from all science fields. The results of all of these factors appear to promise an unfortunate downward spiral of fewer teachers teaching more students. If the promise is fulfilled, then all the trends that can be plotted will mean little or nothing in terms of the future supply of scientists.

To sum up: A population increase reflected in a 50 percent increase in the size of the age group should, in terms of current educational trends, result in a doubled supply of scientists within 20 years. Social trends which may result in more of the abler group going to college and in more of the able college graduates going into science may tend to increase this supply still further. Against these trends is the fact that no one can predict the results that may come from the downward spiral of fewer science teachers teaching more students. If this trend continues, the nature of our instruction in science is almost certain to change, and the change may reduce the numbers of potential science students. Finally, we have no present assurance that our higher education system will accommodate itself to the pressures of a larger group of science students. Our experience of 1945–50 indicates that the system may be flexible enough to work out the problem somehow, but this is not a very firm basis for optimism as to its ability to work out this more difficult problem.

This talk by Mr. Fels is included in this volume primarily because it was by him and is a very good specimen of his early work. It also deals with a plaguey subject. It is virtually impossible to get rid of a test, primarily because the existence of a test somehow certifies that a subject exists.

The larger point in the paper, that curriculums change with the times and the purposes of education, and that tests, too, should change, is not popular with teachers or administrators—either in schools, or colleges, or in the split world of guidance and admissions—who do not like to be disturbed. Hence, as a point, it is usually ignored.

"Who Calls the Tune?" by William C. Fels
Speech delivered October 23, 1953, at Rutgers University before the New Jersey Conference of Admissions Directors, Principals, and Counselors.

Karl Marx was a believer in the withering away of the state. (I hope in saying this that I have not exposed you to guilt by association. You can no longer deny that you were once in a room with a man who mentioned Karl Marx.) I am a believer, not in Karl Marx or the withering away of the state, but in the withering away of examinations. The trouble is that like General Douglas MacArthur's famous old soldiers, examinations never die. Like the state, they tend to become institutionalized, and, like the state, they resist withering with a remarkable tenacity.

The Greek Test of the College Entrance Examination Board is a fine example of persistence. In each recent year the whole elaborate mechanism of the College Board has ponderously revolved and turned out a test for 50 candidates. It is like dropping an atomic bomb on a mouse. The chief purpose of this test is the comparison and selection of candidates. Another is the placement of candidates in college courses. But as for selection, you and I know that the assembled classics departments of all American colleges would trek barefooted across Death Valley to carry these 50 Greek scholars, decked with laurel, to their colleges. And as for placement, a half hour's quiet talk in a professor's study would serve as well or better. Then why is this test retained? Two reasons have been advanced. The first is that candidates usually take Achievement Tests in three subjects they are studying in their senior year. If no Greek Test were offered, candidates might enroll for a tested subject in preference to a third or fourth year of untested Greek. It has been suggested that this possibility could be avoided by the colleges admitting, with only two Achievement Tests, candidates who offered Greek. But that suggestion conjured up fears that other less respectable subjects—driver training and baton twirling are the usual whipping boys—might follow the entering wedge.

The second reason is more substantial. It is the feeling that the College Board has somehow set the *Good Housekeeping* Seal of Approval on Greek, and to remove it would be to deliver the coup de grace to this language, which is not only dead but, what is more to the point, dying.

I happen to be a strong believer in the study of Greek. I have the respect of the ignorant for knowledge. So I would not want you to interpret my fun at the expense of the Greek Test as fun at the expense of Greek. I use the example of the Greek Test to illustrate a point: that a test does not sustain a subject; a subject sustains a test. If a test could sustain a subject, Greek would be a popular one, for it was among the earliest tested and has been tested almost continuously by the Board for 50 years or more. Any one of the modern languages, except Spanish, could equally well be used as an example. Though their cases are not as desperate, all are declining in enrollment numerically and proportionately. Spanish is growing numerically but declining proportionately.

A corollary to the proposition that a test does not sustain a subject is that a subject does not need a test to sustain it. Music and art are examples. Without the support of tests these subjects have been undergoing a remarkable and healthy growth in the secondary schools.

Subjects enter and depart from the curriculum not according to the whims of testers or the demands of educators but according to the needs and aims of society. Tests and college requirements can tug at the heels or get in back and push a little, but they cannot long run counter to the aims and needs of the culture and survive. Subjects must have a cultural vitality of their own. When music and art teachers yearn for tests or college requirements in their subjects they should think on the unhappy teacher of Greek, with his test, and rejoice in their own well-being.

Again a caveat: I do not mean that our culture does not need contact with the language and culture of Greece. I do think it is true to say it has more pressing demands for the time of most of its youngsters when they are in secondary school. The virtual disappearance of Greek and the decline of language study in the secondary schools does not necessarily mean that they are suffering an equal decline in other levels of the educational system.

The curriculum is never at rest, for society is never at rest. Subjects enter and leave the curriculum, move downward from college to school and upward from school to college. Our American curriculum has passed through three principal stages. From 1636 to 1745, for over 100 years, the curriculum was essentially static and the only entrance requirement was Latin. In the second stage, which lasted roughly from 1745, when Yale first required mathematics for entrance, to about 1900, one new subject after another was introduced into the college course and then pushed downward from the college to the secondary school. In the third period, from 1900 to 1953, the schools, coping with the democratization of secondary education, pushed these subjects back to the colleges, while they themselves introduced new subjects. The collegiate cries of agony that the schools were not preparing the students properly and that the colleges were having to do the work of the schools were the verbal marks of this period. The fourth period, on the verge of which we now stand, will, like the second, be one of pushing subjects down from the colleges to the schools. The School and College Study of Admission with Advanced Standing and the School and College Study of General Education, both sponsored by the Fund for the Advancement of Education, are the standard-bearers of this fourth period. The battle cry is "Enrichment!"

Without tracing the mutations of society that have brought about these curricular pendulum swings, it is enough to reflect on how ill-suited the theologically oriented curriculums of colonial days would be to students preparing for the technically oriented world of today. And yet there were values in this curriculum which we retain because their importance remains. A technically oriented world is not a world which can afford to be devoid of humane and spiritual values.

There is another pendulumlike movement of the curriculum: a movement toward stability followed by a movement away from it. For the past 50 years we have gone through two swings, and we are now on the third. At the turn of the century there was an almost chaotic diversity, a sometimes capricious and often niggling individuality. From the establishment of the College Board to an indefinable date between the two world wars the pendulum swung toward unity. From that date until the late 1940s it swung toward diversity. Now it is swinging back toward a new synthesis.

These swings of the pendulum receive their impetus from the ever evolving attempts of our democratic educational system to meet the changing needs of our people and our times. The constant recurrence of initiation and consolidation in education reflect, but do not always exactly accompany, social initiation and consolidation. Rather they follow it with a noticeable and almost measurable lag.

The tester is not free to start or stop these great pendulum swings, but he tinkers with the clock. In times of change one set of tools is forced into his hands; in times of consolidation, another. Syllabuses, definitions of requirements, sale of old examinations, and essay tests with their limited subject-matter coverage are the tools of consolidation. Testing without syllabuses or definitions of requirements, secure administration, and objective tests with their wide subject-matter coverage are the tools of change. We do not choose the tools; we find them in our hands.

The adjustment of the curriculum to social aims and needs is accompanied by similar adjustments within the narrower confines of individual subjects. At the moment there is hardly a secondary school subject which is not undergoing changes. The languages are shifting from an emphasis on the written to an emphasis on the spoken word.

Mathematics is moving in two directions: toward programs leading to its use in liberal studies and toward programs for its practical applications.

Both shifts are being accompanied by a reorganization of subject matter. The sciences are incorporating new knowledge and coalescing. The physics course is going several layers deeper into the atom. The chemistry course is giving new emphasis to organic compounds. Biology, like mathematics, is changing in two ways: toward a humanistic approach, and away from it toward a chemical approach. The social studies are giving new importance to American history, problems of democracy, world history, the Orient, anthropology, and sociology. The older alignment of ancient history, medieval and modern history, American history, and English history is far less common. English literature, while not abandoning *Hamlet*, has left *Silas Marner* far behind.

Are these the effects of changes in testing? Quite the contrary. The testers are hard put to keep up with them. The cardinal principle of teaching and testing is not to teach what is being tested; it is to test what is being taught.

But I would not want to give the impression that testing merely tags along uselessly after social and educational change. It has its important role in effecting it. A program such as that of the College Board has all the usual secondary purposes: The tests serve as an incentive for students, and to a certain extent for teachers. The examinations enable institutions to set and to maintain standards. They are useful for guidance, selection, and placement. But their most important role is social. They make possible that mobility in society which is so necessary to a democracy. They make it possible for students from one part of the country to go to college in another—horizontal mobility. And through the use of tests in scholarship programs, vertical mobility, from class to class, is facilitated insofar as this is effected by education and environment.

In designing testing programs to achieve social aims, we must not overlook their secondary characteristics: time of testing, frequency of testing, length of testing, convenience of testing, cost of testing. Here, too, a testing program can be tailor-made to be inexpensive, brief, convenient, and frequent—hence democratic. Or it may be made expensive, long, inconvenient, and infrequent—hence aristocratic or plutocratic. The College Board has in its time provided good examples of both.

Currently the College Board has in its testing program or its research and development program a whole gamut of tests from the preliminary level to the level of advanced placement. Each is designed to serve some discernible social and educational trend. But which of these tests will be used and which will be stillborn is not within our vision, or in our hands.

To a certain extent, of course, teachers and educational administrators will influence the decisions that are made, but they are the interpreters of the music. It is not they who pay the piper.

The answer to the question which is the title of my paper is, after all, what it always has been. "He who pays the piper calls the tune."

The short paper that follows was prepared from notes I used as a member of a panel appearing before a section meeting within the annual meeting of the Southern Association of Colleges and Secondary Schools.

Its chief interest lies in discussion of the advanced placement activity, which had not yet become an examination program although work had begun preliminary to setting examinations.

It is important to remember that the Advanced Placement Program began outside the College Board and that Gordon Keith Chalmers, president of Kenyon College, its prime mover, opposed its transfer to the Board. Indeed, the Board was not enthusiastic about taking it, though it did so in 1955, owing primarily to the persuasiveness of William Fels, who saw it as very important in the kind of changing educational world we were predicting. He was, of course, right, though its most immediate developments were thumping deficits which continued until the Program was put on a quasi-realistic basis several years later.

The idea put forward in the talk was a feeble alternative to the Program that evolved under Board direction. It is just as well that it was never heard of again.

Memorandum based on a talk given at Memphis, Tennessee, on December 2, 1953, before the Southern Association of Colleges and Secondary Schools.

The Fund for the Advancement of Education has during the past three years sponsored three different projects directed toward some degree of what is called acceleration of education—which, curiously enough, is actually compression, since it aims to compress the present eight-year total of secondary school and college into seven.

The first of these projects, the Pre-Induction Scholarship Program, was originally planned to allow selected male students the opportunity to complete at least two years of college before being called for military service. It was then extended to cover a number of other institutions including women's colleges, in which, of course, the question of induction did not arise. Having run its appointed two-year course, it has now been discontinued.

The second project, the School and College Study of Admission with Advanced Standing, was planned originally to meet the strong secondary school protest against the Pre-Induction Scholarships and at the same time allow selected able students to move through the total school-and-college experience in less than eight years. After a year's intensive work, this study has defined itself as a project for the construction of a series of advanced examinations which can be used for the awarding of college credit, and is now proceeding to the construction of those examinations.

The third project, the School and College Study of General Education, developed as a product of a curriculum revision undertaken several years ago at Phillips Academy, Andover. It was not concerned with either compression or acceleration except as they might prove valid and desirable in furthering better education for the individual student. Its premise was that the schools could do more, particularly with able students, and that, if the colleges would recognize school achievement, the schools in turn could offer more intellectual opportunities to those same able students. The problem of the study group was essentially to set up an atmosphere of mutual trust as between school and college which would allow both parties to offer maximum opportunities to their students. This study group has been relatively inactive since its report, *General Education in School and College*, was published by Harvard University Press in 1952.

Since of the three projects the only one that is now active, and incidentally the only one that has aroused widespread interest as suggesting a possible operating procedure, is the School and College Study of Admission with Advanced Standing, this memorandum will be based on a discussion of it as a probable example of any plan for the allowance of college credit for secondary school work that might stand a reasonable chance of adoption.

The salient feature of this plan, as indicated earlier, is the development of a series of examinations to be administered to incoming freshmen for the purpose of determining placement in college programs and advanced credit. The examinations are to be constructed in terms of definitions of requirements that already have been tentatively agreed upon by committees representing faculties of 12 colleges and 27 schools. Examinations are being developed in 11 subject-matter fields.

The following are to be noted.

A. Previous attempts to grant college credit on the basis of examinations covering work not done in residence, have generally been ended by abandonment. A program of this nature was carried on for many years by institutions admitting on the College Board's "Old Plan" but was of course dropped in 1942, when the examinations of this type were abolished. It was never widely used and neither had, nor was intended to have, any deep educational significance. It was merely allowance of credit for work achieved in excess of entrance requirements. The Chicago Plan, which went a good deal further, set up its degree requirements entirely in terms of examinations which could be passed as rapidly as desired. Neither of these two programs ever achieved wide acceptance or support. The reasons are difficult to get at, but they are probably: (1) limited student interest in breaking out of the usual pattern, which is another way of saying that programs set up for brilliant students are likely to attract only brilliant students; (2) administrative cumbersomeness; (3) requirement on both school and college that they supply individual attention and special programs. Many institutions are not set up to do this, regardless of excellence of intention.

B. Previous examination programs based upon published definitions of requirements and supported by published examinations have been forced out of existence by secondary school protests. The College Boards as they existed between 1900 and 1942 are an example of this. By 1925, the date by which the Boards had accomplished their initial purpose of standardizing entrance procedures, the schools had begun to denounce the Board's control over secondary school curriculums exercised through the definitions of requirements and published examination papers. It is hard to see how any different attitude could in the long run be expected toward a revival of these control measures.

C. The awarding of credit or degrees partially or completely upon the basis of examinations is contrary to our educational practice and tradition and to the English tradition from which our colleges have developed. The principal objection to degree requirements stated in terms of examinations is that they tend to emphasize the minimum rather than the maximum achievement required for the degree and to remove the incentive for achievement in depth. In our English background, degrees rest upon two factors—a fixed minimum of residence and carefully evaluated achievement. So carefully is it evaluated that a double first in an Oxford or Cambridge B.A. is in England considered as the equivalent of our Ph.D. By contrast, those European degrees which are awarded on the basis of examinations only do not have a particularly high standing either in England or in this country, as for example in the fields of law and medicine.

D. Legal definitions, the standards of accrediting agencies, and the admissions practices of graduate and professional schools interpose serious barriers to such a program. While these must be noted, there is nothing much to say about them. They exist; any new program must deal with them.

It is also to be noted that:

E. This program is an affirmative step in emphasizing the educational continuity between school and college. This continuity, once a controlling factor in higher education, has in recent years been, to a great extent, lost. Its necessity needs to be reaffirmed and its existence reestablished.

F. This program offers to secondary schools the first definitive information they have had for some years on the content and requirements of college work. During the distant period when teachers of prospective college entrants were themselves college graduates, the understanding of the nature and requirements of liberal arts programs was taken care of automatically (as it still is in England). Today many, perhaps most, of the teachers in tax-supported high schools are graduates of teacher-training institutions and have had no experience with liberal arts colleges. They have, therefore, no experience that they can draw upon in advising their students or planning their programs.

G. The program offers a definite incentive to able secondary school students. This is so self-evident that it need not be discussed.

H. The program offers a method of avoiding college duplication of work that has already been covered. In doing so, it does not do anything different from what has been done for some years in some of our colleges, but this does not matter. It is still a good thing.

I. The program does not interfere with the normal time-limits of secondary school work. The principal advantage here is that it meets the objections of secondary school administrators who feel that their established residence requirements should not be disturbed. It should be noted that it also puts upon secondary schools the burden of proof that they can offer advanced work suitable for college credit and the reduction of college residence requirements. Again referring to England, be it noted university-level work is there routinely offered in secondary schools.

The success or failure of this plan will depend on the extent to which it can cope with the problems and objections that it raises while preserving its valuable features. As it stands, the plan combines the features of several plans that have, in the past, failed of acceptance. If these features (discussed in paragraphs A to D, above) can be eliminated while retaining its advantages (discussed in E to I, above), the basic idea could assume great importance. There is an excellent possibility that the plan may do just that.

There is a marked tendency for college admissions to move ever farther back into the secondary school experience. To all intents and purposes, most college admissions, at least to the country's leading independent colleges, are now granted upon the basis of the results of 11½ years of secondary schooling plus results of one or more tests. Informal assurances of admission are often given on the basis of 11 years of schooling plus test results. There would be very little strain, either intellectually or administratively, in moving formal assurances of admission back to the end of the eleventh year, a step which would be analogous to the English system of satisfying university matriculation requirements at the end of the fifth form. If this were done, our schools, like the English schools, could continue to hold their students in residence for the twelfth year (in England two years are often required for the Higher Certificate) and during that year could offer courses of college grade. The student who had been granted early admission and was fortunate enough to be in a school which could offer him advanced work could in college follow whatever procedure might be required by the college to establish his readiness to go on in advanced college courses. The college might or might not modify its residence requirements—the tendency would be toward such modifications —but the student would have avoided duplicating or repeating work already covered, the school would have been turned loose to do the best job it could do in teaching advanced work, and the college would have enjoyed the advantage of being able to separate, administratively, two completely different matters: the question of entrance, and the question of advanced placement with its attendant question of advanced credit.

The main requirement of such a plan is a memorandum of agreement between school and college whereby the school undertakes to guarantee that its twelfth-grade program for these selected students would be of a truly advanced nature, and the college guarantees that it will give due consideration to the evidences of accomplishment submitted by the student and attested by the school.

The plan does not, of course, eliminate the individual handling that has in the past proved so troublesome, but it puts it on a more sensible basis by allowing ample time for dealing with each case.

The plan does eliminate the imposition of a twelfth-year curriculum on the secondary school, which is the inevitable consequence of published definitions of requirements.

The plan also eliminates the cumbersomeness of a program of fixed examinations, which are at best based upon a series of compromises between schools and colleges and are therefore not fully acceptable to either party, and which under any circumstances would have to be administered through a central agency in order to provide security. It does so by throwing the examination responsibility onto the college, to be discharged by its own faculty and administration in terms of its own requirements.

The plan avoids the expense of a national organization for the sponsorship of the plan and for assuring the continuity of a national examination program. It is suited to regional and local groupings of schools and colleges, and can be entered into without expense. If it succeeds, as it should, the steps taken and the evidence of its success are clear. If it fails, the responsibility for failure can be ascertained and, it is hoped, remedied.

There can be no doubt that this is, as a plan, more radical than the one which is now being advanced. This, at least, is a positive merit, for it represents, therefore, experimentation in the truest sense of the word.

4. Commitment and Growth: 1954-1957

The four years from the beginning of 1954 to the end of 1957 were a time of great importance for the Board. During that period most of what are now the Board's major programs developed and came into general use.

The Advanced Placement Program was accepted as a Board activity in 1955.

The College Scholarship Service received its first trial in 1954.

The Colloquium on College Admissions was instituted in 1954.

The Scholarship Qualifying Test, forerunner of the Preliminary Scholastic Aptitude Test, was first administered in 1955 by ETS and adopted by the Board in 1956.

Encouraging Scientific Talent, by Charles C. Cole Jr., published by the Board in 1956, was the first book not directly related to the process of preparation and admissions to appear under the Board's imprint.

The Demonstration Guidance Project at New York City Junior High School 43, forerunner of the Higher Horizons program, was instituted in 1956, cosponsored by the Board of Education, the National Scholarship Service and Fund for Negro Students (with the support of the New York Foundation), and the College Board, and with an officer of the College Board serving on its steering committee.

It is not surprising that so many activities came out of the Board's organization, for it was a time of rapid enlargement of American education. The enlargement created new requirements and demands, many of which were within the Board's area of activity. Some, indeed, such as the entry into the field of financial aid, were for a time controversial, and others, such as the Advanced Placement Program, had a potential for controversy yet to come, but most of them were extensions of existing activities and fell into normal activity patterns. Out of them came increased membership and a whole gathering of problems relating to localities and regions, many of them coming down to the understanding and effective use of the Board's tests and publications.

The growing problems forced the Board into a new form of organization with trustees instead of an executive committee, and a president instead of a director. In time, the new organization created regional offices to deal with problems too detailed and, in a sense, too immediate for the New York office to handle. These activities led to more growth, until by the beginning of 1958 the Board had become a sizable organization.

In the midst of this prosperity there was also a certain unease. The basic concern, communicated to the Board from the system as a whole, was over the future of American education. Inadequately financed, facing increasing demands, still bitter over the unchecked fury of the McCarthy period, increasingly criticized for an educational mass slovenliness that did indeed seem to mark some portions of the system, the education system and particularly higher education could not see real hope or encouragement in the future. Under the circumstances the question of how standards were to be maintained was a difficult one—indeed, there was no shortage of critics to say that they were already gone. The national administration was benevolent with respect to education, probably willing to help if it could, but timid in action and uncertain as to its powers. It was not until the Russians orbited Sputnik, the first man-made satellite—in its way, one of the greatest events in the history of American education—that the atmosphere changed. Then, although criticism swelled to a new crescendo, there began to be money and, even more important, political support. From then on, development came with a rush.

The papers that follow reflect the uncertainties, the questions, and the search for directions that characterized the period. The understanding of the depth of demand for education, which had been inhibited by lack of support and the conservatism of national policies, came slowly, but it came. Perhaps we felt it more immediately at the College Board because of closeness to men and women who worked with students. Whatever may be the reasons, the demands for Board support were, in most important respects, met.

The founding of the College Scholarship Service took place under great stress and strain, involving a considerable amount of active opposition to the idea. The obvious problem it was founded to meet was that of a dual competition—one part a competition between colleges to attract certain candidates by use of scholarships, the other part a competition between schools, acting on behalf of candidates, to attract scholarship offers for their students. The competition was further complicated by the recruiting effort of some colleges that were offering so-called scholarships—actually tuition rebates—to all applicants who asked for them.

The actual problem underlying the obvious one was a shortage of students. The supply of veterans had finally run out, and the number of candidates from the schools had not increased sufficiently to take up the slack, so there was a real dearth of applicants. The stronger colleges were using their scholarship funds to fill their classes, often using a form of auction, in which bids would be made and raised over a period of some weeks. The colleges that had less appeal and less money were forced to follow suit, with the difference that they accepted candidates who were less well prepared and gave paper scholarships that were actually only a lowering of the tuition charge.

The CSS was founded on the principle that the financing of college education was a responsibility shared jointly by parents, students, and colleges and that the planning of aid began with a statement of the specific financial problem to be solved. The idea was opposed by some educators on the grounds of invasion of privacy, and by a good many school and college administrators who had been successful in placing or recruiting students under the auction system. But it was so obviously sensible that it finally prevailed.

In actual time sequence, Board actions with respect to services in the scholarship field began with a plan to study the field. A $50,000 appropriation to support a two-year study was voted by the Executive Committee and soon after by the membership in October 1953. This study was planned to prepare the way for the formation of a scholarship service, on the assumption that the Board's membership would not agree to such a step without preparation. However, the appropriation was never used, for the opposition melted away and the membership proved unexpectedly receptive to the idea, once it was formally proposed, supporting the formation of the CSS a full two years before the officers had planned for it.

The following excerpt from the stenotyped report of the October 1953 meeting of the Board's Executive Committee indicates a remarkable degree of readiness for Board action dealing with scholarships but uncertainty about what the action should be.

Excerpt from the minutes of the meeting of the Executive Committee, College Entrance Examination Board, on October 7, 1953.

Chairman Archibald MacIntosh (vice president, Haverford College): . . . I think we will move to the next item, the report of the Scholarship Committee. We had a very interesting discussion at Cambridge on Monday [October 5] afternoon, and the result of this discussion was that the committee moved to recommend to the Executive Committee that the Executive Committee consider a major investigation of the present scholarship situation in the country as a first step in tackling the problem. Frank, do you want to speak about that?

Frank Bowles: The Scholarship Committee was very much an ad hoc committee. It was appointed on the urging of Bill [Eugene S.] Wilson of Amherst, who came in to see us and said that something ought to be done, so our first step was to appoint a committee.

In the course of the discussions of the committee, it became apparent that what was contemplated was substantially the adoption of what we might call the Harvard Plan of calculating family contributions and its publication, along with movement toward a uniform scholarship application blank.

It was my feeling, which I had arrived at in anticipation of such proposals, that the Harvard Plan was very noticeably, as Harvard itself is emphasizing, a plan that is still very much in flux. They are not certain by any means that it is the best method of computing family contribution, but, even beyond that, the Harvard Plan introduces a concept in the entire management of scholarships that is rather new. It is a concept that the university or college has an obligation to make college attendance possible for its applicants. It is the beginning of a movement toward a nationwide flexible tuition figure.

I do not say that this is either good or bad; I just say that it is different. It is a scholarship approach that is quite different from the one inherent in the national scholarships, which were an effort to find talent regardless of need.

The proposal that there be a study of scholarships was made on the basis that a premature adoption of any such plan and of a uniform college scholarship application form would lead to certainly one and probably a series of scholarship conferences that would try to settle the question within a fairly narrow group of institutions and would not help us in solving the question nationally.

I, at any rate, felt furthermore that the adoption of such plans might very well intensify the multiple applications for scholarships—a situation we already know exists. Therefore, to me, at any rate, it was almost an inescapable approach to this problem that the Board should, before doing anything, undertake to try to define what we mean by "scholarships," what the methods of approach to scholarships are, and what the probable results might be of any one of several alternatives that the colleges might adopt to deal with scholarships.

On that point I have a report that tomorrow morning there is meeting in San Francisco a group composed of representatives of all Board-member colleges on the West Coast, and they are meeting to form a scholarship conference. They are talking about uniform application blanks and uniform procedures, definitions of scholarships, and various other things.

It would seem to me to pose considerable difficulties for the future if scholarship policies and procedures were solidified now in terms of what we know about them. I propose a delaying action, which will also have the advantage of producing more information.

The objections to the proposals as they came up in Cambridge were: What will our investigation into scholarships tell us that we do not now know? We know there is confusion. We do not know how much confusion, and there are a good many facts we might learn about the confusion, and some facts that we might learn to allay the confusion, but the fact is that there is pressure—or at least evidences of pressure—for action now, whereas studies such as we talked about in Cambridge would be a not-inconsiderable item.

It would be my objection that such a study would require, to be conclusive and to be worldwide, about two years of work. It would require a separate staff. To be effective it would have to eventuate in some sort of book such as Byron Hollinshead wrote; and it probably would not be conclusive, but it might, like the Hollinshead book, open the door to the consideration of a major problem.

In my judgment it would cost—we would have to figure that it would cost—$100,000. I have very strong reason to believe that if we were to undertake such a study we could expect support, at least some foundation support, for it, specifically from the Fund for the Advancement of Education, who are much concerned with the problem.

The other point, which I mentioned to Archie [Chairman MacIntosh] before our meeting, was that the most I would expect this committee to do about it at this time would be to authorize the officers of the Board to undertake a preliminary study of scholarships and authorize us to spend such money from our contingency reserve fund as we feel necessary for that, in order to prepare a prospectus of a plan, an outline, and present it to you at your next meeting. I would hope that before you would take any action you would really talk about the matter. This is a matter of tremendous urgency, I feel, because it is intimately tied up with the multiple application problem of nonscholarship students.

Edward S. Noyes (chairman, Board of Admissions, Yale University): I would like to add just one word. I happen to know this matter is being brought up before the meeting of the New England College Association.

Mary E. Chase (vice president, Wellesley College): And also in the Midwest by the Big Ten and Big Seven.

Mr. Bowles: I think you should realize that if you think a study ought to be made that this is a major expenditure.

Mr. Noyes: Is there any way by which liaison could be secured with any other groups that might be making similar studies? What I am thinking of is that this is so much in the air in different areas that different groups are already working on it, and duplication or overlapping, it would seem, would be almost certain unless very careful steps were taken.

Mr. Bowles: So far, every time that I, at least, have been called into consultation on any scholarship problem, I have found that the so-called studies upon which the proposals are made are of the most superficial nature. I was really distressed when I attended a meeting called by the National Science Foundation to discuss the scholarship program. They have absolutely no data within their group, although they worked very hard on it. Nevertheless, they were proposing a program that would be in the nature of several million dollars a year.

Miss Chase: One of the points we discussed in the committee meeting on Monday was that there are a number of corporations that are groping for ways to set up company scholarship programs, and that they would undoubtedly welcome the information that we might get out of this type of thing.

Henry Chauncey (president, Educational Testing Service): It seems to me that this is a very important problem, and one that is just the kind of thing the College Board should enter into. There is a vast amount of money in the aggregate that goes into scholarships in a year, but nobody knows exactly what the total impact is on the whole country, and the problem of trying to get those who are able and those who are needy into college is a tremendous one. So it would seem to me that this is a problem that an organization like the College Entrance Examination Board could attack.

I think it would immediately secure cooperation from all sorts of organizations, regional and otherwise, that are interested, and I personally think it is an excellent project.

Allegra Maynard (headmistress, Madeira School, Greenway, Virginia): How much additional expenditure did you think it would amount to in the first phase?

Mr. Bowles: Well, I think, in order to present you with a prospectus, we could do a pretty good job with $1,000. I have in mind two or three people from whom we could pick a man and give him the problem. We could talk with him and make up a fairly brief report of not over five or six pages.

Miss Maynard: If it is as important as this, I think $1,000 would be a very small figure for it.

William K. Selden (president, Illinois College): I thoroughly agree with your initial point, Frank, that it is a subject of profound importance, and, thinking of it from the viewpoint of the independent secondary schools—well, it has implications there as well and not merely on the college level. It has implications everywhere, privately endowed education as well as public education.

Mr. Bowles: Not to mention football. [Laughter]

Mr. Noyes: Please don't! [Laughter]

Finla G. Crawford (vice chancellor, Syracuse University): It also affects your public [Regents] scholarships, for instance, as we have them in New York. [Herbert H.] Williams and I are very familiar with them. That is an examination, but there is a very interesting gimmick, in that, if you happen to live in a certain county, you may get a scholarship on a lower score than if you lived in some other county. The reason for that is that they are given in terms of so many to each county, so that you do not have a statewide standard. You have a county standard which applies, so that again we have no exact measure in terms of abilities, because of the county way of distribution.

Mr. Selden: I would like to make this statement, which has been made to me quite frequently: if you are planning something like this, plan big! My point is that when you say $100,000, at first it is a little surprising. On the other hand, the ramifications and implications are such that if it is thought of on a piecemeal basis, it really will not contribute very much.

B. Alden Thresher (director of admissions, Massachusetts Institute of Technology): I would raise the question of whether a preliminary study by the Board officers is going to bring us into this fast enough and on a large enough scale. I admit we need preliminary exploration on what should be done, but I wonder if that is pushing it fast enough.

Mr. Bowles: You are making the point that John Monro [of Harvard] made. He felt that unless some agency expressed the willingness to move right into the field of scholarships now on a broad front, the situation might deteriorate rapidly.

Mr. Thresher: If I were to choose now between better information about tests or better information about scholarships, I would choose the latter. I would argue for moving in as rapidly as possible.

George W. Mullins (professor emeritus of mathematics, Barnard College): What do you figure we would need to appropriate—$100,000?

Mr. Bowles: Any action now, of course, would involve the immediate search for a man to carry on the study.

Mr. Mullins: That is right; that is important.

Mr. Bowles: Well, I think we could move rapidly enough to have expended, by the end of our fiscal year, about $25,000. This is entirely off the cuff, of course.

Mr. Mullins: It seems to me that this is so important that the expenditure of $100,000 on it is quite justified. It is a big thing that the Board can do, something that it can contribute, and it is a good thing to have a fresh look and a free hand, too. If others want to contribute, all right, but I should say, let us have a fresh look and a free hand.

Mr. Selden: Does it not also have implications in the way of non-Board support in addition? In other words, I would assume the Fund for the Advancement of Education would seriously be interested in this, as it also relates to what they are encouraging with $600,000 in the organization [the Council for Financial Aid to Education] that [Wilson] Compton is now heading; that has a relationship there. Therefore, I would assume that we are not shooting off in the dark insofar as we have other people interested.

Mr. Mullins: I think that is right.

Mr. Noyes: I certainly have no objection to moving fast or moving on a broad front. It would seem to me, however, important to make clear to those interested that our purpose is not to set up some definitive scheme on the basis of information that might become available in the course of a year or so, but that the first purpose was to get the information. Plans or proposals for anything like uniformity would have to be delayed, even if they ever were made—which, in my opinion, seems to be dubious.

Allan V. Heely (headmaster, Lawrenceville School, Lawrenceville, New Jersey): It would not be possible anyway to make a definition until you found and thoroughly checked the facts on which the definition would have to be based.

Mr. Thresher: Well, this thing is still nebulous, but there seems to be a principle in the attraction of nebulae that the larger mass attracts the smaller, and maybe some of these smaller activities could be brought into something like the same scheme.

Mr. Bowles: I think so. I think that if we were to get into this, that we would find ourselves—the director, poor soul, would find himself—the national authority on scholarships in a very short time. [Laughter] And Heaven knows they need one!

. . . .

Archie and I are going to have to go into a huddle here. You moved faster than usual on a matter like this, and I was not prepared for it. However, it seems to me that several questioners here said, "If we approve of your starting a study now, how fast can you move?"

Well, we have no firm proposal to present to you. We can draft a memorandum between now and the time of the Board meeting, if you would like such a memorandum. We could move fast enough so that if you approved of the memorandum, you could recommend action to the Board, looking toward major appropriations—which should, in my judgment, eventually come out of the Custodians' Fund or should, at any rate, be a sum of money that would not go into the Custodians' Fund.

The other alternative is to ask you to vote rather blindly to approve of a scholarship study, and in that case I would assume that you would still wish to have a memorandum before you by the time the meeting came around, so that you could know what it was you voted to approve.

Katharine E. McBride (president, Bryn Mawr College): I would like to see whichever choice is made still empower you to look into the question of a prospectus.

. . . .

Mr. Bowles: With either of the proposals that have been made, it will be necessary to prepare a memorandum. Do you wish to vote now and push forward into an action, or do you wish to defer a vote until a special meeting, which we would have to have just before the Board meeting?

Mr. Thresher: Which alternative would you find more convenient to work under?

Mr. Bowles: Well, I think a special meeting might be rather hard to arrange.

Mr. Noyes: It seems to me that there is enough unanimity of opinion here now, that the thing is important and valuable for the Board to do and that we ought to move into it rapidly, so that we could take a vote and ask the officers of the Board to prepare a memorandum for action at the Board meeting in October. This should not prevent them from taking immediate steps to find someone to head up the study. I wish to make that motion.

Mr. Crawford: Second.

Chairman MacIntosh: Is there any discussion of the motion?

Mr. Mullins: Will that require an appropriation, Frank?

Mr. Bowles: It will require an appropriation. I think that an appropriation ought to be in the nature of authorizing an expenditure of about $50,000 within the fiscal year, with the understanding that any unexpended balance will carry over into the succeeding year.

Mr. Noyes: I shall be glad to add that to my motion.

Chairman MacIntosh: Is that acceptable to the seconder?

Mr. Crawford: Yes, entirely.

Mr. Bowles: Everybody tells me that the Board is a cumbersome and a slow-moving organization. [Laughter]

Mr. Thresher: I should hardly think that this present motion would require an appropriation. Would that not come later?

Mr. Selden: And may I ask, is this the delaying action you were talking about? Frank made the comment that he thought there ought at least to be a delaying action. [Laughter]

Chairman MacIntosh: All those in favor of the motion please say "aye." Those opposed, "no." The motion is carried.

T*his paper by William Fels was only one of a number of talks and papers that he and I produced on the College Scholarship Service. It was not an easy program to explain, but I think that he did it as clearly and gracefully as it could possibly have been done.*

"The College Scholarship Service," by William C. Fels
College Board Review No. 23, May 1954, pp. 428–434.

The College Scholarship Service is the first wholly new activity of the College Entrance Examination Board since its founding 54 years ago. It is the first activity which does not have examinations as its focus. Yet the css is squarely consistent with the purpose of the Board, for it is an attempt to provide a cooperative solution for a problem of transition from school to college.

The problem is a relatively new one. Only recently has the administration of scholarships become an indispensable and inseparable part of the administration of admissions. The appraisal of the ability and achievement of applicants for admission is advanced in technique and partially centralized in administration through the examination program. The determination of need for scholarships and other forms of financial aid is relatively undeveloped and entirely uncentralized.

The desirability of improvement in techniques to determine need and to centralize administration of scholarships was brought home to members of the College Board at its Symposium on Scholarships a year ago. It is unnecessary to repeat the description of intercollege competition and rule-of-thumb estimation of need that have resulted in the uneconomical distribution of scholarship funds and the development of unhealthy attitudes toward scholarships. But two constructive proposals that were introduced at the Symposium should be recalled. John Monro, of Harvard University, described Harvard's method of arriving at an amount the parents of an applicant might be expected to contribute to the applicant's higher education.[1] Mr. Monro warned that the Harvard procedure was experimental and called upon other colleges to join with Harvard in the refinement of the technique. J. Edward Sanders, of Pomona College, pointed to the desirability of cooperation in the administration of scholarships.[2]

Shortly after the Symposium, Eugene Wilson, of Amherst College, and Donald Eldridge, of Wesleyan University, urged that these two sugges-

---

1. John U. Monro, "Helping the Student Help Himself," *College Board Review* No. 20, May 1953, pp. 351–357.
2. J. Edward Sanders, "Are Scholarships Improving Education?" *College Board Review* No. 20, May 1953, pp. 358–364.

tions be taken up and carried forward, through the establishment and operation of a central scholarship service. Since then, several college presidents, among them James S. Coles, of Bowdoin, Charles Cole, of Amherst, John S. Dickey, of Dartmouth, and Nathan M. Pusey, of Harvard, and a great many admissions and scholarship officers have given thought, encouragement, and support to preliminary plans for the css.

Functions of the css

Details of the plans have changed and continue to change, but the essential features of the css are now clear. It will perform the following functions.

1. The css will prepare and distribute directly and through the colleges a form called Statement in Support of Application for Financial Aid,[3] to be filled out by the parents of applicants.
2. The css will receive these forms at the offices of Educational Testing Service in Princeton and Los Angeles, acknowledge their receipt, scan them for omissions and obvious errors, conduct such correspondence as may be necessary to obtain complete and correct forms, duplicate the original form submitted by the parents, send copies to the colleges designated by the parents, and file the originals.
3. In sending copies of the form to colleges, and in later communications, the css will report to each college the names of all colleges to which copies are being sent and the amounts which parents expect to provide toward the expenses of their children at the colleges.
4. The css will prepare and distribute a manual for the computation by the colleges of the amount to be expected from parents.
5. In the fall, after the applicants have enrolled, the css will collect from the colleges reports of financial tenders and awards to their applicants.
6. Also in the fall, the css will prepare and distribute to the colleges consolidated reports of tenders and awards made to their applicants by other colleges to which their applicants applied.
7. Using these data, the css will undertake to refine the method of computation.
8. The css will also conduct studies of the factors affecting the ability

3. Now known as the Parents' Confidential Statement.

of parents to contribute to the education of their children for the further refinement of the method of computing the expected contribution.

Colleges which participate in the css will be expected to require the parents of all freshman scholarship applicants to file the form. The colleges will also be expected to submit reports of tenders and awards to the css. In cases of unusual types of scholarships, special exceptions to the requirement that the form be filed may be permitted, but all aid tendered and awarded will be reported by the colleges.

Strictly confidential

The confidential nature of the financial information reported will be respected. Copies of the form will be sent to colleges only at the request of the parents. If the css is later extended to scholarship sponsors other than colleges, copies sent to them will also be authorized by the parents. After they receive the statements, colleges will be expected to exercise the same discretion they now use in handling information obtained on their own scholarship application blanks.

The css will begin operation in the academic year 1954–55 by distributing and receiving forms in support of applications for financial aid to be awarded in the academic year 1955–56. For the first year, at least, it will be limited to forms in support of applications for aid submitted by students who expect to enter college as freshmen.

The form which the parents are to fill out will be a critical factor in the success of the css. On the one hand, it must obtain accurate and ample information; on the other hand, it must be susceptible to economical and legible reproduction. Preliminary drafts of the form have about narrowed the possible types of reproduction to the dye-transfer process, which the familiar Ozalid and Bruning machines use, and the photographic-facsimile process, used by Recordak and Dexigraph. If the dye-transfer process is used, only one side of the form may be written upon; if the photographic-facsimile process is used, both sides of the form may be written upon, but this would require photographing both sides, and the photographic process is more expensive. In any case, the final form will be selected with the assistance of a committee of scholarship officers. In doing so, we will not sacrifice the collection of accurate and ample information to the cost of reproduction. We are fully aware that a satisfactory form is the minimum essential to the success of the css. It will request financial information only, of course, and leave the collection of all other information that may be desired to the individual college.

The proposal to supply the names of all colleges to which statements are to be sent may raise a question of whether this information may not be used for the determination of college choice. To a certain extent, it can be and perhaps will be. When the "college choice rule" was in operation, however, its critics pointed out that scholarship applicants could have no real preference until they knew what scholarship aid would be offered them. This fact minimizes the possibility of using this information for college choice purposes. We will also take care to ask the parents to list the colleges alphabetically, and to provide spaces for the parents to insert the amounts of expected contributions at different colleges under different conditions of residence and nonresidence.

Since the names of colleges to which statements are sent will be supplied, it may be asked whether colleges might not use this advance information to raise their offers and to press the candidates into early replies. The answer must rest partly upon confidence in the ethics of the colleges, but, lest this be a shaky ground, there are four other deterrents to misuse: the inadequacy of scholarship funds (which reduces colleges' ability to "bid" against each other), the uniform computations, the consolidated reports of tenders and awards, and the Candidates Reply Date Agreement. A fifth deterrent would be agreements entered into by the colleges themselves, which, of course, are matters for the colleges, not the College Board, to arrange.

My own feeling, after talking to many persons about supplying the names of colleges, is that this is an essential feature of the css, that it has more possibilities of benefit than of harm, and that it certainly should be given a trial.

Estimation of need

At the outset, the manual for the computation of amounts to be expected from the parents will follow the Harvard procedure, which Harvard has generously offered to share, possibly somewhat modified by experience with data from other colleges to be collected and analyzed this summer.

The figure estimated with the Harvard method may well prove to be low for colleges with smaller scholarship funds; it is, in fact, usually low even for Harvard, which does not have all the scholarship funds it would like to have or needs. But this will not make the estimated figure less useful. The actual award is always the result of two compromises, first between the computed amount expected from the family and the parents' offer, and then between the result of this compromise and available scholarship funds.

In its first year, the css will undertake to make computations experimentally for only a small group of colleges, but each college participating in the css will receive the manual and directions for making its own computations.

During and after the first year of operation, the css will refine the computing procedure through the analysis of parents' statements and tenders and awards made by the colleges. An important feature of the css is that it automatically collects many of the data necessary to its own purpose. The css will further refine the method of computation through studies of factors affecting the ability of parents to contribute to the education of their children. We have been calling these projected studies "pinching studies" because they are designed to find whose shoes pinch and where.

The collection and distribution of reports of tenders and awards has presented us with a difficult decision. The css will request reports from colleges after the applicants are enrolled. It will consolidate these reports and send to colleges a list of all tenders and awards made to their own applicants. The original thought was to confine this service to groups of colleges which had entered into agreements concerning the administration of scholarships. Our present feeling, held strongly by the Executive Committee, is that this service should be provided to all participating colleges. It should be pointed out that no college will receive a complete report of the scholarships granted by any other college. It will receive only the complete report of tenders and awards made by other colleges to its own candidates. These reports should in themselves in the long run identify the college's principal competitors and, at least in part, automatically ameliorate competition. If further improvement of this situation is considered desirable, the colleges will, of course, be free to enter into cooperative agreements to achieve it.

Service to start in fall

This fall, the css will collect and distribute reports of the current year's tenders and awards, even before the statement clearing procedure goes into effect. This will give the css a chance to work the "bugs" out of the procedure and to obtain data for the refinement of the computing procedure. It will also give the colleges an opportunity to see how their own offers and awards compare with the offers and awards of other colleges.

As with the supplying of names of colleges to which copies are to be sent, the award-reporting procedures, we feel, have in them more possibilities for good than for evil, and we would like at least to start with them.

The css has many possibilities that cannot be used at the outset. The most obvious is the central determination of the accuracy of the information submitted by the parents, that is, credit checking. To do this once, centrally, for each applicant would be much more economical than to do it many times, at the colleges, for each application. There is a good chance that parents who might be tempted to "fudge" the information on the form will be discouraged by the knowledge that they are submitting the form to a central agency and by the fact that copies may go to several colleges. We hope next year to make credit checks on a sample of the statements to see just how accurate they are and to test various methods of verifying their accuracy.

Possibilities for the future

Another possibility is the extension of the css to scholarship sponsors such as corporations, unions, and fraternal organizations, which will almost certainly want to use it. For them, as for the colleges, the css will provide a means to determine need objectively and thus to stretch their scholarship dollars. Reviews of scholarships in upper-class years and determinations of the financial needs of graduate fellows (though the latter would require somewhat different procedures) are other purposes to which the css could be adapted. Not beyond the realm of possibility, but certainly remote in time, would be the use of the css to appraise the financial resources of applicants for admission as well as of applicants for scholarships. This would enable the colleges to set sliding tuition and expense scales, should they ever wish to. The central filing, copying, and distributing features of the css might be extended to a uniform school transcript form with much saving in clerical expense to the schools and in eyesight to the colleges. But all these possibilities are for the future.

For the present, we shall have to hope for narrower but still solid benefits from the css. The improvement of the technique of assessing need and the centralization of administration would make it possible for the colleges to administer scholarships more equitably and more economically. The latter could mean either more scholarships or less expense. No less important to the colleges would be improvement in public understanding that scholarships are grants-in-aid for needy students, necessarily limited to the ablest by the shortage of scholarship money, but not mere unearned increments for ability. If there is a reduction of what seems to the students to be competition among the colleges for the ablest among them, there should also be a lessening of the collecting and parading of scholarship offers. The clerical burden of administering scholarships would be lessened.

Parents can hope for an informed appraisal of their finances and a reasonable offer of aid. They will be saved the filling out of many forms. Students can look forward to awards of scholarships, loans, and student employment in accordance with their needs, neither so large as to unnecessarily deny funds to others nor so small as to place an impossible burden of employment upon them. In addition to these specific benefits to colleges, parents, and students, we hope for an increase of the general fund of knowledge about scholarships, which is now pitifully small, and for the dissemination of information on awards available and the conditions upon which these awards are granted. It is not unlikely that the css will come to the publication of a College Scholarship Handbook as a companion volume to *The College Handbook*.

Fee necessary

One unfortunate aspect of the css is that we must charge a fee, even a small one, to scholarship applicants, who are the least able to pay. We believe that the advantages to the applicant will outweigh the cost and have kept the fee as low as possible, $1 per copy of the statement. In fact, using this fee, it is not at all certain that the css can break even with fewer than 10,-000 applicants, though the cost of consolidated reports of tenders and awards and of computations (when the css is ready to provide these) will be borne by the colleges. The duplication of statements is relatively inexpensive, varying from a few cents for a one-page statement by the dye-transfer process to 50 cents for a two-page statement by the photographic process, but there are many other expenses: the printing and distribution of forms, the receipt and scanning of statements, correspondence on incomplete or incorrect statements, the notification of the parent that the statement has been received, filing, preparation of additional reports, administration, and the ubiquitous "overhead." However, even if the services could be provided free or at the expense of the colleges, it would be necessary to charge a fee to deter unreasonable multiple applications.

Economy of effort

Some idea of how large the css might be if all the colleges of the Board participate and of the economy of effort that will be effected when it is in full operation is suggested by a few basic figures. The 122 of the 155 College Board member colleges that responded to a questionnaire reported that they received 151,000 completed applications for admission in 1953. Of these, 39,000 were applications for scholarships. Twelve thousand of these "applications" (we cannot say "applicants" because of multiple applications) were offered scholarships, and 9,000 applicants enrolled with scholarships. The 39,000 applications for scholarships constitute a measure of the number of copies of statements the css might be called upon to send out. The 9,000 enrolled is the minimum number of statements the css might be called upon to receive if all the member colleges participate. The difference between the 9,000 enrolled and the 12,000 "applications" offered scholarships is interesting, because it shows that, even if it is assumed that there was no multiple application, 75 percent of the "applications" offered scholarships enrolled with scholarships at Board colleges. Since we know there is multiple application, the percentage must be even greater. The difference between the 12,000 tenders and the 39,000 completed applications suggests that the increase of public knowledge about the administration of scholarships would do much to reduce unwarranted applications or, if the applications are warranted, to substantiate the colleges' claim that more scholarship money is desperately needed.

Limited to members at first

Though it will be necessary at first to limit the css to member colleges, this should not prevent it from making a significant contribution to the solution of the scholarship problem. The 155 member colleges award 41 percent of the approximately $30 million awarded in undergraduate scholarships by colleges each year. The remaining 59 percent is scattered among some 1,650 institutions. If the css is successful, we would expect member and other colleges to follow the same pattern with it that they have followed with the examination program—that is, we would expect them to come into the css when they are in a position to find its services useful to them, just as member and other colleges come into the examination program when they find themselves in need of more accurate selection procedures.

This paper, which undertook to describe patterns of admissions, was actually the first of a number written over the next six years, describing various cross sections of the college entrance universe. The universe itself changed during the period in two important respects that show up on a reading of this paper.

The paper places heavy emphasis on the shortage of space in colleges and the wastefulness involved in filling a certain number of spaces with students who will fail, while at the same time there are able students who do not get to college at all but who presumably could be recruited and who presumably would not fail if recruited.

The second emphasis was on the need for economy in the use of space because of the nonexpansible nature of higher education. It seems odd in 1967 to point out that no new colleges were being founded, that existing colleges were not being expanded, that private colleges were in despair over inability to find new money, and that the whole fear of higher education was of being trapped in a financial bind in which standards would have to be lowered in order to promise enough income to maintain operations. The time of rapid expansion, of rising tuition, of government grants, of effective support for educational improvement programs (such as National Defense Education Act summer institutes), and of new cur-

riculums (the College Board's Commission on Mathematics was to be formed the following year) was still in the unseen future.

Within five years, of course, virtually every condition lamented in the paper had been changed, either by federal intervention, or by funds brought in by tuition increases or money raising, or by new kinds of activity—one example of which was the intervention by colleges and universities in the curriculums of the secondary schools.

"College Admissions—Present and Future"
College Board Review No. 22, February 1954, pp. 400–406.

This year about two million young Americans will meet the first of four elementary requirements for college admission. They will reach the age of 18, and, in the language of the demographers, or what Will Cuppy might have called "the populationologists," they will constitute the 18-year-old age group from which all the freshman classes of this country's colleges and universities will be chosen.

About half of the group will fulfill the second requirement for entrance, graduation from high school. Half of the high school graduates will have satisfied the third requirement by studying, or in any case following, a combination of courses which can be very loosely described as college preparatory. Slightly more than two-thirds of these will want, or at least be willing, to go to college.

The approximately 350,000 souls in the age group who meet these basic requirements will go to college with very few exceptions. Some will undoubtedly find it impossible, but only a small number of these will be able to cite financial reasons. Even the most impoverished high school graduate of today, if he does not have others to support, can have a college education in one way or another. Thousands of people who could not have attended college 25 years ago because of the cost are registered in the evening sessions of the great city institutions, and thousands more are receiving scholarships for full-time studies. It is also true that very few will fail to gain admission for academic reasons, unless they are very dull indeed, for a determined high school graduate who can read and write almost certainly can find a college which is willing to accept him. There are many others, of course, who are not quite determined enough and who rationalize their lack of determination by speaking of money, family obligations, or military service.[4]

The 350,000 who will go to college may be further characterized as having a mean ability between 110 and 115 on the IQ scale. They are, in other words, a selected but not a brilliant group. They will include most of the really able secondary school graduates but far too many of the less promising students, for the mean IQ indicates that 175,000 of the group will be below 112 on that scale.

The types of colleges

The hundreds of colleges which the students will enter may be roughly divided into three groups according to their functions in the admissions process. At the top of the pyramid there are about 50 institutions, most of them located in or near large cities, which offer superior facilities and instruction in a wide choice of programs. These are independent institutions, plus a very few state universities that act as if they were independent institutions. They have an oversupply of applicants drawn from stable sources which include a large number of feeder schools. They are also characterized by a recruiting policy aimed at finding students of exceptional ability with the use of liberal scholarship funds, by a requirement of early application (usually in February), by the use of entrance examinations, by careful selection of admitted candidates, and by early admission (usually completed by May). These colleges attract a total of about 75,000 applicants who rank, for the most part, in the highest quarter of their school classes and who among them submit about 175,000 applications in order to be sure of finding a place. About 50,000 of the students are registered, many if not most of them after having been admitted to at least two institutions. About 10 percent of the freshman class is lost through various causes, of which downright failure is relatively infrequent. Better than 75 percent of the admitted students are graduated.

The colleges in a second group, numbering about 350, are not as large on the average as the top 50 and include a higher percentage of rural and suburban institutions. Predominantly independent colleges, they are charac-

---

4. Of the age group of two million, about half are boys who will be liable for military service six months after their eighteenth birthdays. They will be required to serve but may be deferred long enough to complete their education.

terized by a barely adequate and at times inadequate supply of students drawn only in part from stable sources. Their recruiting is intensive and continues until school opens, with scholarships used fundamentally as a recruiting device, not just as a means of locating exceptional students. Though the students come in large part from the second and third quarters in ability of the secondary school classes, entrance examinations are not used regularly in spite of the fact that they are sometimes recommended and always mentioned in the college catalogs. These institutions attract a total of about 100,000 applicants, including some overflow from the 75,000 applicants described above. About 125,000 applications are submitted by these 100,000 candidates, of whom about 75,000 are registered. Freshman attrition is at the rate of about 20 percent, and from 50 to 60 percent of the entering students are graduated. It should also be noted that about 100 of these 350 institutions follow as closely as they can the philosophy and practices of the top 50, and that at least 25 of them can now very nearly qualify as members of that company.

The third and largest group, about 1,400 institutions, includes a number of struggling independent institutions which are usually very small, a number of urban institutions of the service type, and a great many tax-supported institutions. Their freshman classes have no fixed size, but are dealt with late in September according to the enrollment. They have no steady sources of students, but of course draw heavily upon the large urban and suburban high schools. These colleges indulge little in recruiting, have few scholarships except those occasionally awarded to athletes, do not select their students, require very little in the way of formal application, and close their rolls at the last possible moment, usually a week after classes have begun. Their students come from all four quarters of secondary school classes and do not take entrance examinations. They register about 225,000 from an application group which may be as large as 250,000, counting overflows from the other two groups of colleges. Freshman attrition is 30 percent or higher, and fewer than half of the students that enter as freshmen are graduated.

Only a few of the figures presented above are supported by research, and most of them probably include a considerable error of estimate, but as generalizations they do serve the purpose of describing college admissions very roughly.

Wasted money

Among the major problems which arise within that general situation, perhaps the first and most obvious has to do with the makeup of the 350,000 students who will enter college. One of the most striking things about this group is that 150,000 of them have not demonstrated the ability and do not have the capacity to do college work. This is implicit in the earlier statement that the mean IQ of the applicant group as a whole is between 110 and 115, from which it follows that about 175,000 of them are below 112 and about 150,000 below 110 on the IQ scale. By no coincidence at all, about 150,000 within any given freshman group will fail to finish college.

If we say 150,000 fast, it may not seem a large number, but translated in terms of colleges it becomes more impressive. It amounts to no fewer than 150 fully equipped colleges, each with a student population of 1,000, a president, faculty, dormitories, classrooms, libraries, and laboratories. Each institution has 500 freshmen, 300 sophomores, 150 juniors, 50 seniors —and no graduates. There are alumni organizations, however, since an alumnus may be defined for fund-raising purposes as anyone who ever walked in the front door. Presumably they will have athletic teams, probably pretty good ones.

These 150 "institutions" do not exist as identifiable colleges, although a few colleges barely escape belonging to that category, but their component parts are scattered among colleges throughout the land. They represent, in fact, nonproductive investments in education. Assuming a capital investment of $2,000 per student, which is far below present costs, and an expenditure per student of $400, which is low, this means unused capital to the extent of $300 million and wasted expenditure to the amount of $60 million a year. In addition, family support of these students amounts to at least $75 million a year. This, be it noted, could purchase a lot of good education. It is a high price to pay for the slogan that everyone should have his chance.

Wasted talent

A second big problem revealed by the general admissions picture concerns those competent students who never get to college. As against the 150,000 who will be admitted only to fail, there are about 200,000 individuals of superior ability in the age group who will not go to college. The 350,000 group, it will be remembered, is composed of persons who have in common a desire, or at least a willingness, to attend college. The importance of the factor of motivation, when applied to this consideration of large groups, becomes all too apparent. The top quarter of the age group of 2,000,000, measured in terms of ability, consists of a group of 500,000 persons, each with an IQ of 115 or better and capable of good college work.

Of the 500,000 not over two-fifths, or 200,000, enter college. About 100,000 in the remaining 300,000 of the group do not finish high school. Of the other 200,000 who do graduate from high school but do not go to college, we know only two facts: that more than half of them are girls, and that many of them go on to some form of short-term schooling in preparation for employment. We do not know, however, *why* this large number does not go on to college. Sampling studies have shown that about half of them frankly do not care to go and that the other half, when pressed, talk about financial difficulties. When the financial problems are investigated, about half of them turn out to be serious, but there are very few, even of this type, that cannot be solved. Certainly these troubles do not appear to be any worse than those faced by many students who are in college. The essential problem, then, seems to be one of motivation, although it must be acknowledged that many in the ability group have no particular reason for going to college. A striking example of the role of motivation in determining college attendance is the fact that among the children of those farmers who have high incomes, the percentage who go to college is smaller than that of any other occupation group of equally high income. The fact remains, however, that there are 200,000 able potential candidates whom we do not reach, and 150,000 actual candidates whom we would rather not reach.

Duplication of studies

A third problem originates in the duplication and overlap between high school and college studies, a subject that has come into a good deal of attention through projects sponsored by the Fund for the Advancement of Education. Students who do their work well in secondary school often find themselves repeating, in their required freshman courses, the materials they had already covered in the twelfth-grade program. This is a triple loss, for it is a negation of high school efforts, a useless expenditure of student time, and a waste of college facilities. Studies now under way are trying to provide incentive and programs to eliminate this waste. Although the suggestions that are being considered are not in themselves new, they have never been applied on a wide scale and have never been used with real success, perhaps because the problem has never before been seen so clearly. The reason that it is now being recognized and dealt with is, ironically enough, not an educational one. It originates in the fact that male students who meet the entrance requirements for college also meet the entrance requirements for military service. Because of this, it is to the interest of both college and student to get as deeply as possible into the college course before the student is called. There are good chances that, under the present law and the present administration of the law, the student may then be deferred until he finishes college, and in some cases may even be permitted to finish professional school.

Application pressure to increase

Having dealt at length with the present group of actual and potential candidates, let us consider the future. If we continue at the present rate and keep on doing the same things, we shall some time within the next 15 years find ourselves dealing with an application group of 700,000 instead of the present group of 350,000. Of this group we shall be admitting, only to lose them before graduation, some 300,000 individuals instead of today's 150,-000. To accommodate this group we shall have to exactly double the system of higher education. The only thing wrong with this statement is that if we continue to do things as we are now doing them, the job is flatly impossible. The support, the facilities, the equipment, and above all the teachers not only are not now available, but are not even a gleam in the eye of the most optimistic college or university president. Something comparable was done during the veterans' rush, of course, and we are all familiar with the wartime cliché: "The difficult we do immediately, the impossible takes a little longer." But if we are going to consider inspirational mottoes it might be better to remember one that a Marine colonel had erected over the pile of papers he was pushing around: "Think—there must be a harder way." The point is that the problem cannot be dealt with by either mottoes or history. It has to be dealt with by us, and we had better begin now.

Multiple applications

A fifth problem refers to multiple applications and competition for students. This is a serious administrative difficulty caused by the tendency of applicants to apply to the best institutions they can afford, and then to place other applications as a form of admissions insurance. It is the result of poor advice in both school and college, of the ease of making duplicate applications, and of faulty administrative practice in both colleges and schools. It is not really an educational problem, because it is not affecting standards in any except rather far-fetched ways, but it is a terrible nuisance and has to be recognized as such. Multiple applications certainly create one of the barriers to smooth administration of admissions.

Having defined the controlling facts of admissions and the most serious of the admissions problems, at least as they appear to the writer, we may now ask what can be done to improve this situation. The answer, perhaps a trite one, is that we had better start by using the facilities we have. After our present resources and operations are put in order, perhaps we can do a better job of planning for the future.

Finding the remedies

The first two problems relate essentially to poor use of resources and facilities. Both the 150,000 candidates who are admitted each year only to fail and the 200,000 high school graduates of superior ability who never get to college represent a net loss to higher education and to the country. In order to remedy this we must begin in the school and then carry the school's influence directly into the home and to the parents. Such action means, of course, a new role for the advisers and guidance officers, but it is a role that school and community must accept if they are to look for a maximum return from their education dollars. Ways of doing this kind of job have been tried out to a limited extent, but they are outside the present pattern of operations in which advising usually occurs in the twelfth grade. If we are to do anything about influencing motivation, we must begin much earlier, probably in the tenth grade, for most of what is known about the making of decisions to go or not to go to college indicates that those decisions are made and firmly fixed by the time the high school student has reached the twelfth grade.

In general the decisions are based on factors the school knows little about; often they are made through fear or ignorance of what college is. Counseling that is begun in the tenth grade should be general in nature, consisting of approaches such as comments on ability or exceptional work and conversations with parents about college plans. If this is done, by the time the student reaches eleventh grade a trial run can be given on the American Council on Education's Psychological Examination, or the Scholastic Aptitude Test, to give a definite measurement of the student's college potential. This should complete the worst of the advising job, leaving only the selection of a college to be done. An unanswered question, of course, is how this can be accomplished in a school where the guidance officer has no office to work in and who also teaches a full load and coaches glee club and debating. The fact is that this school has no guidance program and no guidance officer. The school which can support a three- or four-year college guidance program with time, facilities, and perhaps a little money has possibilities which are genuinely exciting and challenging.

The colleges, too, have a major responsibility in guidance and selection and must be ready and able to help a program which is directed to a group of tenth-grade students. In addition, they must be ready to change their pattern of recruiting. Far too much recruiting is directed at the large urban and suburban high school in the upper-middle-class residential areas, and far too little time is spent in the nonfeeder schools. There are high schools, not only in the rural areas but also in our large cities, that are never visited by college representatives and that produce able students who would go to college if the opportunity were brought to them. The colleges also have an obligation not to admit a student whose chances of success are negligible. Even a college which is trying desperately to fill a freshman class for budgetary reasons is hurting itself by admitting poor students, for this sets up a vicious spiral of mediocrity which results in inability to attract any good students and finally in inability to attract any students at all.

In the area of selection and guidance there are no panaceas or easy solutions. Success requires hard work, intellectual honesty, and careful attention to the individual. If we can do a better job by using these as our tools we will be taking the first step toward meeting the situation.

The third problem, duplication and overlap between school and college, involves a very knotty matter—the customs and traditions of American education. These are all opposed to allowing college credit for work done in secondary school and even to some extent against excusing a student from any college work on the basis of secondary school achievement. Yet all of the proposals for dealing with this problem embrace one or both of these alternatives. The writer is prejudiced on this matter as the result of personal experience at Columbia, where for 25 years students have been allowed to pass over subjects they know to get at subjects they do not know. A particularly striking case concerned a student who passed off his calculus and differential equations in the first week and registered for vector analysis as his freshman mathematics course. This student's degree requirements were not reduced because of his achievement; he still took the full 124 semester hours, and he and everyone else felt that he had gotten the most out of his 124 hours. General adoption of some such pattern as this will probably be the first widely taken step in avoiding college duplication of secondary school work. It seems reasonable to expect that this will be followed some years from now by allowance of college credit for secondary school work.

The ready, willing, and able

The studies and projects sponsored by the Fund for the Advancement of Education look toward the granting of academic credit somewhat sooner, or to acceptance of an alternate plan to admit students to college as soon as they are intellectually ready. These proposals, given the safeguards with which they have been worked out, have much to recommend them, but their general adoption is problematical. A pet scheme of the writer which is a good deal more radical would be to grant assurance of college admission at the end of the eleventh grade—something that, given present tests and our knowledge of how to use them, is perfectly practicable—and then let the student remain in secondary school to take an advanced program of the school's own making. This would leave the question of schooling up to the school and the question of recognition up to the college. This division of labor would work pretty well and be less cumbersome than the present proposals, but its adoption cannot be anticipated. In any case, whatever is done needs to be done soon, for we must devise more economical ways of using college facilities if we are to take care of the population bulge which is now well on its way to high school.

Problems of numbers

This brings us to the question of how to handle the population bulge, a question that has no apparent answer. Unless facilities are increased this bulge can only mean that our colleges will be forced into a selective admissions basis. There is, of course, room for considerable expansion in our colleges today, and there are in various stages of growth the beginnings of about 100 more colleges, most of which will expand into four-year institutions. One of our great troubles, however, lies in the area of teacher supply, and as matters stand now, our graduate schools are not producing prospective college teachers at anywhere near the necessary rate. In fact, there are not enough good graduate schools to produce college teachers at the rate required to maintain faculties of double their present size. This means that unless there is some miracle not now foreseen, we will not be able to expand our freshman vacancies beyond 450,000. If we could do a first-rate guidance job in our schools, and this is a very large "if," the number of vacancies would be almost enough. But if we do not, then the colleges must handle the selection job alone, and the results will be rather unfortunate from a secondary school standpoint.

Finally we come to the problem of multiple applications and competition for students. The problem should not be underestimated, but it does seem to be primarily an affair of educational bad manners all around. The colleges are greedy in grabbing for the best students and much to blame for bidding against each other with scholarships and other inducements. The schools have a regrettable tendency to encourage multiple applications and to join in pushing and bidding for scholarships. The pupils appear to regard scholarships as a right and also as a prize, with the brass ring going to the student who can collect the largest number of offers.

In recognition of this situation a number of colleges have suddenly and simultaneously decided that the situation is getting out of hand. They will probably take drastic steps which will include placing all scholarships on a financial assistance basis only, which will be determined strictly on need and require that the size of grants be held confidential. Schools will be asked not to make any public announcement as to scholarships granted to their candidates. A movement is under way for a uniform scholarship application blank to be passed through a clearinghouse, with awards to be processed in the same manner. It may well be that applications for admission will also be passed through a clearinghouse. The approximately 85,000 candidates who take College Board tests for admission are filing an average of about 2.5 score reports, which represents a great deal of work for the colleges and the schools. Much of this is wasted effort because the standards of the Board member colleges are much the same, which means that a candidate admitted by one will be admitted by the others to which he applies and vice versa.

The responsibility of guidance

It would be rash, indeed, to go beyond these comments and prophecies. It is enough to indicate that the problems of college admissions at present, and even more so in the future, are startling in their number, complexity, and size. Most of them are being studied and worked on, but it is clear that some of the greatest burdens and responsibilities are going to be thrown on the school. Every guidance officer has a major share in molding the future, and the sum of the individual efforts will in large part shape the course of higher education in our nation.

William Fels presented this paper with the purpose of encouraging the tiny flickers of cooperation with the professional secondary school administrators that had begun to appear.

The speech was a difficult one: the audience was composed of men who were fundamentally opposed to any form of external testing. Mr. Fels was required therefore to rest his entire talk on a philosophical defense of testing—which meant that he could not deal in any detail with the causes and products of educational expansion, which he would have preferred.

"How Tests May Be Used to Obtain Better Articulation of the Total Educational System," by William C. Fels
Speech to the National Association of Secondary-School Principals, February 22, 1954.

The title of this discussion is open to various interpretations, but since I am a representative of the College Entrance Examination Board and you are school principals, perhaps the two most fruitful aspects to explore are, "How can the leverage of tests be used to bring secondary and higher education into better alignment?" and, assuming that perfect alignment will never be possible—which I believe is the case—"How can tests help the student pass easily and economically from one level to the next?"

Tests undoubtedly have what one English examiner, Leslie T. Brereton, calls "mobilizing power." They can exert leverage. The degree of mobilizing power or leverage is dependent on the method of test construction, the nature of the test, its degree of externality, its degree of security, and the actions which depend on it.

Let me give you examples of tests that exert weak and strong leverage. The weakest of all is an unannounced short test, with several optional questions prepared by a classroom teacher and administered to his class. At the opposite extreme would be a test which was part of an announced testing program for some important purpose, which was prepared cooperatively by teachers on the sending and receiving levels, which was based on a published syllabus and sold after use, which was long and contained no options. In the first case you can see that no pressures bear on either teacher or student. In the second, it is clear that both will be under considerable pressure.

The present College Board program is another example which falls somewhere between the other two. The tests are constructed cooperatively by college and school teachers. They are external; there are no options; and they are taken for an important purpose, college entrance. But on the other hand they are secure; no syllabus is published; no old tests are sold. They are broad-based, objective tests. They are designed to place the minimum restriction on teaching within the broad scope of subdivisions of knowledge.

Clearly, a testing program does have the means to exert some influence toward better articulation. But those of us who have studied the matter feel that the influence cannot be very great, either for good or ill. A testing program can reinforce a trend; it cannot long buck one.

Why is this? Well, largely because there are other conditions in existence or forces at work which are more pervasive or stronger than any testing program. Look at the conditions and forces which militate against articulation.

First is the staggering diversity of American education. There is no national system of public education. Rather we have 48 state systems, each subdivided into a myriad of local systems controlled by local school boards. There is a parallel system of Catholic education controlled by the Church. A hundred Protestant sects have founded schools and colleges. And there are hundreds of independent schools and colleges, by-products of that American propensity to associate for benevolent purposes that de Toqueville remarked in the early nineteenth century.

The organization of education is as diverse as its control. The 16-year space of elementary, secondary, and higher education is almost everywhere split into three levels, but this first break may come at grades 6, 7, 8, 9, or 10, and the second change at grades 10, 11, 12, 13, or 14.

Our curriculums vary from the vocational to the academic, from the terminal to the interminable.

Our philosophies stretch from John Dewey to Canon Bell and lately to Canon Betts.[5]

Then there are the strong economic and social influences on the curriculum. Subjects move in and out of the schools in answer to much stronger dictates than those of any tests.

We are the most mobile people in the world. Last year 40,000 Puerto Ricans caused quite a stir by migrating to New York to find employment there. But the Puerto Ricans were less than a third of the "immigrants" to New York last year. Two-thirds simply moved there from other states.

This diversity I have described; these social and economic forces, this mobility of population make articulation extremely difficult and make tests only a minor force in the process.

---

5. "Canon Bell" is Bernard Iddings Bell, who has been warden of St. Stephen's College (later Bard College). "Canon Betts" refers jokingly to a Mr. Betts, a high school principal in Rochester, New York, who had denounced vigorously some of the recent changes in teaching mathematics. —FB

What then holds the system together? Why doesn't it fly apart like a shattered flywheel?

First of all, there is the integrity of subject matters. It is man whose problems we deal with: man's relations with the natural world, with other men in groups, and with himself, with his humanity. These relations are treated in the broad fields of science, social studies, and humanities. No matter how superficially or deeply we deal with those subjects, how elementary or complex the subject itself, we are always somewhere on the same continuum of knowledge.

Then there is the common culture. America is not a conglomerate of cultures, it is a composite culture. Our people share a body of beliefs, customs, views. Our educational system cannot stray far from these without public criticisms and pressures, as you know.

There is also the phenomenon of lag. Change is accomplished slowly and discontinuously. The College Board, for example, is still receiving orders for tests and syllabuses 20 or more years old.

Associations of educators, such as the one meeting here this week, exert a centripetal tendency. They hold things together.

So we have a system which is constantly trying to fly apart and constantly trying to hold itself together. As I have said, in this pulling and hauling, tests can make a difference only in reinforcing, not in bucking, trends.

The 50-year history of the College Board illustrates this fact. In 1900 there was an almost chaotic diversity of college entrance requirements. The schools objected strongly and called for a closer articulation of school and college. The Board, founded to achieve this end, pulled out the whole bag of examiners' tools and was able to draw the secondary schools and colleges into a line because they wanted to be pulled into line. Forty years later the schools found themselves too restricted, and the Board released pressures by withdrawing the definition of requirements, by refusing the sale of old tests (which could be used to build up syllabuses), by shifting to broad objective tests, and by other means. It wanted to do this, but it also had to do this.

Today we find a strong desire for closer articulation—but not too close —and we are under constant persuasion to exert influence to reinforce this or that trend.

Later I will describe some experiments with tendencies in this direction, but first let me consider where the present situation leaves the student.

He is called upon to make some pretty difficult transitions, some pretty long, hard jumps—say from a rural high school which cannot demand as much as it would like to of its best students to a first-rate college or university.

Tests can be used to articulate the individual and the system even when they are exerting little influence to bring the parts of the system together.

The whole procedure of testing, cumulative records, guidance, and placement, which you can find described in any textbook on measurement and guidance, can be brought to bear. I need not describe it to you here.

But it is important to make two distinctions: between aptitude and achievement tests, and between measurement of achievement and prediction of achievement.

Aptitude tests did not develop in this country by chance. They were an outgrowth of the need for classification of individuals whose education could not be compared and whose abilities had to be predicted, in a political and social system which wanted to give play to the talents of the able.

Aptitude tests arise from diversity. They do not improve the articulation of the system. In fact, they subvert it—and I'm glad they do, because I think diversity is the genius of the American system. They make it possible for individuals to jump gaps where, in a perfectly articulated system, no gaps would be.

Achievement tests are sometimes used in the same way: for example, they are combined with aptitude tests in the prediction of college success. But more often they are used as measures of status—for example, in sectioning and placement. In these uses, too, they can avoid the need for closer articulation between the parts of the system.

Now, having described with rather broad strokes the way tests can exert leverage and the way they can be used to help students jump gaps in an imperfectly articulated system, let me describe the new tendencies and trends tests are being called upon to reinforce. These I think are three: the desire to strengthen or enrich the college preparatory programs of the secondary schools; the desire to avoid repetition at different levels of the system; and the desire to shorten the span of education for able students who may be expected to go on to professional or graduate work. All these tendencies are reflected in different degree in three experiments sponsored by the Fund for the Advancement of Education, an offshoot of The Ford Foundation.

The first of these studies, in point of time, was first called the Pre-Induction Program and is now called the Program for Early Admission to College. This program takes able young students who have not finished high school and places them in college. No attempt is made to articulate school and college. The predictive power of both aptitude and achievement tests is used to make possible a jump over a long gap.

The second of these studies, the School and College Study of Admission with Advanced Standing, takes the opposite approach. Students jump the first year of college. But this experiment uses syllabuses to encourage schools to prepare the students so that the jump in time will not be a jump in subject matter. Achievement tests are used to measure status. Placement is their main purpose, not prediction.

The third study, with the similar name of School and College Study of General Education, aims at a directly articulated program covering grades 11, 12, 13, and 14, but will encourage jumping either a year of school or a year of college—not both—for those who appear qualified to make the jump.

A fourth experiment in Portland is a cooperative effort of Reed College and the Portland schools. It is working in other soil, the encouragement of able students with other than strictly academic talents.

The College Board is cooperating with the first three of these four studies. It is also preparing a new series of tests called the Tests of Developed Ability. The name will probably be changed, but it is intended to express the fact that these are combined aptitude and achievement tests. All tests are to some extent, but the effort before this has been to separate aptitude and achievement. Here the desire is to combine them. They will test developed ability, that is ability upon a base of achievement. There will be three tests, one in the humanities, one in the social studies, and one in the sciences. From the point of view of articulation, they are designed to give the schools a maximum of freedom in the selection and treatment of subject matter while encouraging them to develop the students' abilities in the major fields of knowledge.

Now, what will all these developments mean for you and for the student transferring from school to college? We foresee a somewhat closer articulation between college preparatory programs in the schools and college programs. We also foresee a new pattern of admissions testing. Perhaps there will be three stages.

1. Scholastic aptitude testing—this is shifting to earlier and earlier dates.

2. Tests of Developed Ability, plus school records, used for admissions.

3. A flexible battery of placement tests used after admission for students moving from grades 11 to 13, 12 to 13, and 12 to 14.

The paper on the admission of foreign students was given first as a paper and then rewritten and expanded for publication. It was one of the products of a small foundation grant to the Greater New York Council of Foreign Student Advisers, made to assist that group in a study of foreign student problems in the New York area.

I notice, in going back over it, that it deals with many day-to-day problems but never gets to the statement of the central problem, which is that the universities and colleges have never organized themselves to work cooperatively on problems of evaluating foreign credentials or of the admission, guidance, and education of foreign students. None of the agencies in the field speaks for the universities and colleges in the sense that the College Board speaks for them in the field of the admission of American students, and the lack of such an agency constitutes a real problem.

"The Admission of Foreign Students"
Written in January 1955 for the Greater New York Council of Foreign Student Advisers.

The admission of foreign students, by complete agreement of all those concerned in the process, is the most trying, difficult, time-consuming, and esoteric of the administrative arts as practiced today in American higher education. There can, in fact, be no doubt that this is so, for foreign students combine and compound all the problems of communication, application, evaluation, placement, counseling, and program making that are common to all students, and add to them problems of language, regulations, passports, and visas that are peculiarly their own. Whether it needs to be so is another matter and one which can be settled, if at all, by a consideration of the factors that today control the process.

First, and by all odds the most important of these factors, is that the entire business of foreign students is government-dominated and to a large extent government-controlled.

Although it was not always thus, the foreign student today is often selected by the government of his own country to study in the United States. Furthermore, when so selected, he is usually committed to a specific subject field, if not a specific program. To leave his country, he must obtain currency permissions which involve further scrutiny, must obtain his passport and an American visa, both procedures involving still other investigations including loyalty clearances. His admission to this country and his stay after arrival are controlled and regulated by the laws of the land in a status which involves careful compliance with a complex law. His placement as a student is often aided or accomplished by the Institute of International Education, which, though an independent agency, handles so much of government business relating to student exchange that it can be considered as virtually a government agency and maintains close contact with government agencies. In many cases, the United States government, through its Office of Education, makes recommendations as to evaluation of credentials which are in many institutions considered as sacred as an income tax ruling. Finally, if the student, having arrived and been placed, fails to behave (either academically or personally), the United States government, acting as a kind of grand-scale Dean of Students, will arrange to have him shipped home.

The point of this exposition is not to erect an argument against government control; it is merely to point out that with respect to foreign students, American higher education institutions have for the most part only the very limited admissions function of picking among candidates who have already been selected on criteria that are partially political, and the limited educational function of carrying out a program that is prescribed before the student reaches the institution. The results of such selections are in the main satisfactory as to the students and their acceptability, but sometimes embarrassing and sometimes disastrous. It does not require any striking feat of memory to recall the shiploads of Indian students who arrived in this country with all necessary clearances and strong support from United States governmental sources to study subjects that were not taught in any American colleges or universities. It is not inconceivable that some of the present lack of sympathy between India and our nation dates from the experience of some of these students, who were so hastily, and sometimes so badly, handled. Of the same order is Columbia's well-authenticated story of the three boys from the Asian highlands who pursued with patience and determination their government-inspired goal of M.D. degrees for each, stimulated by their government's assurance of decapitation as the penalty of failure.

A second problem touching foreign students, which is closely related to the practice of government sponsorship but which also existed before government sponsorship became as prevalent as it now is (about 50 percent of foreign students are, to judge from the statistics, under direct government sponsorship), has to do with the tendency of institutions to waive normal admissions procedures in favor of foreign applicants. These waivers include such fundamental changes in procedure as (1) acceptance of minimum credentials, or even of statements in lieu of credentials; (2) admission at a late date and without sufficient time for program planning or any but the most perfunctory exchange of correspondence; (3) waiver of quality requirements for foreign students, while maintaining them for other candidates; (4) blind acceptance of selections made in other countries by individuals not connected with the institution to which application is made. It is worth noting that while all of these academic sins are committed annually by a great many institutions in favor of foreign students, very few of them are committed by any self-respecting institution with respect to their regular and normal group of American applicants.

The third important problem relating to foreign students has to do with our—that is, American—lack of understanding of the educational concepts, ideals, systems, and programs of other nations and with the equal, and equally damaging, lack of understanding by others of the concepts and programs of American education. This discussion of problems and policies is no place for a discussion of comparative education, but a full discussion is not required to point out that the guiding principle of American education is opportunity for everyone willing and able to try for it with relatively few barriers to be hurdled, while the guiding principle in virtually every other nation in the world is limitation of opportunity to those who can surmount numerous and rigorous examinations. The difference in principle has two main results: the first, that in our country about 20 percent of any given age cohort has the opportunity to try higher education, whereas in other nations, including Great Britain, not more than 5 percent of an age cohort has such opportunity; the second, that the average standards applied to the American 20 percent are lower than the standards applied to the 5 percent of the other nations who have survived several eliminations and siftings. From this difference in average standards flow two different and damaging sets of conclusions: one, on the part of nationals of other countries, that American education is inferior to their own; the other, on our part, that American education is the same as that in other countries and can be equated subject by subject and year by year. Both of these assumptions are incorrect. American education is inferior when it deals with inferior students, and of these we get more into our system than do, comparably, the other countries of the world. In general, it is fully comparable to English and continental education and superior to education in South America and the Middle and Far East. But, since other countries deal with fairly homogeneous groups of high-ability students, their primary and secondary education programs are compressed, as compared to ours, and, when these programs are translated into our "credit" terms, they deserve more credit than a straight year-by-year equivalent.

Obviously, the solving of such an equation as this one offers great opportunity for misunderstanding, an opportunity that is regrettably enriched by the great variety of different specialized schools, each with its own purposes and requirements and rigidly maintained standards, that exist in other nations, and the contrary tendency in American schools to draw specialized programs under the single umbrella of higher education but to permit wide variation in quality as between apparently similar institutions.

There does not seem any obvious solution for this problem unless it is that of establishing the not unreasonable expectation that American academic people who deal with foreign students should be able to master the elementary facts of comparative education. These facts are not, as it happens, difficult to obtain or hard to learn. Reference material is plentiful, and the files of our institutions are full of records which provide actual case studies. The prescription, however, is easier to write than to follow, for it is all too often the case that the governmental aura which hangs over the foreign student inhibits attempts to understand and evaluate his education, or, alternatively, supplies a predigested evaluation and program. Indeed, the efforts of the United States government through its Office of Education to supply evaluation of foreign credentials, while always helpful and useful, actually operate to encourage our academic people to laziness with respect to the task of understanding foreign education.

A fourth set of problems that arises in connection with foreign students is that of objectives. Most students come to this country with firmly fixed goals that are likely to be based on a narrow definition of studies to be followed, a disinclination for any of the required courses which are so prominent a part of our system, a limited budget of time and money, and a determination to obtain a recognized academic credential. Since, in general, our foreign students are mature individuals, they pursue their goals with a firmness of purpose and an unwillingness to either accept advice or to change their plans, which comes as a shock to us who are accustomed to our own easier-going fellow countrymen. We could understand these objectives, and the firmness with which they are held, more easily if we could understand the structure of the professional, academic, and social life of the society from which these students come, and could realize that the opportunity to study in this country is for most foreigners a make-or-break opportunity, sometimes—though rarely—even to the life-or-death urgency of the Asian students referred to earlier.

The importance of these objectives to foreign students and the urgency of the task of reaching them tends, in American eyes, to render these foreign students difficult to deal with and impatient of our ideas and methods. It is of little importance to a foreign engineer to study, as do our engineering students, some broad aspects of American political and social life. A knowledge of our English idiom he will accept, both as an end in itself and as a necessary tool for his ends, but he will not accept as a comparable necessity any study of our institutions, which are to us inseparable from our language. The tight schedule of our required courses in undergraduate and professional curriculums is for foreign students an unreasonable method of delaying their pursuit of their goal. Hence, it is only natural that they should seek constantly to change those requirements to achieve greater specialization in less time.

A further confusion is introduced by the fact that foreign students do not understand either our hierarchy of degrees or our hierarchy of institutions. A foreign student who comes to follow a particular program is often dismayed to find that it does not lead to the degree he wants in the time he wants it; a student who comes to obtain a degree is often equally distressed to find that it does not represent the program he wants. Further confusion arises from the fact that the same degrees are given for different courses—such as the B.S., which covers everything from occupational therapy to economics, or the M.A., which covers everything in the academic spectrum—or that different degrees are given for similar programs, sometimes in the same institutions. Similarly, the vast range of institutions in our country, all giving just about the same degrees, represents to the individual foreign student a problem in evaluation which is peculiarly difficult to solve. These problems, which we have learned to take in our stride, tend to force the foreign student into a good deal of intrainstitutional and interinstitutional movement, much of it actually unnecessary, but resulting from the student's personal plan to reach his objectives as rapidly and as easily as possible.

A still further complication for the foreign student arising from our academic structure is the misunderstanding that arises from our category of "special student." We understand this to mean a student who has not complied (or does not care to comply) with our degree requirements, but who can be permitted to follow courses suitable to his needs. The fact that no such category for students (except for summer programs) exists in universities outside of the United States tends to lead the foreign student into a trap. He comes to this country to study, let us say, personnel management. Since he has appropriate credentials, he is admitted and elects to be a "special student," since only in this category can he avoid requirements which seem to him unrelated. A year later, having completed his program, he finds—to his dismay and, in his judgment, unfairly—that he cannot get a degree, even though he has covered all the personnel management courses that are in the degree program. The attempt to explain why he cannot usually leads nowhere, for such an attempt must reach back into the sometimes elusive logic of degree requirements and must dismiss the fact, so obvious to the student, that he has done the important part of the work and should therefore get the important recognition of the degree.

The failures, the difficulties, and the grief brought about by this lack of understanding of the American system of higher education are all the more tragic because they affect individuals where it hurts the most—at the point of recognition and reward for effort. The worst of it is that much of the trouble is avoidable and could be remedied if those who are responsible for sending foreign students to this country would put in the time and trouble necessary to understand the system with which they are dealing. And, on the other hand, much of the trouble that foreign students encounter in handling our system could be avoided if they could be brought to understand our system and if our administrators could understand the basic facts as to their educational backgrounds. In part, at least, this is our responsibility, but only in part, for nothing can exempt any student from the common-sense responsibility of trying to learn what he is getting into and how to get along in his environment.

A fifth and insistent problem in foreign student admissions is that of their command of English. This is a problem on which many a foreign student and many an admissions officer have foundered—the admissions officer because he is disposed to place overmuch emphasis on ability to command English; the foreign student because he is disposed to consider that ability too lightly. Both of these viewpoints miss the crux of the matter, which is that the real problem in foreign student admissions is to assess the student's ability to complete his planned program in the time he has set aside for it. Each student coming to an American university can, if he has requisite abilities—and most of them do have—learn English and use it as a language of instruction, but very often they cannot do this and complete their program in the time they have scheduled. It is entirely proper for an admissions officer to insist upon good reading, writing, and speaking knowledge of English, but only if he does so by way of making clear to the student that without that knowledge he cannot achieve his objective within the institution's scheduled minimum time. Conversely, it is entirely proper for an admissions officer to admit a student without inquiring into his knowledge of English, but only if, in so doing, it is made clear to the student that the time required for him to complete the work in which he is interested cannot be determined until after his skill in handling English has been determined

—and that even then the time required is merely an approximation, as it is even in the case of American students.

It is not proper for an admissions officer to admit a foreign student with an unqualified promise as to the length of time required to complete a program without having a firm understanding of the student's ability to command English. Likewise, it is improper for a foreign student to conceal or misrepresent his ability in English in order to obtain a firm promise from an institution as to the time required for his training.

It has to be recognized that there are at the moment no tests of any real value in determining from a distance a student's ability to read, write, or speak English. Such tests can be devised, but their administration requires skill and standard conditions and is likely to be expensive. Furthermore, they usually have to be paid for in hard currency. It has proved very difficult to obtain the standard conditions, skill in administration, and hard currency all with respect to the same student. At one time it was expected that our several government agencies would take care of this matter of testing foreign students for their ability in English, but so far this has not worked out.

A sixth distinctly touchy problem with respect to foreign students, and one on which it is easy to make unpleasant generalizations, has to do with their quality as academic performers. Here it is well to remind ourselves that we as a nation have not, since the development of our own graduate schools—that is to say, not in the last half century—had the tradition of sending any substantial number of our best students abroad for study, although the Fulbright Scholarship Program has recently begun to reverse this trend with very satisfactory results in foreign appreciation of American education. The same thing has been true of foreign students. The prewar foreign students in America were not an outstanding group, although within their number there were outstanding individuals. Often they were mediocre students who came to America in pursuit of the distinction of having studied abroad, very much as some American students have gone to Europe to obtain the export models of continental degrees.

Since the war the situation has been different in that, as remarked earlier, a good many students are now seeking the advanced training in skills and techniques which our universities offer. These students are at any rate purposeful, and many of them are able. But, even so, their quality is not outstanding and too often fails to justify the amount of special attention these students require, unless this special handling is accompanied by a tolerant attitude based on the understanding that we are still not receiving the best products of foreign institutions. It is, of course, only natural that this should be so. The best individuals have immediate opportunities in their homeland, and it tends to be the second best who are selected for training as technicians.

Within this problem of quality of foreign students as a large group, there is another and persistent problem which can be described as the "professional foreign student," a category which has three important subdivisions: the veteran, the floater, and the weeper.

The veteran foreign student is one who pursues, often displaying a great deal of academic ability in the process, the goal of life tenure as a foreign student. If he handles himself well he goes from degree to degree, from scholarship to fellowship to research grant, and from student status to assistantship and finally to research associate and even to authorship, always using his foreign student status as a fulcrum to help him in his next move and always finding one more haven to shelter him for one more year.

This type of student is a good cut above the second type, the floater, who drifts from one institution to another, usually without finishing anything, perpetually in difficulties, and forever escaping them.

The floaters in turn overlap the third type, the weepers, or the helpless ones, who, like their American cousins in the same category, are unable to understand any of the requirements or regulations with which they are expected to comply and who propel themselves through their programs as nuisances to be passed on and on, until they finally are given degrees to get rid of them—a process which, considering the number of institutions and degrees available in the nation, can be prolonged almost indefinitely.

There is another group of professional foreign students who are tragic. These are the political exiles and the stateless ones who have become, through no act of their own, genuinely homeless and too often genuinely penniless, yet who cannot find the loopholes in the law to permit them to escape into the stream of American life. This group is too large for comfort, but the fact is that no man knows how large. They are, in a political sense, an American problem, and so far one with which we have not dealt properly.

The seventh set of problems touching foreign students has to do with the laws under which they are admitted and under which they remain in this country. In discussing these laws it is well to point out that they fall into two general categories.

The first of these categories is the general law of the land—that is, the civil and criminal codes and pertinent federal legislation which touches everyone residing within these United States. There are certain aspects of this general law of the land that are rarely, if ever, explained to foreign students. The first is that there are in the shape of states, counties, cities, and smaller subdivisions, as well as the District of Columbia, innumerable civil and criminal jurisdictions as contrasted with the national jurisdictions to which they are accustomed. This means that a student in trouble with the local law may suffer deeply from sheer ignorance of what law he is in trouble with and be hopelessly entangled before help can come to him. In particular, civil law as it relates to automobile accidents may be a fertile cause of trouble, unless the student has spent at least as much on insurance as he has spent on his 1946 jalopy. The second aspect of the law of the land that requires attention is that certain federal legislation affects all maintaining residence and receiving income within the United States, in particular the income tax law and the Selective Service Act. Furthermore, it is easy for a foreign student in an institution that has a compulsory Reserve Officers Training Corps program to become confused between required ROTC and the provisions of the Selective Service Act.

The second general category of law which affects the foreign student covers those laws which are specifically directed at the foreign student, and the administrative regulations that have the force of law so far as the foreign student is concerned. These laws and regulations make in themselves quite a sizable body of legal materials, and foreign students may well be pardoned for not knowing them in detail, since very few foreign student advisers can claim this distinction.

The real problem for the foreign student in complying with the law is not the complexity of the law (that is bad enough, but a well-behaved individual may have a lengthy residence in this country without ever encountering the true extent of that complexity) but the fact that we who are charged with the responsibility for advising and working with foreign students do not discharge what is in fact one of our important obligations—

that of explaining to the students the general processes of American law, the points at which everyone is likely to come in contact with the law, the specific provisions of specific laws which touch foreign students as foreign students, and finally the reasons underlying the laws and rules. In this connection, it is well to quote a remark of Paul Chalmers, which appears in an article in the November 1954 *Newsletter of National Association of Foreign Student Advisers:* "The regulations that seem just and reasonable are those which have been written particularly for the foreign student. The regulations that cause misunderstanding, annoyance, and even injustice are those that address themselves to all aliens, without consideration of the peculiar characteristics of the alien student, researcher, or teacher."

Implicit in all the problems described above is the problem of deciding whether a foreign student is a student or a foreigner. This is a decision for both the foreign student and the institution that receives him.

When the foreign student is treated fundamentally as a foreigner, or thinks of himself primarily as a foreigner, the results are nearly always unfortunate. From the institutional side, the student is either given privileges or put under handicaps that result in an abnormal education. And from the student side, the results tend to be equally bad, for the student becomes a professional foreign student, trading on his status rather than his ability.

On the other hand, when both the student and the institution can view the foreign student as an individual coming from an unusual background and perhaps pursuing an unusual goal, then the problems that arise can be handled on their merits, if both sides will give or take a little in their opinions and requirements.

The formulation of policies to be followed in the admission of foreign students is now and must always be controlled to a large extent by the factors listed above as well as by other factors which may have been omitted or which occur in special situations. Therefore, in the last analysis, these policies can only be changed or modified as our understanding and the understanding of our foreign students, as well as those who send them to us, develops. Ways of achieving this development are:

1. The publication of a handbook for foreign students which, beginning with a chapter on comparative education by way of orientation, goes on to describe, in sufficient detail, the American system of higher education. It should also include a summary of laws relating to foreign students. Such

a handbook should help a great deal in getting foreign students settled intellectually in their institutions.

2. The production of a handbook, probably loose-leaf, for admissions officers and foreign student advisers which would enable those who deal with foreign students to understand their background and to make simple evaluations of credit, particularly the common evaluations dealing with secondary school credentials.

It is, of course, recognized that there is nothing new in these suggestions. They are nothing more than ideas for another presentation of material that is already available. But these materials, or something like them, are required to establish an understanding between student and institution.

Beyond these suggestions, the development of policies in the handling of foreign student admissions comes down to a series of suggestions for procedure within the policies that already exist and are in many cases required by the situation. These suggestions come under the following headings.

1. Gather full information as to preparation and insist on complete credentials. Foreign students, particularly when they are government-sponsored, are prone to rely on a written statement of their studies which is sometimes misleading. Only when credentials are in hand can a student's readiness to undertake his proposed program be assessed.

2. Develop self-reliance in evaluation. Government services are often delayed and are prone to use pat evaluations. Admissions officers should be able to make all the standard evaluations. Then government services could be relied on for help in the difficult ones.

3. Get a clear statement, not only of announced objective, but of the levels that the student has in mind. Students who want to study chemistry may be planning on a laboratory technician's course, and engineering very often means study of maintenance and repair. A study of the American labor movement is likely to mean nothing at all. Only if the objective is explained, matched to preparation, and understood can an admission be made on valid grounds.

4. Do not admit save when a program is obviously available at the level the student is ready for. Programs to be worked out on the basis of evaluations to be made after the student arrives are likely to be unsuitable.

5. Do not admit on poor preparation. A poorly prepared foreign student does damage all around.

6. Always strive to admit to a degree program, even when the student doesn't say he wants one. Odds are 10 to 1 that he will be asking degree status within a month after arrival.

7. Spell out every step in advance, using if possible a prepared registration guide. Foreign students are accustomed to informal registration procedures and do not understand our precise and formal methods.

8. Be sure the student understands our system of attendance, recitation, required courses, examinations, and residence and degree requirements.

9. Get a clear statement of the student's sources of support, living conditions, available resources, and personal plans. These are essential to proper advisement.

10. Insist on maintenance of institutional standards.

11. Treat the foreign student as a student.

I have always considered this my best paper.

It will be recalled that in 1955 a "student bulge," which was the result of the large number of children born in 1940, was apparent in the high schools, and everyone's eyes were focused there. Some colleges were woebegone with fear of overcrowding; others looked forward eagerly to increased enrollment as a form of financial salvation.

The paper developed out of an attempt to find out, from the enrollment and population figures, what had happened in the past as a result of population increase. The findings made interesting reading, and they led to forecasts that, at least to me, were totally unexpected.

I have reason to think that the paper had a good deal of influence. At any rate, the Board distributed hundreds of copies of it, it was published in College and University, *and it was quoted in many papers and speeches.*

The paper is actually two papers, for it changes direction in the middle to discuss probable future developments in several fields. These forecasts, reviewed in 1967, seem ambiguous and a bit obvious, but they are left in this version because they were part of the assignment.

"Facing the Increasing Demands for Higher Education"
An address at the annual meeting of the New Jersey Association
of Colleges and Universities, at the College of St. Elizabeth,
Convent Station, New Jersey, on March 26, 1955. Printed by
the College Entrance Examination Board, 1955, 21 pp.
Published in *College and University*, the journal of the
American Association of Collegiate Registrars and Admissions
Officers, Vol. 31, No. 1, October 1955, pp. 5–22 (entitled
"Form and Direction of Growth in American Higher
Education").

Our topic today is in fact the predicted form and direction of growth of the American system of higher education. We bring to the discussion of this topic one fact and a good deal of experience.

The fact is that there has been during the last 15 years a tremendous growth in the population of the nation. To be precise about it, this growth has produced 18-year-old age groups of 2,300,000 for 1955, 2,800,000 for 1960, 3,600,000 for 1965, and 3,700,000 for 1970. This, I emphasize, is a fact, because all of these individuals are now on earth and have been counted, perhaps not with complete accuracy, but at any rate counted.

The experience is that college enrollments increase when population increases. This has been the case, and we may assume it will continue to be, but since we do not know the coefficient of increase we cannot cite firm statistics. But we do know that college entrants in 1953 were 572,000 and in 1954 were 581,000, and we have reason to predict that they will number 600,000 next fall.

Assumptions concerning college growth

During the 18 months since this topic first came under discussion, we have been building up a structure of assumptions relating to the results of the increase in and growth of college population, which can be stated as follows.

1. Enrollments in institutions of higher education will increase in proportion to the size of the age group.

2. Virtually every institution of higher education in the nation will have an unlimited supply of applicants from which to pick and choose.

3. This constantly increasing pressure will bear equally on every part of our entire structure of higher education.

4. Enrollments will be limited only by the colleges' facilities, equipment, and faculty.

5. The enlarged student bodies will choose programs of study in about the same ratio as students are now choosing programs.

6. These students will be prepared for college in the same patterns and to the same extent that students are now prepared.

7. The mean ability levels of these student bodies will be equal or superior to the mean ability levels of present student bodies.

These assumptions add up to the belief that the increased demand for higher education will change the size of our system, but will not affect materially its form or structure—in other words, we will keep on doing what we are now doing, but it will be on a larger scale. My thesis today is that these assumptions do not supply a firm basis for planning and that we will be on much safer ground if we anticipate that both the size and the structure of our system will be altered, that we must in the next 20 years expect to change the form of many of our present institutions, must develop some completely new institutions, and perhaps must cease operating some of our existing institutions.

These assumptions challenged

I feel that the assumptions that I have alluded to are inadequate because we have failed to account for the wide fluctuations in the growth of American higher education shown by the history of the past 80 years, and because we have failed to consider that the factors that contributed to these fluctuations are now present in our society and will probably result in similar wide fluctuations in the growth of higher education over the next 20 years. In other words, I believe that what we have assumed to be *the* law regarding the growth of colleges in relation to population increase is in fact only one of two laws regarding the growth of colleges.

To make my point clear, let me state both of the laws that I have in mind. The first law is that colleges grow in relation to population increase. The second law is that, in addition to growing in relation to population increase, college enrollments grow in response to the current needs and demands of society.

These laws derive naturally from the operation of society. The simplest form of organized society has need for only three kinds of educated men—priests, chiefs, and witch doctors. If within this simple organization the population increases, there will be a proportionate need for increase in the number of these leaders, and so long as this society remains stable and structured in that pattern, the ratio will hold constant, at least until a witch doctors' association is organized for the purpose of raising professional standards. But if the society becomes complex and needs specialists, such as soldiers, engineers, and scribes, the number of educated men will have to increase in proportion to the population.

This is exactly what has happened in America.

Basic statistics

The statistics on which I base my remarks are figures showing population growth and numbers of college graduates during the period 1870 to 1950.

In the first half of this period—that is, from 1870 to 1910—our population grew from 40 million to 92 million, or 130 percent, while the number of college graduates increased from 9,300 to 34,200, or 260 percent.

In the second half of this period—that is, from 1910 to 1950—the population rose from 92 million to 151 million, or 65 percent, while the number of college graduates increased from 34,200 to 434,000. Since the latter figure is skewed by veteran enrollment, we can correct it conservatively to 260,000. This leaves us with an increase of 660 percent in the number of college graduates.

To recapitulate these figures, we have one 40-year period during which population increased by 130 percent, while college graduations increased by 260 percent, followed by another 40-year period during which population increased by only 65 percent, while college graduations increased by a whopping 660 percent.

You will note that during the period from 1870 to 1910 the increase in college enrollment was directly related to the growth of the population. A one-to-one correspondence between the two factors accounts for half of the growth of the college population, leaving half to be accounted for by social change. During the second 40 years there was no discernible relationship between population growth and college enrollments, for a one-to-one correspondence between the two factors would have accounted for only one-tenth of the change in the size of college population. We cannot, therefore, rely on population figures in predicting the increases in demands for education, since, as I have already pointed out, population is of itself only a contributing factor and not a determinant. Therefore, in order to make our predictions as to the form and structure of American higher education, we must examine the changes in the form and structure of our society and consider the effect those changes had on our educational structure. Once we have done this, we are in a position to undertake some predictions as to the form and structure of that society over the next 20 years.

Social change in America

If we apply this method to the figures I have just quoted and go back in American history to 1870, we find a society much more firmly structured than our society is today, at least as to its leadership. Nicholas Murray Butler [president of Columbia University from 1902 to 1945] once remarked that the two great nineteenth-century professions in America were the law and the ministry. Had he added medicine as a third, he could have stated with complete accuracy that the task of our nineteenth-century colleges was the production of men for these three professions.

This is not conjecture. It is provable by facts adduced by Dael Wolfle in *America's Resources of Specialized Talent,*[6] wherein he shows that, during the decade 1901 to 1910, 85 percent of all who received either bachelor's degrees or first professional degrees were in the liberal arts, which was the area of ministerial preparation, the health fields, or law, with only 5 percent in engineering and 10 percent in all other fields in which degrees were offered.

But while it is true that this period in American history was one wherein no great change in society actually took place, it is also true that it was a period during which great changes were in the making. The country was making the transition from an economy based on manpower applied to agriculture and limited industry to an economy based on the power of steam, electricity, and the internal combustion engine applied to the ex-

---

6. New York: Harper & Brothers, 1954, 318 pp.

ploitation of raw materials and their manufacture into marketable products. This was a technological revolution which produced great social changes, such as the beginnings of the great American fortunes, agrarian unrest (which was actually a form of counterrevolution), and the beginnings of the formation of labor unions (which were in effect the first step toward achieving a wider distribution of the profits of these great developments). As an important result, this technological revolution produced a major change in the function and structure of American education.

Changes in education

The striking nature of this change is shown by the fact that by 1951 liberal arts, law, and medicine represented only 42 percent of the total product of our higher educational system, instead of the 85 percent they had accounted for. The remaining 58 percent trained in technical or professional fields must be compared with 15 percent in all of those fields 40 years before. In fact, this change was so great that education and related fields, which do not even appear in the tabulation in 1910, were by 1951 accounting for over one-fifth of all college graduates; business and commerce, which likewise did not appear in the 1910 tabulations, accounted for one-sixth of all college graduates; applied biology, which did not appear in the 1910 figures, accounted for one-twentieth of all graduates; and engineering, which had accounted for one-twentieth of the 1910 graduates, had risen to one-tenth.

It seems clear to me that this rather bewildering array of figures proves not only that it is not possible to predict college enrollments from population figures, but proves also that the changes in American society during this century have been even more striking than we had realized.

I think that we have not realized that one of the greatest of the changes has been the shift in leadership from the generalist, the man trained in the humanities or the law, to the technician, the specialist, the man of competence, trained and experienced in the management of men and affairs.

As a striking example of the acceptance of this shift by the American nation, I cite the history of the American presidency from 1800 to the present. During the nineteenth century, almost all of our presidents were lawyers, and many of them noted lawyers. The only ones not learned in the law were soldiers—Taylor, Harrison, and Grant. I think I am safe in saying that every other president had legal training, and some—Van Buren, Jackson, Lincoln, Hayes, and Cleveland—were well known as lawyers. But in this our twentieth century, the last president of acknowledged legal distinction was Taft. Since he left the White House, we have had political scientists, editors, professional politicians, engineers, and soldiers, but none of legal distinction, while we have as a nation repeatedly rejected distinguished lawyers of both parties—Hughes, John William Davis, Willkie, Dewey, and Stevenson. Here, I think, is clear evidence that the requirement for the skilled technician and manager, be he engineer, politician, or soldier, has come in our minds to replace the requirement for the generalist and the learned man.

Four types of specialists

Actually, we have in America been so successful in producing technicians and specialists that we can classify them under broad headings and determine their relationship to each other, to society, and to our educational structure. There are four such headings: engineering for the design, building, and operation of industry; management for the subordinate commands in our economic structure; merchandisers to dispose of the products of our corporate structure; and service technicians such as nurses, pharmacists, accountants, social workers, and others, who exist to meet the immediate needs of the consuming public or to assist our relatively small professional groups in doing so. Somewhere in these categories come the educators, who were absolutely indispensable in the provision of the numerous and varied types of professional, nonprofessional, and technical training required to maintain this great structure.

These figures, facts, theories, and laws with which I have been belaboring you are, as you will have noted, based on the history and present state of our educational structure. They do not supply any basis for predicting the incidence of increased demands for education, except as they relate to those aspects of our present social structure that we can expect to find in the structure of the next 20 years. As it happens, it seems reasonable to believe that many of our requirements for training men during the next 20 years will be similar to our present requirements. However, we cannot launch off blithely into prediction on that basis alone without considering other variables that may exist.

Changes in the liberal arts

The first of these variables has to do with the nature of the firm core of our program of higher education—the studies in the liberal arts and sciences.

I have already commented that technical specialties have drawn a tremendous number of students away from the liberal arts. It might be just as correct to say that many of the students now in technical fields would not have come to college at all merely to follow the liberal arts, but this in a sense is beside the point. The point is that the A.B. degree has changed so completely that no single subject as studied in the course of the ordinary A.B. program of today would have been a part of the ordinary A.B. program of 1870. That program, as we all recall from our occasional forays into the history of education, was based almost entirely upon the classics and the study of the history and thought of ancient times. Today, the A.B. degree is based primarily upon the study of contemporary materials or of materials that are designed to explain the contemporary.

As it happens, this does not bother me, and I hope it does not bother anyone else, but it does indicate two things: first, that changes in education have not been confined to the introduction of technical and occupational programs; second, that our A.B. programs are tending to become introductory or preprofessional programs followed either by preparation for some other program on the professional or graduate level, or by preparation for some one of the advanced inservice training programs offered by our large corporations or by a governmental agency.

Changes in secondary education

There is yet one more fact which we must consider before we can undertake predictions of the form and structure of American higher education in the foreseeable future. It is that during the first 50 years of this century, we have essentially completed the development of our educational system through the twelfth grade; that is, we have adopted the principle that all Americans within a given age group are entitled to the opportunity to finish secondary school, we have built a substantial part of the plant which is necessary for them to be able to do so, and we are in the process of increasing the size of that plant. We have trained the administrators, have trained many of the teachers and are in the process of training more, and are in the process of agreeing on a curriculum that will probably be controlling for at least the next 20 years.

There are, I think, some comments to be made about secondary school systems which are important in terms of planning our colleges and universities. The first is that the educational and cultural opportunities available today in secondary school are on the whole vastly richer than were the educational and cultural opportunities available in college at the beginning of this century, and they are better than the opportunities now offered in some colleges. In other words, our secondary schools today, while overcrowded, are well-equipped, are manned by trained teachers, are supervised by experienced administrators, and are able to offer preparation for a wide variety of careers. By contrast, at the beginning of this century our secondary schools were almost entirely oriented to narrow college preparation, as is evidenced by the fact that, in 1900, 75 percent of all secondary school graduates went to college. Today, as we know, the percentage is nationally about half of that, although it is obviously tending to increase.

The second comment is that the very breadth of the secondary school curriculum is forcing, as a simple matter of administration, a comparable breadth in the college curriculum and has also tended to foster a tremendous spread in the abilities of our college-going students, since many students can now move through the broad spaces of the secondary school program without ever having their abilities evaluated, or without ever reaching a point where they are forced to choices or decisions.

The third point is that in the course of their development during this century the secondary schools have discarded certain tasks that they formerly performed. One of these tasks, most important of all from the standpoint of the colleges, was that of exact preparation for the college program. Another of these tasks was the introduction of the study of certain of the more exacting disciplines, such as the foreign languages, mathematics, and science.

These several changes in the role of the secondary school in our educational system have been so thoroughly and completely deplored over the last 20 years, and particularly over the last 10 years, that I can see no point in adding to the literature of mournfulness. Instead, I would like to point out that the secondary schools are doing on their level much the same thing as the colleges have been doing on their level. The difference is that in the main the colleges have been able to insist on and maintain the principles of specialization within the many programs of studies that they offer, while the secondary schools have brought all of these programs into one comprehensive curriculum where they have offered them on a sampling basis. Since I can see no possibility that the secondary schools will turn back to their former role as institutions subordinate to and preparing for the colleges, I have mentioned this variable because I believe it to be one of the most important in our educational planning.

The controlling factors

Since I am at this point about to launch myself fearlessly into the future, I think I should, before doing so, stop to draw together the variables that I have set forth as the controlling factors in determining the shape of the future.

The first is that social structure is the determining factor in the structure of higher education.

The second is that the development of our social structure in America has been a development based on the use of technicians and the applications of technology, with a concomitant growth in the training of educators to assist in turn in the training of technicians, and another concomitant growth —which is still only in embryo stages—of the training of service technicians who assist us in myriad ways in dealing with the problems of living in our complex society.

I have also commented that the A.B. degree, which has been the bench mark of standards in American education, is no longer serving the purpose which it once served and has in fact become a generalized preparation for specializations into which all of us are now inevitably forced in American life.

Finally, I have commented that our system of education has been substantially completed through the twelfth grade in terms of its structure, its purposes, and its philosophy. In very broad terms, the secondary diploma is now serving somewhat the same purposes that the A.B. degree serves, that is, a very broad and general preparation for later specializations. That being the case, there is no reason for us to expect or hope for any change in the preparation of college students or in any other of the functions of our secondary schools, at least within the generation with which we are now concerned.

In making our plans to meet the increased demands for education, we need not, I think, concern ourselves with an overelaborate prediction of the form of American society in 1975 so long as we bear in mind that it is the form of society rather than the size of the population that is the ultimate determinant of the structure of education.

What we do need to concern ourselves with is a sensible projection of current demands for educated people combined with a dispassionate analysis of the ways in which we are now meeting those demands and a search for better methods of meeting them.

We can go about this by working down the several broad lines along which we are now educating people and seeing what changes are likely to come and what they are likely to be.

The future of liberal arts colleges

For historical reasons, let us start with the so-called traditional A.B. degree, which, as I have remarked, no longer follows the traditional pattern although it is still labeled the A.B.

We depend on the A.B. as basic preparation for nearly all of our most highly trained specialists including research scientists, college teachers, physicians, lawyers, and high-level government officials. We also depend on the A.B. to furnish preparation for service professions that have been placed on the postbaccalaureate level, such as social work, library science, and public administration. In addition, we expect that a very large number of responsible posts requiring long inservice training rather than graduate and professional education will be filled from the ranks of holders of the A.B., as well as, of course, an even larger number of positions in the medium-income brackets. Yet, despite the fact that all these tasks are loaded upon the A.B. program, the demand for A.B. graduates is now being met without utilizing all of the available facilities. It is true that perhaps 50 of the country's strongest liberal arts institutions are under heavy pressure, and that perhaps 50 or 100 additional such institutions, not quite as well known, are managing to stay comfortably full. But there are a sizable number of institutions that can offer an entirely respectable A.B. that are not full and that have no immediate prospects of filling up unless they develop a much larger clientele than they now possess. I believe that many institutions in this latter group are presently basking in the comfortable assurance that the rush of students will fill them and that they will once more live in security. I believe that many who think so are going to be terribly disappointed.

As I have already pointed out, the popularity of the A.B. programs has declined steadily for 80 years, and in addition the nature of the A.B. programs has changed completely, which is another way of saying that the A.B. program has stayed in existence only because it has executed a complete change from its traditional pattern.

These changes have taken place because of the development of technical specialties and the development of professional programs to service them. This has affected the A.B. programs in two ways. First, they have served as development grounds for certain professional programs which are then removed and set up as separate programs, as in the cases of business and social work. Second, many of the resources formerly assigned to A.B. programs have had to go to strengthen professional programs that have developed from subprofessional levels, such as nursing, medical technology, and journalism.

We have therefore a contradictory situation in which the liberal arts serve as general-purpose programs, thereby tending to increase the pressure on liberal arts colleges, while at the same time certain professional programs are being developed by drawing teachers and students away from the liberal arts. I suspect that the long-term result of this will be to strengthen the strong liberal arts institutions which can adapt themselves to the general-purpose task, and to weaken institutions which cannot do so. I think the results of this will come out about as follows.

1. The institutions now under heavy pressure will continue to be under heavy pressure and will expand their facilities about 25 percent overall, with the state universities and the large urban institutions expanding far more than the residential colleges that are at the top of the prestige list.

2. The institutions that are now comfortably full and prosperous will come under moderate pressure and will expand from 10 to 25 percent to meet that pressure.

3. The institutions not now under pressure will be affected in one of two ways. Those institutions that are now located reasonably near to growing urban centers will expand as day colleges and will develop into small or medium-sized universities. Those institutions not now well located with respect to population centers will continue to struggle to stay alive. They will face the alternatives of closing their doors or of accepting a new role

in the training of what I have described as service technicians, or in the training of teachers. Many of them are in fact now doing just that, under the elastic covering of what is called an A.B. program.

In addition to these considerations as to the future of the liberal arts institutions, there are some important considerations with respect to the nature of those programs. I suggest that changes in those programs will continue. One of the most important changes I believe will be the slow disappearance of the required study of foreign languages. This disappearance is already well under way, and I can see nothing to arrest it. The facilities for language study will, of course, remain, as indeed they now remain for Latin and Greek, but with language study now disappearing from the secondary schools, and college requirements already at a minimum, I suspect that many colleges will give up the struggle. Another important change, I believe, will be the introduction of strong courses in the arts, emphasizing participation rather than history, theory, and appreciation. Still another development will, I expect, be the general formalization of reading programs, particularly if we can arrive at some reasonable method of evaluating the results of such programs. I will note as an aside that courses in these areas rate so high in student popularity that I have never known a college which did good work in these areas to be in serious trouble on account of student morale or student support, though I have known some of these colleges that had developed serious financial ailments as a partial result of introducing such programs.

The future of science study in our strong arts colleges has become a matter of grave concern. I believe it will continue to be until our teachers of science and mathematics can undertake a courageous overhaul of their offerings and eliminate the ridiculous concentration requirements which tie up two-thirds or more of the students' time during the four years that are advertised as being a broadening and enriching experience. I suspect that if such an overhaul is made, the natural attractions of science will hold many students who are now abandoning the field in protest against the grinding hours of labor that are attached to it.

Although I am gloomy as to the future of the A.B. degree in any but the strongest institutions, I am not at all gloomy as to the development of liberal arts studies. I think that the trend, already well established, of adding humanistic studies to professional programs will continue, which is another way of saying that these studies will continue to be the core of our system of higher education by spreading their influence through all parts of the system, rather than concentrating it in the traditional pattern.

The future of teacher education

Numerically, the second most important area of education today is that of teacher preparation. Here we are faced with the fact that it has taken a long time for teacher education to gain recognition as higher education. I am not of course talking about the education of college teachers and scholars, but about secondary, primary, and specialized teachers. It is only within the last 20 years that the majority of teachers' colleges in the land have acquired the right to give bachelor's degrees, and even today these degrees are often held in low esteem. I have suggested earlier that the acquisition of status by the teaching profession is related to the need for large numbers of educated people to serve in our commercial and industrial structure. Partially for the reason that this structure will continue to need the services of teachers and will therefore continue to support teacher education indirectly by supporting schools, and partially because the teaching profession is generating its own dynamic of self-improvement, I believe that we can expect a steadily increasing interest in teaching as a profession and a steady improvement in the quality of the education of teachers.

The increasing interest will, I think, come about as a consequence of the successful effort to make teaching attractive as a profession by paying a living wage, providing social benefits such as broad insurance coverage and pension benefits, assuring job security, and regulating the work load. If we add these items to the long vacations, we have an unusually attractive and secure work situation compared to the average office or factory job. This fact is being realized, particularly by children of families that are taking their first steps up the social scale.

As to teacher education, it must be said that it still has a long way to go, but that it is well started toward improvement. An important part of this start has been contributed by the strong liberal arts colleges that have integrated teacher-training programs with their regular programs. Unfortunately, the teachers' colleges and graduate schools for teachers have been slow in taking this hint and have not yet taken the drastic step of overhauling the dreary and repetitious courses in the principles and methods of pedagogy. If this can be done so that youngsters can enter teacher-training institutions with reasonable assurance of finding good libraries and laboratory equipment (which are unaccountably missing in many teachers' colleges) and of following a lively and interesting curriculum under teachers who combine a sound knowledge of subject matter with an understanding of pedagogy, then the popularity of teaching as a profession can be assured, and we shall have gone a long way toward meeting the teacher shortage.

One of the great questions in teacher education has to do with the conversion of struggling independent liberal arts colleges into teacher-training institutions. There have been surprisingly few successful independent teacher-training colleges, but there is no reason why there cannot be many such. Certainly, it would be a near tragedy if the small liberal arts colleges that I referred to earlier as facing a certain struggle for existence in their present form were allowed to go out of existence without making an effort to use their faculties, their libraries, their facilities, their plants, and their respected position in their localities for the purpose of teacher education. There are admittedly administrative difficulties in the way, including the serious ones of providing practice schools and critic teachers, but these are not insuperable, particularly if some way can be found to provide partial tax support. I have no idea how many colleges could be converted if the means were found, but judging from the known difficulties of some colleges today, I would suspect that it might be upward of a hundred, which would certainly supply an important addition to teacher-education facilities.

The future of business education

Third in order of numerical importance today in American higher education are the programs in business and commerce. While it is reasonable to expect that the popularity of programs in these fields will continue to grow, it is difficult to predict the form and direction that this growth will take. Courses in business give an outward impression of going in several directions at once and of being unable to decide which direction is best, which is certainly strange when it is considered that a prime purpose of such courses is training in decision making. One direction is that of accountancy, which is becoming increasingly technical and has been steadily extended as a course of study. Another direction is that of management, where one school of thought advocates a broad course in what is essentially applied economics combined with a strong admixture of liberal arts courses, while another school of thought advocates a quasi-technical course with a strong admixture of basic engineering courses. Still another direction is that of merchandising, which, like education, suffers from the repetition of detailed courses based on a common content and the overloading of the curriculum with methods courses and so-called laboratory experience at the expense of the broad preparation which could be approached through a judicious inclusion of liberal arts courses. Still another direction taken by business schools is that of training service personnel, such as secretaries and office managers; and on the opposite end still another is the erection of graduate programs and research and consulting activities.

This uncertainty as to direction is not altogether the fault of education in business schools. The fact is that these schools are very sensitive to the requirements of business and commerce, and that these requirements tend to change rapidly according to the condition of the economy. A shift from a seller's market to a buyer's market may mean a large-scale and long-term shift from emphasis on production, management, and quality control to merchandising and cost accounting, and may completely upset the placement process which is the lifeblood of any professional school.

But, regardless of these problems, there can be only one conclusion as to the demands for business education. These demands can only go up. It seems entirely reasonable to suppose that schools of business, which are now, as mentioned earlier in this paper, granting one-sixth of the college degrees given annually, will within 10 years be granting one-fifth of all college degrees. Their ability to expand beyond that point may well depend upon their ability to develop and present a reasonable controlling philosophy for business education, and to utilize such a philosophy in the organization of business schools into something approaching universities that will build the specialties in business education on a firm foundation of core subjects, including essential offerings in humanities, social studies, and science drawn from the liberal arts fields.

The future of engineering education

If the business graduates are indispensable for filling the subordinate command and some of the command posts in corporate enterprise and banking and for handling the merchandising and advertising chores, the engineers are no less indispensable for the design, operation, and maintenance of our industrial plants. However, despite their present indispensability, the growth of engineering as a profession has been curiously slow. You will remember that I remarked earlier in this paper that engineering graduates, in proportion to the total of all college graduates, have doubled in the last 40 years. This is a considerable growth, but it is the smallest growth recorded by any profession that has grown. As of today, the future growth of the profession depends on several factors: first, the extent to which the subprofessional technicians now being trained in technical secondary schools or by inservice training programs will take over duties now performed by engineers; second, the extent to which engineering schools can prepare their graduates to take leadership in the research and development work which has become so important in our industrial pattern; third, the financial support for engineering education. As of this writing it appears that the long-term health of the engineering profession depends upon emphasis on research and development, even at the cost of lengthening the engineering program, rather than upon competition with subprofessional technicians. The emphasis on research and development is closely tied to the support of engineering education, for at the present time many of our major engineering schools are supporting themselves by selling their research skills to industry, a condition which cannot possibly be to the long-term benefit of those schools, although the present crisp sounds of folding money are undoubtedly attractive. It is to me most puzzling that the talk about corporate support for higher education has not produced sizable direct grants for our engineering schools. Certainly industry has a great stake in the future of engineering education, and certainly it has, so far, dismally failed to recognize the obligation which goes with that stake.

Taking into consideration the facts that engineering education may have to go through a period of program readjustment and that its present support is lagging behind its needs, I can see no reason to expect that engineering will in the foreseeable future enroll more than its present 10 percent of college-going students.

The future of the senior professions

Since I have already touched upon what we may call the senior professions of law, medicine, college teaching, and research scientist in my discussion of the A.B. degree, I do not feel that I need to labor them further in a separate section. However, I do think it is worth commenting that the relative importance of these professions has declined farther than it should and that a swing back to them is due and perhaps overdue. At present, 80 medical schools, the superior graduate schools numbering about 60, and the superior law schools numbering perhaps 40 are carrying most of the burden of advanced training for these professions. Except for about half of the medical schools, which are under heavy pressure, these institutions are not overcrowded. Should they become overcrowded, some additional strong graduate and law schools can be developed from existing institutions, and the need for more doctors can be met by the foundation of new medical schools. This last process is indeed already under way, for two new medical schools will open within the New York metropolitan area during the next year.

I would expect, though I know of no figures or studies to support the expectation, a slow relative growth in the number of students planning to enter these senior professions in addition to the normal growth attributable to population increase. My main reason for suggesting this is that shortages in all these fields are becoming noticeable and that attention is being focused upon them, even to the extent of considering specific financial inducements. As some of you know, the College Board is conducting for the National Science Foundation a study of the possibilities of increasing enrollments in scientific fields. No findings are available, but the mere fact that a fact-finding operation is under way is an encouraging sign.

New demands

In this latter section of my paper I have not touched upon the possible development of new professions and specialties, with consequent new demands upon our colleges and universities, and I am going to do so now only by suggesting areas wherein such developments may come.

One such area is that of medical services, which have already expanded greatly by reason of the upgrading of all sorts and varieties of technicians and assistants, and which will probably continue that expansion with the further development of health insurance and group practice plans.

Another area is that of power utilization, dealing with the development and use of nuclear and solar energy, which are still in the laboratory stage so far as day-to-day use is concerned.

Still another area is that of heat transfer, which may well require the development of an entire branch of technology dealing with air conditioning, refrigeration, and the still rudimentary use of heat pumps.

In the area of social and political science, we still have a long way to go in the training of career government servants and another long way to go in community organization and planning, made necessary by the relentless expansion of the cities into the country, and the progressive abandonment of our cities for all purposes other than the transaction of business.

The training and employment of technicians to work in other countries, as a part of the cementing of the loose political grouping that we call the free world, may be a minor task numerically, but it will be of great importance politically.

It is by no means improbable that methods of controlling and operating airborne transportation will be developed which will bring such transportation within the reach of millions of Americans and thereby bring about another revolution in American life comparable to the one for which Henry Ford and the Model T are held responsible.

As you will recognize, these are speculations, not prophecies, but, as you will also recognize, no one can review the history of American education during the last 50 years without noting that its startling developments came about in a brief span of years, and that none of the developments could have been predicted from the evidence available at the beginning of the 50-year period. Hence, lacking the wisdom for prophecy, we can at least speculate with the knowledge that it can do no harm and may do some good.

The facts, conjectures, interpretations, and suggestions that have been presented in this paper do not begin to exhaust the possibilities bearing on this topic. As I reread it before presentation I could not fail to note that areas of major importance have been left completely untouched, and that in other areas the presentation is subject to interpretations almost diametrically opposite from those that have been offered. But these areas will be explored by others, and the interpretations and misinterpretations are open to challenge and correction by others.

What to me is important is that we view our tasks in education and the great rambling system in which we work, not as a thing apart, but as a vital part of the social organism that is our nation. If we can hold to this view and approach our tasks with dispassionate understanding of our role, we can view the future not as a fearsome specter of toil and improvisation, but as an area of opportunity such as has been offered to few men in any period of our history. Surely none of us can ask more than this.

T*he following talk, given before the Nassau Club (which functions in many respects as a kind of Princeton Faculty Club), was a continuation of the line of inquiry opened up by the previous paper on increasing demands for higher education.*

In an evolutionary sense it is an interesting talk. It discusses the relationship between the number of youths being educated and the size of the labor force, but does not yet establish a connection between education and productivity. Also it discusses the generalization of secondary education during the twenties and thirties without making explicit the need to broaden the high school curriculum in order to proceed with the democratization of secondary education. Both of these concepts were, at the time, latent and did not emerge into full public view until the Sputnik Revolution focused such attention on our education system as it had never before received.

"Who Enters College?"
Talk before the Nassau Club, Princeton, May 23, 1955.

The suggestion that I talk to you today resulted from a talk made early this spring to the Engineering Manpower Council. That talk was concerned with manpower—or, better, brainpower—in two contexts: first, how much of it is still available that we have not drawn upon; second, how much of it gets away under any circumstances. There was also involved some discussion of what might be done about it.

Since this concern with manpower is held in colleges and universities, as well as by hunters of engineering ivory, it seemed reasonable to accept an invitation to use the same topic again in this talk today. This I have done. I have also used the same facts, which seemed to be about as good as any available. The only changes I have made have been with respect to the reasoning, the order of presentation, the emphasis, and the conclusions.

Let me at the outset disclaim any intention of talking about the brainpower that gets into college. I don't know what becomes of it either. Apparently it goes underground immediately after freshman registration, never to manifest itself again until the day after commencement. I have never fully understood what there is in the interaction of faculty chemistry and student chemistry that serves within one week to transform the sparkling, bright-eyed, bushy-tailed new freshman class that entered the door into the dull, confused, illiterate mass that flows in a gelatinous tide into the freshman classrooms. Nor do I know what it is that transforms the struggling seniors, still grappling with patient faculty minds, into stalwart, alert, and capable alumni, advancing in their business and prospective donors to the alumni fund. And, while I would like to learn, I feel that today may better be devoted to problems that can at least be quantified even if they cannot be solved.

There are several ways of looking at the brainpower shortage we now hear so much about. One, which is very popular just now, is to assume that it is a new phenomenon. This is a comforting assumption, for it makes it possible to find out what is going on that causes the phenomenon, order it changed, and settle back with the problem solved. This, in effect, is what has been done. It has been discovered that the cause of the phenomenon is the failure of the high schools to teach adequate mathematics and science courses.

This fact having been proved, and there is no doubt that it has been proved, appropriate orders have been issued by government officials, military officers, corporation executives, scientists, university presidents, and others that the high schools should mend their ways and resume teaching mathematics and science. Therefore, as soon as the laboratories in some 12,000 high schools have been brought up to date and reequipped, as soon as the wage scales for science teachers have gotten to the point where promising young teachers can be held in teaching instead of drifting off to better-paying jobs elsewhere—in other words, as soon as there is direct support from tax sources for secondary school science, plus the people necessary to man the program—the situation will be remedied.

While we are waiting for these things to happen, we might ask the scientists and the mathematicians, particularly at the senior level, to cast a professional eye over the whole continuum of science and mathematics education and inquire as to whether it is being done as economically with respect to time and money as it can possibly be done. If this were done, the contribution in terms of the students salvaged—students who are now being driven out of science by excessive requirements—might be unexpectedly high.

As you gather, I don't think very much of this as a way of dealing with the problem, unless the logical solutions to the problem in the form of direct support and overhaul of the program are also considered along with the fault finding.

We would, I think, be a good deal farther along if we would take a look at what has happened to bring about this and kindred situations in the hope that we may learn a little bit about the future from the present and the past.

I think the first thing that happened was that we have in 50 years in America completed an education revolution, and before that was complete we started on the second one. The revolution that we completed was that of moving substantially all of our youth into secondary school. At any rate, there were only about 700,000 out of a little over 6,000,000 children between the ages of 14 and 17 in secondary school in 1900, while today there are 7,200,000 out of 9,000,000. In 1954, this meant that we would have had just under 80 percent of all possible secondary school students in secondary school. Now, the general belief is that it is a little higher, although nobody is quite sure of the statistics. This was the educational revolution we completed.

The second educational revolution that we started was that of moving into college the 18-to-21-year-old age group. This movement actually didn't begin until after 1910, for by that date we still had less than 5 percent of the age group in college. In actual figures, it was 355,000 out of 7,300,000.

By 1940, the operation had been tripled. There were 1,500,000 students in college out of a possible 9,700,000, amounting to 15 percent. Since 1940 this has doubled again, so that by 1954 we had 30 percent of that age group in college. Actually, this has gone up noticeably since then and is probably at the present moment reaching toward 35 percent.

Now, while it is very interesting to note these transfers of whole age groups into educational status, it is of some interest to inquire as to where they came from, what they were doing where they came from, and what effect they had been having on the state of the nation in their previous status. The answers to these questions are not very easy to come by, and they have to be sketched in rather than affirmed. However, it is clear enough that the majority of the students who came to school and college came from the labor force, that is, from the group of gainfully employed.

At any rate, in 1900 there were apparently about 8 million of the labor force who were under 21—this being 8 million out of the 11 million who were not in school or college and also 8 million out of the total of 30 million then in the labor force. By 1950, there were a total of 17 million between 14 and 21. Nine million were students, 8,300,000 were not in school or college, and 5,700,000 were in the labor force. The labor force then amounted to just under 60 million. In other words, statistics on the transfer of people from the labor force to student status have indicated that perhaps the most striking transformation of all in America during the 50 years, and certainly a major factor in the educational revolution, was this reconstitution of our labor force, by removing youth from it. The youth was a little more than one-fourth of the labor force in 1900; in 1950 it was a little less than one-tenth.

From this fact alone, several things follow. Obviously, the labor force had a higher mean age in 1950 than in 1900. It is probable that this led to increased stability and probable, in turn, that this had some effect on the ability of labor leadership to command an organized labor group. But this is pure speculation. What is not speculation is that the students, after they finished school, were sent back into the labor force, and there has therefore been a steady upgrading in the educational quality of the labor force. Or is it speculation to note that there has been a steady increase in per capita productivity of the American labor force? The increase has been going on since about 1870, so far as the labor statisticians can discover, but then, for that matter, the roots of this educational revolution can be traced back that far also.

Still another thing that follows from these facts is that the burden of education as a tax-supported activity has become tremendously heavier than it was 50 years ago. Obviously, there was relatively little tax burden involved in education in 1900, and obviously, too, with a labor force largely uneducated, there had to be a certain amount of on-the-job education through apprenticeship or inservice training programs. These burdens, which were probably never very heavy on the employers, have been shifted to the taxpayers along with the rest of the burden of developing and supporting public education.

Still another thing that followed as a result of this revolution was the transformation of the secondary school system from a fairly special-purpose organization into a general-purpose one. In 1900 the meager 11 percent of the age group that went to secondary school were largely destined for college. The secondary school curriculum was directly connected to the college curriculum. The subject matter was the same, differing only in level; teachers were drawn from the same sources; and the same standards were maintained. After 1900 this changed very rapidly. By the time our secondary school system reached the 1920s, it was no longer predominantly college preparatory. Hence, the college preparatory curriculum began to disappear as the dominant curriculum, and finally the college preparatory philosophy began to disappear from the administration and development of the school system. If we are searching for devils who destroyed the high school curriculum and thereby reduced our chances of obtaining scientists and mathematicians, we had better look back to the 1920s and to those educational leaders who were forced to adapt a single-track, college preparatory secondary school system to the needs of industry and economy and to the needs of a population that was being driven by the requirements of industry and economy into the securing of a general education.

The fact that these needs existed then is the root of our secondary school preparation troubles now. In a larger context, the fact is that our secondary school system is in the process of a second transformation and is once again edging toward becoming a college preparatory enterprise. It will never be so to the extent that it once was, but it may eventually hit the point where over 50 percent of all high school graduates will be going to college. In this case, the dominant secondary school curriculum will once again become college preparation, and the problems of specific courses and methods of preparation will become much easier to deal with.

The final thing that follows from these figures is that there is at least enough evidence, or at least enough coincidental fact, to suggest that there is a relationship between the level of education of the labor force, productivity, and the expansion of the economy—a relationship which sets up some sort of cycle in which the expanding economy requires better-trained and better-educated individuals, who are in turn obtained by expanding the educational system so that it will accommodate more individuals, and these individuals in their turn go into the economy, assist in its further expansion by being better workers, and place still further demands upon the educational system.

Whether the theory is true or not, it squares with certain facts to be observed in secondary and higher education. These facts are that both secondary and higher education have been increasingly assuming burdens of specialized and technical training. Originally such programs were introduced on the secondary level, and the college programs were kept relatively close to the pristine liberal arts condition. However, times have changed now, and half of what we are doing in education today percentage-wise would not even have been considered to be higher education in 1900.

A good deal of the explanation for this development of all kinds of specialized programs under the general umbrella of higher education has to do precisely with the discovery that higher education, like secondary education, can make a direct contribution to training people for positions in the economy. Hence the tremendous development of specialized programs, the tremendous development of new professions, and, during this century, the development of a whole new species of higher education institutions. You will recall the urban university offering innumerable service programs on almost every conceivable standard and level.

There are, I think, two general problems which must now concern us. One is about the result of all this educational offering upon the education-seeking group. The other is about the effect of the demands of the education-seeking group upon higher education.

The result of the education offering upon the education-seeking group, which is roughly the 18–21 age group, is that while a steadily increasing percentage of that age group has been brought into higher education, this bringing-in process has not been conducted in an orderly fashion insofar as native ability is concerned. It has rather, and as we might expect, been affected by economic status and social status, by location, and by opportunity. This has meant that while a good many people have been going to college who shouldn't have gone, as witness the 50 percent attrition figure in our higher education structure as a whole, a good many people have not been going to college who should be going. The actual numbers of such people, as well as the proportion that they constitute of the age group, have been a matter of speculation for several years, ever since the shortage was discovered and made politically official. The estimates made, based primarily upon selective service test data, suggested that about half of the top quarter of the age group in ability did not go to college. These estimates, of course, did not attempt to arrive at the reasons why these individuals did not go to college, nor was there any way of verifying the estimates. Two years ago the National Science Foundation asked the College Entrance Examination Board to do several things on this specific problem: to undertake a study which would verify the estimates as to the number of people lost per year; to find out the reasons why the people were lost; and to find out how many of them could be affected by the inducements of a scholarship program. We did this study, and we have some results from it that are germane to the whole question of manpower utilization.

The study itself consisted of a questionnaire prepared by Educational Testing Service, accompanied by a very short aptitude test. Using the aptitude test, the group sampled was subdivided by picking out the top 30 percent. The questionnaires of these students were then investigated. Expanding the figures on the sample to a national basis, we get the following results.

The top 30 percent of high school seniors makes a group of about 365,-000 students. One hundred and sixty-five thousand of these are planning on college immediately. Another 96,000 are planning on college later. Twenty-one thousand were interested in college but had no plans. Fifty-one thousand had no interest. Another 10 percent of the sample, in other words, 36,000, did not make useful replies and probably should be added to the 51,000 having no interest, which, in that case, would set up this grouping as 87,000.

This, however, was the distribution in terms of interest. It did not seem to be, so far as we could determine from the responses, the distribution of what is actually going to happen to the group. We took it for granted that those who said they were going to college immediately were, in fact, going to college immediately. We took it for granted that those who would like to go to college but could not go immediately were being held up for financial reasons, that perhaps half of them would get to college and the other half would not. We took it for granted that the 21,000 who were interested in college but had no plans would probably not go to college, that all of those who were definitely not interested in college would not go to college, and that all of those who were unable to answer the questionnaire intelligibly would not go to college. This meant that we got 215,000 out of the 365,000 constituting the top 30 percent of the high school class who will go to college and 150,000 who will not go to college.

Now, if we have 150,000 students a year at the present time who have ability but who are not going to use it in higher education, there are two questions that arise: first, how great is our loss; second, what are the prospects for the future?

The greatness of the loss has to be considered in terms of the fact that a sizable portion of this group of high school graduates who will not go to college have immediately found other careers. Assuming that the majority of the group are women, on which most people seem to agree, they will either get married shortly after high school, or take a short postgraduate course to prepare for specialized work, or go directly into employment, or, eventually, they may do all three. As for the men, we can speculate merely that most of them will have little or no difficulty in finding employment, and it is reasonable to assume that a good many of them will go on and get further training, usually in company schools.

So much for the present loss. The evidence is pretty clear, if you will recall the remarks I made along toward the beginning of this speech, that we have been steadily increasing the percentage of the age group going to college. This probably means that we are steadily drawing into college a larger and larger percentage of this group of 150,000 that is presently counted as lost ability. We will never get them all into college, and, in fact, we might even be in a rather bad way for leading mechanics, foremen, chief clerks, top sergeants, headwaiters, and other useful personnel were we to do so.

This brings us to the other question. What is to be the effect upon the system of the numbers of those seeking education? Here we come up against a problem which is best expressed by the fact that the 21-year-old age group was almost exactly doubled between 1940 and 1954, and, so far as is known, is still growing. This means, obviously, that the schools have a doubled burden to look forward to. Actually, this is understating it. They have even more than a doubled burden to look forward to, for the percentage of the age group that is going to school is continuing to climb as well as the numbers. It seems probable that these numbers can be cared for. New school buildings are appearing, and, what is even more important, some of the raw material in the shape of teacher-training candidates is beginning to appear in the colleges in some quantity.

However, we need to be clear that it is just about impossible to double numbers and to improve quality at the same time. Both operations call for the same resources and methods of procedure, but, as of this moment, it does not appear that we have the resources to spread over both. Obviously, therefore, we are going to have to concentrate on the quantity rather than on the quality.

I make this judgment, realizing that it is completely against the current doctrine, which calls for quality, excellence, and a return to the intellectual integrity of our forebears. This doctrine is, in my view, romantic and nostalgic. We are no longer dealing with 5 percent of an age group in college, as we did when the legends of intellectual greatness were made. We are dealing with a quarter of each generation. In time we shall deal with a third, and, before the end of the century, with a half. The pressures to be created will change curriculums, methods, support, the choice of students, the values of students, and, in time, the very purposes of college.

In the face of such changes it is a reasonable estimate that Princeton and its sister Ivy League institutions will still be here, but I suspect that they will change in both form and function. If they receive the kind of support that enables them to control the manner of change, they will be able to hold their quality. If they do not, they will be forced into the role of service institutions. My guess is that they will continue to be well supported and will thus be able to retain control of their own destinies.

Τhe following excerpt from the 1955 Report of the Director *deals with an activity that was to be important for the Board within a very short time. The interest of the National Science Foundation in improving the flow of science students into colleges and graduate schools took the form of a good deal of pressure on the Board to study the factors affecting the recruitment of science students. The fact that the Board did not have enough staff to undertake the study was finally overcome by enlisting Charles C. Cole Jr. of Columbia College and subcontracting the testing and statistical work to Educational Testing Service.*

One important aspect of the undertaking was the consideration of a recommendation that the National Science Foundation support a major national scholarship program for the recruitment of science students to college. The decision against such a recommendation finally rested on a concern over specialized recruiting programs, which, it was feared, would merely breed other specialized programs. Whether or not this was right is an open question. However, it is interesting to note that this decision left the field clear for the launching of the National Merit Scholarship under private auspices. This was a move far more important than it seemed at the time, for these scholarships—along with the General Motors Scholarship, which appeared at the same time—developed a public emphasis on scholarships and achievement, which, I am convinced, played a real part in supporting the rapid shift in undergraduate values away from security and corporate employment and toward research, advanced study, and intellectual accomplishment.

"Study for the National Science Foundation"
54th Report of the Director. New York: College Entrance Examination Board, 1955, 107 pp., pp. 6–8.

As reported a year ago, the Board accepted in the summer of 1954, at the request of the National Science Foundation, responsibility for studying the flow into college of students interested in science as a career. The problems involved in the study were those of determining the factors affecting the choice of science as a career, the conditions under which a secondary school student actually makes a tentative choice of science as a career, and the extent to which forces external to the student, such as an extensive scholarship program or a guidance program strongly oriented toward science, may conceivably affect the choice of science as a career.

The Board was fortunate in making its plans for the conduct of the study to obtain on a generous time-sharing arrangement with Columbia University the services of Charles C. Cole Jr., assistant dean of Columbia College, as director of the study. Mr. Cole, working closely with the staffs of the Board, Educational Testing Service, and the National Science Foundation, and under the guidance of an excellent advisory committee, planned the study in terms of the factors outlined above. A group of consultants were asked to contribute working papers on factors affecting the choice of science as a career. The consultants and the papers which they submitted were as follows: Dr. Jane Blizard, New England Institute for Medical Research, "Increasing the Effective Number of Women in Science"; Paul F. Brandwein, chairman of science, Forest Hills High School, "Stimulating the Development of Students with High Ability in Science"; Herbert A. Deane, assistant professor of government, Columbia University, "Political Science in the United States"; Robert J. Havighurst, professor of education, University of Chicago, "The Role of Motivation in Attracting Boys to Science"; Mrs. Allaire U. Karzon, associated with the law firm of Hodgson, Russ, Andrews, Woods, and Goodyear, of Buffalo, New York, "A Tax Revision Proposal to Encourage Women into Professional Careers."

Mr. Cole himself supplemented the work of these consultants with a review of the literature on factors controlling plans for college attendance with particular attention to the interrelationships between ability, educational background, choice of career, and financial position. While this material was in process of collection and compilation he worked out, in consultation with members of the ETS staff and with representatives of several government agencies, the details of a sampling based upon seniors and sophomores in 5 percent of the public high schools of the nation. Plans for the sampling included a brief ability test used to supply a basis for distribution of the respondents in terms of their scholastic aptitude and a questionnaire to elicit information on the student's family and educational background, financial position, college and career plans, and specific interests in studies. Also included in the questionnaire were questions concerning the extent to which plans for further study might be altered by the existence of a scholarship program which would be open to students electing a science major in college. Finally, the study included a section describing a scholarship program that would be appropriate to the purpose of encouraging the choice of careers in science of a sizable group of high school seniors. It will be noted that the study plans did not consider students in independent secondary schools. This was a decision based in part upon the assumption that financial considerations did not loom as large in the college plans of such students, in part upon the additional time that would be required to study them, and in part upon the assumption that they are more likely to be college-bound than are public high school students.

The study was, by a narrow time margin, completed during the year under review, a remarkable achievement considering the complexity of the problem and the fact that Mr. Cole continued his regular work in Columbia College. In its final form, entitled *Encouraging Scientific Talent*, the report included a discussion of the problems affecting college attendance and the choice of careers, prepared on the basis of the consultants' working papers supplemented by Mr. Cole's own interpretation of other literature dealing with those matters; a section on the factors affecting college plans of high school students, which involved careful analysis of the questionnaire responses; and an outline of the specific scholarship program to be recommended in the event that the decision was made to proceed with such a program.

The report of the study, in addition to being an important contribution to the literature on the subject of factors affecting college and career plans, is of absorbing interest by reason of the factual information brought to light by the combined test-questionnaire sampling of high school students. It is noteworthy that although there have been several careful analyses of gross statistics on the relationships between ability, financial position, college attendance, and college graduation, among them an earlier study done by the Board at the request of the Commission on the Financing of Higher Education,[7] there have not heretofore been any studies of these relationships which produced verified facts based on a sizable national sample. The study revealed, for example, that almost half of the senior boys of high ability included in the sample would have preferred to take more mathematics and science than they actually studied in high school, and that only slightly more than half of the seniors interested in the study of mathematics and science felt themselves in a position to plan on college attendance immediately after high school graduation. Extrapolations based upon the findings of the study verified Mr. Hollinshead's estimates that not over three-fifths of high-ability high school graduates would actually get to college, although the returns from the sample did indicate that among those who were unable to plan for college a somewhat larger group than had been estimated in the earlier study could be induced to enter college if financial resources were made available.

---

7. Byron S. Hollinshead, *Who Should Go to College*. New York: Columbia University Press, 1952, 190 pp.

Since it is obviously impossible for this report to include a complete resume of a study so detailed and far reaching, it is necessary to refer the interested reader to the report itself for further information.

This paper on the superior student was part of a conference at The University of Michigan in the fall of 1956. My two colleagues on the program were Clarence H. Faust, head of The Ford Foundation's Fund for the Advancement of Education, and Russell Lynes, managing editor of Harper's Magazine. *Our joint task was to tell all that was then known about the superior student in higher education—or, at least, all that we knew. My paper, and indeed the other two papers, reflected accurately a great current concern over finding the potentially superior student and arranging for him to receive a superior education. At the same time, the papers make it clear that we had, at the time, only conventional measures and conventional programs to use as our operating elements.*

In fact, I do not feel that matters have changed much during the 10 years since the paper was delivered, save that we now have more resources to devote to the superior student and more programs to attract him.

"The Description of the Superior Student"
Addresses Given at the Annual Conference on Higher Education in Michigan, University of Michigan, 1956, pp. 7–21.

The guidelines for this paper consist of a series of questions suggested to me at the time I was invited to participate in this conference. Since they were a good set of questions, I think it appropriate to begin the paper by offering them for your consideration.

Who and what are the superior students? How many are there? What are their motives and goals? What becomes of them? How can they be identified? How soon can they be identified? What interest should the colleges take in them before they are eligible to enter college? What evidences of their talents and achievements do we need in addition to their school marks?

It will, I think, come as no surprise to an audience composed of individuals who have all, at one time or another, struggled to find reasonable answers to some or all of these questions, to hear that the preparation of a paper dealing with them has presented certain difficulties.

I believe that a good many of these difficulties come as the natural consequence of our philosophy of education and the system we have developed to implement the philosophy. Therefore, I think it worth our while to spend a few minutes considering the problems that this philosophy and system have set for us in dealing with our present concern for the superior student.

The first set of difficulties has to do with the definition of superior students. These difficulties arise because there is no one definition of the superior student valid for all times and places—there is only the definition created by a given school system. And I think it would be not unfair to say of our system of secondary schools that it has for 50 years devoted itself, with much singleness of purpose and notable success, to a broadening of our educational base. I base this statement on a brief series of statistics, plus a certain amount of observation.

This series has to do with the development of secondary education in this country. In 1900 our secondary schools enrolled 11.4 percent of the 14-to-17-year-old age group. By 1910 the figure was 15 percent, by 1920 32 percent, by 1930 51 percent, and by 1940 72 percent. Since 1940 the rate of increase in this percentage figure has slowed down as the figure approached its theoretical limit of 100 and what is probably its practical limit of 90. At present, it is probably around 82 or 83 percent.

It is, of course, obvious that this development has been accomplished by changing the purpose and the method of operation of the American secondary schools, but the question is from what to what and how.

In 1900 the primary purpose of all American secondary education appears to have been college preparation. I have seen a number of attempts to state a figure showing the extent to which this purpose dominated the schools at that time. They have all been approximations or guesses, but they all suggest that in 1900 between 60 and 75 percent of all high school graduates entered college.

This college orientation of the secondary schools had three results.

First, that the secondary school curriculum of 1900 was necessarily predominantly college preparation, stressing, as did the colleges themselves, the study of language and mathematics.

Second, that since a college goal could only be entertained by students whose financial means were adequate, the secondary school population was largely, though not necessarily exclusively, drawn from children of those who could look forward to covering college costs, namely the middle and upper-middle classes.

Third, that since there is a rough equation between cultural and financial advantages, and our imperfect tests do give a weighting to cultural advantages, it is almost certain that the 11 percent of the age group in school in 1900 was drawn from the upper 50 percent of the ability represented in that age group, and probable that it was largely drawn from the upper 25 percent of the age group.

The statistics show that the somewhat exclusive nature of the secondary school population broke down, slowly at first, and then with a rapidity that became a tidal wave. The figure of over 50 percent of the age group in secondary school by 1930 is evidence that the ability level of secondary school students was approaching the mean of the ability level of the population—the theoretical 100 IQ. The figure of over 80 percent enrollment for the age group today shows that we are now very close to that mean.

This drift toward the mean has had large implications for both the secondary schools and the colleges.

The secondary schools have been forced to adopt a variety of curricular expedients in order to carry on their educational job over the wide range of abilities offered by their students. These expedients have been made all the more difficult by reason of the American insistence upon the single education track along which all students followed a broadly similar pattern of studies. It would, for example, have been easier to have followed the European system with its elaborate series of selections, special schools, and dead-end programs, but to do so would have stratified our social system along European lines. We did not do this, but instead have managed, by following our own pattern, to establish an equation between education and opportunity, by making it clear that both are open to all. This we have done by evolving the comprehensive secondary school which, with all of its administrative compromises and semantic expedients, does manage to provide the opportunity for a complete secondary education, on a level suited to individual ability, to all who wish to pursue it.

However, this opportunity was not purchased without cost, and I think it is not unfair to say that the cost was borne by those at the upper end of the ability spectrum. There were four reasons for this. First, the higher ability group became a relatively small proportion of the school population, even though it became absolutely larger; consequently, their demands became a smaller portion of the total demands. Second, the higher ability students could get along with less supervision than most of the other students, a fact which in time came to be rationalized with the statement that such students prospered with a minimum of teaching, supervision, and guidance. Third, the subjects which were the core of the 1900 secondary school curriculum had little practical value for those preparing for early employment, and were, in addition, difficult for those who lacked cultural advantages. Fourth, the secondary schools could not get enough college-prepared teachers to take care of their rapid expansion and had to turn to supplying their own teachers through a system of normal schools and teachers' colleges. These teacher-training programs necessarily placed great emphasis on method at the expense of subject matter because of the need for developing methods to take care of the growing school population.

At this point, result began to pile up on result. The end product was a frame of mind among secondary school administrators which emphasized the task of dealing with large numbers of non-college-bound students, rather than the task of dealing with smaller numbers of college-bound students. From that point it was a short step to the establishment of a concept of secondary education which recognized college preparation as an option. And this establishment in time changed the requirements for entrance to college.

It is, I think, demonstrable that college entrance requirements follow the dominant secondary school curriculum. I realize that this statement is diametrically opposed to the common belief that college entrance requirements determine the secondary curriculum, but I would point out that if this were so, we would probably still be back with the old 16 Carnegie units, for certainly these were abandoned over college faculty protests that, on occasion, can still be heard. If entrance requirements do not follow the secondary curriculum, it is a remarkable coincidence that every change in college entrance patterns has followed a major change in secondary school patterns. The coincidence dates back to the establishment of the academies at the beginning of the nineteenth century, which introduced a broadened pattern of study in secondary schools; crops up again during the period when the public high schools began to take hold during the latter half of the nineteenth century; and comes up for the third time in 1930, when our secondary schools began enrolling more than half of the eligible students. Shortly after that happened, college entrance requirements began a retreat from the specific statement to a general, even vague, statement which permitted an emphasis upon ability and an implicit interest in motivation.

Although it would be possible, and even tempting, to go on discussing the development of our school system in these rather general terms, I think the discussion has now been carried far enough to make it clear that it is my view that this pattern of schooling has controlled our methods of identifying and counting students, and particularly superior students, by the very fact that it has not permitted the erection of a single standard program. Where there is no agreed program of secondary studies, no agreed standards to be applied to secondary school performance, and no genuine paths marked out which could be followed in the development of superior students, there is no clear-cut way, through the appraisal of academic performance, to identify a superior student, much less to assure him of a program of studies to match his abilities.

This in its turn has meant that the only generally understood and applied measure for identifying students has been the measure of ability provided by objective, impartial, ability tests. In other words, a superior student almost necessarily has been defined as a student who was to be found above a certain reference point on the ability scale. The use of this reference point has required that formal studies of superior students—at any rate, most of the longitudinal studies that have undertaken to tell us something about their performance over an extended period of time—have started with a selection made in terms of ability tests. This is to say that the words "gifted," "talented," "exceptional," "superior," and "able" have all been roughly equated to high ability as measured by a standard ability test. They have then all come to be used interchangeably as constants connoting capacity to perform.

In our attempts to introduce some modifying elements into the definition of the superior student, which have been forced upon us by the necessity to rely on the only available common denominator, ability tests, we have introduced a whole host of variables that are attributes, such as imagination, skill, interests, motivations, and ability, which—together with emotional, environmental, and personality factors having to do with the student's maturity and adjustment—control his use of his capacity.

This method of definition has been inherently unsatisfactory for three reasons.

First, as we know, there are errors of measurement in all ability tests, and, further, as we know, most of these tests do not differentiate between individuals above certain ability levels.

Second, some of the students identified by tests fail to have certain traits that would enable them to perform as superior students.

Third, some of the students who fail to be identified by ability tests do in fact turn out to be superior students by reason of attributes and traits that enable them to use their ability to the maximum.

Nevertheless, unsatisfactory or not, this is the method we have used as the basis for our definition of a superior student. At this point, I offer this definition as follows: a student with an IQ of 130 or better who is doing superior academic work. This is, of course, pretty flexible, as it needs to be because of the errors built into it. Therefore, it is natural that the count of the number of students in a given age group should have to be stated in terms of limits rather than a specific number. This number, allowing for all major errors of measurement, is not less than 30,000 and not more than 60,000 in any present-day 18-year-old age group of about 2,500,000.

The errors inherent in this method of identification and of counting make it inevitable that a sizable number of individuals of superior ability will escape from this small group—that is, will not be educated to their maximum capacity, and that a much larger number of students in the range from good to superior will escape from their group.

We are all more or less familiar with these loss figures, so I will not repeat them here. But I will note that the really superior group suffers the smallest losses—perhaps 10 percent. Yet this small percentage of loss is important in concrete terms, for it represents the equivalent of the total undergraduate enrollment of one or two large universities, and, of course, the equivalent of the total enrollment of quite a number of graduate and advanced professional schools—enough to make a sizable difference in the annual production of teachers, scholars, and professional men.

The realization that this situation was inherently unsatisfactory was first borne in upon us by the manpower shortages induced by the war and, of course, reinforced by current critical shortages of educated manpower in many fields, as well as by the realization that in some fields there is no visible end to the shortages.

The statement that this was an unsatisfactory situation began almost immediately after the war with the report of the President's Commission on Higher Education. Since then there have been a number of noteworthy books. Dael Wolfle's *America's Resources of Specialized Talent*, Byron Hollinshead's *Who Should Go to College*, and Ralph F. Berdie's *After High School—What?*[8] have all dealt with various phases of the problem and are, in effect, required reading in the field. From these and other statements, it is, I think, sufficiently clear that a sizable number of individuals of superior ability are not educated to their maximum capacity, some because they do not wish to be, some because they cannot get the education they want. In addition, we all assume that an unspecified number are never effectively identified.

Recognizing these three categories of educational failure, we have developed four forms of effort to deal with them.

First, a sizable increase in financial aid to students to remove financial barriers. Though we cannot pretend that these efforts have been sufficient, I think it is a fair judgment that scholarship funds now available are sufficient to care for the needs of superior students. But this would be true only if we disregarded all other students, and this we cannot do. Therefore, these efforts are only partially successful.

Second, the development of special secondary school programs for superior students. These range all the way from offerings of single courses for a few students selected by an individual teacher, to the development of complete secondary schools such as the remarkable Bronx High School of Science in New York City. In general, these programs have been notably successful, but they are still too few in number or in the number of students they affect to stand as anything more than pilot activities.

Third, special college recognition for superior students. This has taken

8. Wolfle—New York: Harper & Brothers, 1954, 318 pp.; Hollinshead—New York: Columbia University Press, 1954, 190 pp.; Berdie—Minneapolis: University of Minnesota Press, 1954, 240 pp.

several forms. A few colleges have, through admissions and scholarship programs, transformed themselves, in effect, into colleges for superior students. What the long-range effect of this will be on the superior student problem, we do not know, but the short-range effect, judging from the pressures to gain admission to these colleges, seems healthy. Other colleges have started, or are considering, programs of advanced credit for secondary work and are finding these remarkably successful in encouraging and attracting superior students.

Fourth, special admissions programs which allow intellectually mature students to leave secondary school before graduation and proceed directly to college. These programs have had limited appeal, since many secondary schools and some colleges oppose them for reasons having to do with the maturity of the students concerned. These reasons may or may not be valid, but they do express the administrator's distaste for departing from established patterns and probably in the end will tend to eliminate this type of solution.

The nature of the attention to the problems of superior students—books, conferences, reports, and programs—makes it clear, I think, that the fundamental effort is to break out of the restricting framework of established school and college patterns into a new area where the superior student will become a major concern of both school and college, instead of being taken in stride by both.

The work that is going on is based on the belief that a superior student is made, not born. This doctrine holds that identification through testing has achieved its purpose when it has revealed ability potential and that from then on the task of development is up to the school. In this doctrine, identification is not a single act to be accomplished in an afternoon by an act of academic magic, but a continuous process which may be affected by any number of factors but which always requires a deliberate and coherent shaping process.

The process of identification, when carried on as part of development, has, necessarily, two components which must be maintained in balance: the first, instruction to meet the needs of the individual; the second, observation to evaluate his progress and development.

On the question of the kind of teaching required by superior students, the theory of nurture splits sharply into two segments. There is unquestionably one school of thought which holds that the mission of the school with respect to the superior student is to force him to make his own identifications and achieve his own development through the trial and error of freeing him for independent activities. This theory is perhaps more widely held in college than in secondary school, and it is certainly almost universally held and followed with respect to advanced graduate study. It is a severe test and a mature one. It is perhaps too severe and too mature for the young student who is still developing his habits of learning and methods of study. The fact that a few individuals of exceptional ability have developed themselves through this method does not prove that it should be generally applied, even though the idea that superior students require a minimum of teaching may be an attractive one for administrators who are facing a teacher shortage.

The opposing theory, which is generally followed, states that the superior student is the one who is likely to make the most demands on the teacher, and therefore requires more and better teaching time than any other student. On this point, observations made by Paul F. Brandwein in his excellent book, *The Gifted Student as Future Scientist*,[9] on the performance of potentially gifted students in science are clear and pointed. The teacher is, in his phrase, the "activating factor." But he notes that even good teaching in a given area cannot stand by itself. "Successful work with students of high-level ability on the school level does not usually go on unless successful work with the average student and the so-called slow learner goes on as well." In other words, in one school where a major effort was made, under good conditions including a goodly supply of high-quality students drawn from an upper-middle-class background, and in which a good program offering plentiful challenge to the individual student was available, the single most important contribution offered by the school was superior teaching—and superior teaching was characteristic of the entire school, not just of the gifted student program. I have only referred to one school here in pointing out that good teaching is basic to the development of superior students because I think there is no disagreement with this thesis. But there are other studies, including the "30 schools study"[10] of 20 years ago, which establish this point beyond a doubt.

---

9. New York: Harcourt, Brace and Company, 1955, 107 pp.

Here are no new or startling facts. Most of us in education have known or suspected that the teacher was an important person, and it is not news to learn that he is even more important for the able student than for the average one.

There is, however, one set of observations that emerges from these remarks that is important for the college. It is just this. A school which is willing to use its information in the form of measurements and observations, and its resources in the form of teachers and facilities, to set up programs for the identification and nurture of superior students, can achieve successful results, provided its programs are all of a piece. For example, a strong science program must necessarily involve a course in the calculus. This can be and is taught in secondary schools, but it is an idea that would not be readily adopted by all schools. As another example, a strong secondary school course in the humanities would require superior offerings in foreign language, English literature, and work in the history of thought and culture. Again, this can be done in terms of students, staff, and school resources by many schools, but it has not been tried extensively.

Obviously, there is much more to be said about programs for the teaching of superior students, but there is so much available literature in this field that I think I can leave it to be read rather than said, and go on to the need for maintaining the activity of identification through observation.

In his book, Brandwein notes that all superior students observed showed a marked willingness to spend time beyond the ordinary schedule in a given task, a willingness to withstand discomfort, and a willingness to face failure. These he notes as "persistence traits." I think most of us would feel that these traits are outward evidences of motivation, which we agree is a necessary attribute for all superior students. However, persistence is not all of motivation. Perhaps even more basic than persistence is the quality which produces inquiry and challenge—what Alfred North Whitehead has described when he says: "He [meaning the man of science] does not discover in order to know, he knows in order to discover." This is probably the same attribute as persistence, but it is intellectual, not physical, persistence, and can only be inferred, not observed. However, there are certain

10. The "30 schools study" was undertaken by the Progressive Education Association, financed by the Carnegie Corporation, in the late 1930s. Its findings were published as the "Eight-Year Study." —*FB*

observations of a general nature which can aid in such inferences. Brandwein notes that gifted students with science potential rarely sought political office, that they were faithful in attendance, that they avoided extremes and student fads, that they tended to be more quiet, more reflective, more inward-looking, and that they exhibited in general a tendency to introversion.

Beyond this level, in the discussion of the identification and development of the superior student, it is difficult to penetrate. The final definition that we can arrive at is, in fact, not a definition but a series of observations. The superior student is an individual who has the capacity to score high on ability tests, has a record of superior work, a studious mien, a conservative deportment, an inquiring mind, an interest in books, a willingness to accept intellectual responsibility, and a quality of persistence and determination. Added to this is the fact that he must have made full use of his opportunities for education. If, out of this series of observations, we take all of the qualifying adjectives, we have a simple statement which will apply to any student. The differences between superior, ordinary, and inferior students are then differences of degree. There are, in fact, only two points in this series of observations which allow for the intervention of formal education—the initial identification through measurement of ability, and the provision of educational opportunity—and it is only through the kind and quality of the provision of opportunity that the school has the chance to play its part in the creation of the superior student.

It will by now be clear that I believe that superior students could do with less identification and more education. An observation made by an anonymous writer reporting some years ago to the Scottish Department of Education to the effect that English composition tends to be tested rather than taught, is in point here.

Such being the case, I must remark that the role of the colleges in joining with secondary schools for the identification and nurture of superior students is one that must be handled carefully. On one point I am certain. I hope that no colleges will take up the public posture of talent searching and send their admissions officers flitting from school to school carrying quickie forms of so-called talent tests to be administered to high school freshmen and sophomores for the alleged purpose of program guidance, but for the actual purpose of early recruiting. While I hope that this will not happen, I also hope that if it does show signs of happening, the schools approached will dismiss the talent searcher, preferably head first. I speak firmly on this point, for in this search for able students I am concerned about the results of such a program. In the first place, I doubt if the student would gain any benefits, tangible or intangible, from such testing. Any school which lacks either the initiative or the know-how to identify its own able students is unlikely to act on the findings of a college admissions officer, untrained, as too many of them are, in the use of tests for measurement and counseling. A pupil in such a school who is tested as potential talent knows only whether he has been "identified" or not, without knowing anything about the validity of the "identification." The college which has made the identification has nothing to offer in the way of benefits except a half-promise of a scholarship several years hence.

Now, by contrast, let me suggest the best that a college can do. This "best" can be done in terms of a school–college relationship providing not only college assistance in planning the work that is to be done in the identification of superior students, but in going farther to assist with the work, and finally going even farther to participate in the instruction. Planning of the work involves joint school and college effort in arriving at the definition of superior students for administrative purposes, in devising the methods to be used in applying this definition, and, if necessary, actually setting up the instrumentalities to be used in applying the method. Such an instrumentality, in its simplest form, might be an annual regional, or even local, school and college conference on the subject of the identification and nurture of the superior student. Carrying this conference idea one step farther, it might develop into a workshop wherein ideas as to the identification and programing of superior students are actually presented and discussed in terms of their use or possible use. And, going one step farther, such an annual conference might be transformed into a continuing form of superior student clinic to which individual cases might be carried for appropriate testing and guidance.

Such school and college cooperation would take care of two of the three elements that appear to be essential in the identification and nurture of superior students—the testing and the observation. However, they do not take care of the problem of instruction. The instructional problem has, as has been noted earlier in this paper, a long and on the whole negative history, negative in the sense that provisions for the instruction of superior students were for a long time pretty well dropped out of consideration as a job for the secondary school. As a result of this, the single most important element—at least according to studies and efforts that have been made in the past on the development of superior students—has been left out of their development. Recently, attention to this problem has produced ample evidence that schools can give college-level courses, and some evidence that colleges are willing to admit that this can be done. For example, 15 percent of Harvard's present freshman class have college credit for one or more courses taken in secondary school. Thirteen of these same Harvard freshmen who entered in September were granted sophomore standing on the basis of such courses. So the evidence, although based on a small sample, is pretty clear that it can be done.

This, then, raises the question as to whether colleges can offer direct assistance to secondary schools in the offering of courses which will provide an adequate challenge to superior students and give them a chance to move forward academically at a rate commensurate with their ability. This possibility moves the offering of advanced courses in secondary schools from the level of theory to the level of administration. It puts it squarely up to the colleges to consider whether or not they can join with secondary schools in the development of courses appropriate to superior students. As far as I know, there are no reasons, except administrative reasons, why this cannot be done. In fact, in such an idea, I can see possibilities of a genuine instructional continuum in which students may move forward in their studies as fast as their time and their abilities will permit.

I want to make it explicit that I am not here discussing closed circuit television or sound track films of classroom situations. I am sure these are admirable for some purposes. What I am talking about is methods of bringing teachers into classrooms in which they may have the potential of acting as catalytic agents. And, while we are on the subject of college self-interest, can anyone imagine that a college which had worked actively with a secondary school superior-student program would fail to benefit from that program insofar as its drawing power was concerned?

But the role of the college in assisting in the development of superior students cannot stop at the door of the admissions office. The whole idea of superior educational opportunity for superior students rests on the basis that such opportunity is a continuum which reaches all the way from the point when such opportunity can first be provided—usually the ninth grade —to the end of the college course. If such a continuum is to be provided, then the college has the obligation to clear away some of its own administrative underbrush and to be willing in its turn to provide open educational opportunity, superior teaching, and the chance to the superior student to move at his best pace.

Indeed, unless this happens, the promising stirrings of interest in secondary schools which indicate that they are now preparing to remedy their long neglect of the superior student will go unencouraged and a new and even more tragic age of neglect will be upon us.

This next paper is an excerpt from the annual Report of the Director *for 1956. I worked over it long and hard and in the end felt that it was a clear and specific statement of proposals for dealing with the most urgent problems in the business of college entrance. Note particularly that no curriculum problems were mentioned here. The Board was not unaware of curriculum problems: the whole activity of trying to establish the ill-fated Tests of Developed Ability was a form of recognition of one curriculum problem, and the formation of the Commission on Mathematics was an explicit recognition of the need for a new mathematics curriculum. But these problems were not pressing either the schools or the colleges (and they were not to do so until Sputnik went into orbit). The matter of handling candidates was the problem.*

Seen in hindsight, the problem was not quite as it is presented in the paper. Much is made in the paper of the wastage involved in failing large numbers of students, and the solution that is suggested is to reject them before entrance in order to make room for swelling multitudes of better-qualified students. Ten years later I realize that these failures helped pay for the education of those who succeeded. Now, with a new order of finance for all forms of higher education, I see the problem as that of providing education better adapted to the potential dropouts, thus giving them a real opportunity to succeed rather than the opportunity to fail, which is all that we used to give them in the past.

This paper, though it adds very little to this book in the way of either ideas or discussion of problems, does serve to demonstrate process—in this case the process

*of identifying problems in the public domain and transferring them into the
Board's own realm of action. The process did not always produce results, but it
can at least be established that it existed.*

"Prospects Ahead — A Look at the Future"
55th Report of the Director. New York: College
Entrance Examination Board, 1956, 133 pp., pp. 64–71.

To remark that American education is in process of change is to utter a
truism that is by now so banal that its very use constitutes a solecism in
educational conversation. Yet, paradoxically, to undertake to define and
quantify the change in any terms except in terms of numbers is to attempt
a task which has so far baffled our best analysts and the most clear-sighted
of our philosophers.

A large part of the problem inherent in the definition and quantification
of change has to do with the fact that we are in time very near to the forces
which are bringing about this change. There are, as the writer sees them,
three such forces.

First, the tremendous expansion of money and credit, amounting to the
equivalent of an explosion, that has taken place since the close of World
War I. This expansion is essentially a mortgaging of the future, based on
the assumption that this future is best served by building now the physical
and economic structures that it will require. The result of this expansion is
to create both opportunities for growth and development in every phase of
our national life, and a tremendous demand for knowledge, skills, and manpower to keep pace with the opportunities.

Second, the literal explosion of scientific knowledge which has been in
preparation for most of this century but which actually occurred only when
controlled fission became an actuality. This explosion of scientific knowledge will, as it is understood and controlled, supply the knowledge to
match the opportunities created by the explosion of money and credit.

Third, the explosion of population. Latest in point of time, this explosion was probably unrelated in its original causes, which had to do with
psychological factors growing out of the second war, but in its continuance
is pretty obviously related to the fact that there is now available to every
man a vision of opportunity for himself and his children such as has not

been known since the golden days of the Renaissance. This explosion of population provides, in effect, the human material for the operation and management of the society built upon the expansion of credit and of knowledge.

The effect of these forces has been felt progressively by American education, first in a swelling demand for what might be termed unspecified educational opportunity—in simple terms, the right of access to secondary schools and to colleges—and now in another form of demand for trained and specified products of American education—engineers and scientists, technicians and teachers, physicians and social workers, agriculturists and administrators, in fact, all the vast array of professionals, specialists, and generalists required by contemporary society.

It is in one sense a long step from this broad statement to the specific problems that now face the schools and colleges at this meeting-point in the area of the movement of students from one phase of our educational system to another, but in another sense the step is a short one.

The future management of transition from school to college is inescapably controlled by the broad problems of society. The clerical and administrative problems that are to be faced, the devices to be employed to solve them, the very assessments of individuals that are to be required are ultimately determined by the force and interaction of the three explosions which have taken place in this century and which are shaping our future. The nature of our problems is now fairly clear.

The main task ahead is to create an educational system responsive to the needs of expanding social and economic structures. This problem is not directly within the Board's purview, but it is the central problem with which the institutions that comprise the Board's membership must deal. It is the problem of establishing an educational system based on diversity in which opportunities are available at all ability levels, established in accordance with the known and anticipated requirements of the social and economic structure. This is a problem to which there is no final solution. There are only intermediate solutions—successive steps in the development of the educational system, each to be followed in time by another.

American education, and particularly higher education, is in its present form the result of a series of such intermediate solutions which have had in common the fact that each of them has brought new concepts or new elements into the makeup of the total enterprise. The prime example of the effect of a new concept was the development of our system of secondary education to the point where it now serves nearly 90 percent of the students of secondary school age. Another new concept now being introduced is the extension of the forms and methods of higher education to cover programs that are essentially noncollegiate, as in the community colleges and adult education centers which offer courses of a level and scope that are well outside of the usual college or university program.

The results of the introduction of new elements in education have been felt most widely in professional fields, particularly through the establishment during the past 15 years of programs in business administration and teacher education as a part of higher education. At present a number of new college-level professional programs are emerging from courses that until recently have been classified as semiprofessional and subcollegiate.

Although these problems of change and expansion of educational opportunity are not directly within the Board's purview, the solutions that are found, such as those mentioned above, have tremendous effects upon the Board, for each new set of solutions creates problems which have direct effects upon the Board's operations.

There are two sets of such problems.

The first set has to do with the placement of students within this system as it grows in size and simultaneously expands its tasks. This, in essence, is the problem of selection, and it is a relatively new problem. This is not to say that selective admission to college is a new idea. Many colleges have in fact for many years undertaken to select only those students who had a reasonable chance of college success. But it is to say that since the close of World War II the structure of American education has reflected the increasing stratification of American society along professional lines to such an extent that all our colleges and universities, regardless of whether or not their admissions policy is a selective one, are now engaged in a continuous process of selection. The writer has remarked before that all institutions select their graduates, even though not all institutions select their freshmen. But today the process goes further. The selection that goes on within an institution is now controlling the students who have professional and graduate studies as their goal beyond the first degree. The importance of this control is clear in the fact that it is those institutions which have the largest percentage of their graduates going on to graduate and professional studies that are working under the heaviest pressures of applications, and those with the smallest percentage of graduates continuing their studies that are least concerned with admissions pressures.

This trend toward the establishing of the criterion of excellence in undergraduate education as based upon success in studies beyond the bachelor's degree is placing increasing emphasis upon effective initial selection of students. There can be no doubt as to this point, nor any doubt that the Board's tests must be responsive to this emphasis. Therefore, a major Board concern must be to develop tests which will yield the largest amount of information as to the capabilities of a given candidate, and to introduce these tests into its program, supplementing and, if necessary, replacing tests now in use.

At present the Board's program, based upon the Scholastic Aptitude Test and the Achievement Tests, is meeting the demands for selection instruments. However, it has been recognized for some time that advances beyond this level of testing were within the bounds of possibility.

The work on the experimental program which has been named the Tests of Developed Ability (described elsewhere in this report) has, in fact, been carried forward for some years with the express purpose of providing an admissions instrument which would yield more and better information on candidate abilities than any college entrance testing program now in operation. This work is now in its penultimate stage of tryout as an actual admissions implement. If the results of this tryout measure up to expectations, then it will be possible to introduce the program as a regular Board offering with confidence that it will meet the need for an improved selection instrument.

Another Board program, now in operation, must also be viewed as a step already taken to provide better admissions information. The Advanced Placement Examinations, also described elsewhere in this report, although dealing for the present with relatively small numbers of candidates, do so in a manner that supports careful individual judgments and makes possible a genuine improvement in the total process of selection and placement.

These two programs are at the moment the frontier of Board activity in the development of new tools of selection and placement. The Board, of course, cannot rest upon them, however successful they may ultimately prove to be, but the directions in which it may go beyond them are not presently to be known, for they are dependent upon speculation, investigation, and research.

The second set of problems has to do with the clerical difficulties involved in handling large (and increasing) numbers of candidates within a relatively short space of time. This, while perhaps not as difficult in an intellectual sense as the creation of new selection instruments, is immediate for the very simple reason that we must assume that if application pressures on colleges in general, and particularly on Board member colleges, continue to increase at the rate at which they have been increasing over the past five years, then we must expect that the admissions process as we now know it will suffer a clerical breakdown by 1960.

The reasons for this statement are fairly easy to derive from an analysis of the admissions process. A count reveals that all candidates for Board member colleges require from 7 to 10 admissions operations, and that the candidates for scholarships, amounting to about 20 percent of the candidates, will require from 5 to 8 additional steps.

Considering the fact that each of these steps requires clerical operations involving either the candidate and the college, or the candidate and the College Board, or the candidate and a scholarship granting agency, or the school and the Board, or the school and the college, or the school and the scholarship granting agency, or the Board and the college, or the Board and the scholarship granting agency, or the scholarship granting agency and the college, it will be seen that there are many possibilities for multiplication of clerical activities. And, since each additional candidate offers the possibility of generating up to nine different lines of correspondence on any one of the stages, it will be seen that the clerical load is likely to increase, not only arithmetically, but in proportions approaching the geometrical.

Clearly, then, the clerical problem is a major one which can be solved only in one of three ways.

First, by reducing the number of applications to college. This, as a solution, can be rejected as out of the question. Neither schools nor colleges are disposed to be a party to such reductions, and even if they were there is no practicable way to accomplish it.

Second, by improving the handling of applications. Here the opportunities are tremendous. At present the college admissions system permits only a relatively short time between first application and final decision, and, furthermore, stipulates that all candidates must go through all stages of the system.

Yet the colleges could, with relatively little effort, get in contact with all or nearly all of their candidates months earlier than they now do, could use a preliminary screening test to make advisory judgments on preliminary applications, and could begin to make certain types of final decisions, that is to say, negative decisions, shortly after receiving the January or February test scores. These two steps alone would save a tremendous clerical load now carried in behalf of thousands of candidates whose applications can be quickly categorized as submarginal.

If the colleges were willing to go one step further and make final decisions on the basis of information contained in 3½ years of school record, plus preliminary test scores obtained in the eleventh grade, plus a second set of test scores in January or February of the twelfth-grade year, some thousands of additional candidates would benefit from an early decision which would allow them to know that their problems were settled, or alternatively, that they must make additional applications.

It must, of course, be said that there might be reasonable objections to giving up subject-matter tests, which do provide a valuable check on secondary school records, even for a purpose as praiseworthy as streamlining the admissions process. Here it should be noted that there are possibly two modifications of the admissions process which either singly or together would minimize the pain of such surrender. The first modification is implicit in the Board's work on new testing instruments. If, in fact, the Tests of Developed Ability, which are now undergoing trial, do prove effective, then the Board's membership will be able to obtain information about candidate ability in subject fields without having to wait for a March administration of subject-matter tests. The second such modification would follow naturally from the introduction of the Tests of Developed Ability as an admissions instrument. It would be the introduction of an *admitted student* series of placement examinations consisting of the same Achievement Tests that are now so widely used for admissions purposes. This would differ from the present practice in only two respects: the tests would be administered in May (a far better date from the standpoint of accurate assessment of subject-matter achievement than the present March date), and the students would take as many tests as might be required by the institution instead of being limited to three.

To sum up these observations on application handling, it is possible, through the use of programs now in existence or in the final stages of development, to reduce the number of steps in the admissions process without any essential sacrifice of information, and to do so at less cost to the candidate and to the institution. Furthermore, this will result in a saving of time which will permit the unsuccessful candidate ample opportunity to apply elsewhere and allow the successful candidate to complete in the spring the program of placement testing which ordinarily has to be sandwiched into registration activities in a last-minute rush before program making.

A third possible solution to the clerical burden lies in an entirely different area. This solution would involve the design and administration of a central clearinghouse operation which would leave to the colleges the full exercise of admissions discretion, employing whatever combination of information and judgment they would wish to employ, and would collect from the colleges their decisions on admissions, in rank order of preference for candidates. It would also involve collecting from the individual candidates the names of the colleges to which they had applied, accompanied by their statements, also in rank order, as to their preferences. With such information, a matching of choices could be conducted by a central agency with far less confusion and delay than now attends the annual admissions operations, and both candidates and colleges could be assured of obtaining the most desirable match of choices.

A clearinghouse operation of this magnitude would, of course, be difficult to schedule and to operate. It would involve the collection and collation of hundreds of thousands of items of information from candidates and colleges. Furthermore, it would have to take into account the related problems of scholarship awards. Nevertheless, and despite all difficulties, it is probable that modern high-speed equipment could deal with most of the problems at a cost considerably lower than the costs that are incurred by the institutions in the conduct of their present operations, and with results far more satisfactory than are now achieved by present methods.

The prospects ahead, to return to the heading of this section, are perhaps more interesting, and even exciting, for the profession of education than they have ever been. But they are prospects which call for adaptability, change, and new decisions. It is hardly fitting to contemplate that the vital process of transition from school to college should be entrenched behind slow, costly, and outworn methods when there are already at hand the methods, the knowledge, and the skills to free it of crippling handicaps and to make it a doorway to opportunity rather than an obstacle race.

This was a very typical commencement assignment—to mix wisdom, humor, admonition, and comment in exactly the right proportions.

So far as I know, the perfect commencement speech has never been written. This one is as near as I ever got to it. I liked it and enjoyed giving it, and the audience liked it. One could not ask for more.

Talk to the graduating class of Westminster Schools, Atlanta, Georgia, on June 3, 1957.

It is always good to be able to begin any talk on a note of reassurance and with the suggestion that a time of trouble has ended and that a new day has dawned or will dawn shortly after the speaker has stopped speaking.

I am glad to say that I can give such reassurance to the graduates of the Westminster Schools here assembled. You are through with your troubles with the College Entrance Examination Board. When you have heard me out, your relationship with the College Entrance Examination Board is complete for the rest of your life, with perhaps one small exception. This exception may be expected to turn up during the 1980s, when you will begin to worry, with your children, about the College Boards and the college entrance problems of that time.

Furthermore, I am glad to remark that the College Board is through with you. There have been a great many of you this year—nearly 500,000 —and the problems you have brought, not to mention the sheer bulk of the work load, have made it quite a year. Now that it is over, we too can relax for a little before we turn to the new year.

This time of quiet gives us jointly a chance to review the past and speculate—or, if you prefer, prophesy—about the future. I could wish that we had enjoyed the chance earlier, for there are things to be said that might help us both to better understanding of the experiences we have had and those we will have.

In undertaking to say some of those things, I want to begin with my own field, which is college entrance, and then go on to discuss college in its broader context, as the continuation of the educational process you have been experiencing.

Tests and test taking are familiar to all of us. Yet there is always a disposition to consider that tests are something apart, something extra, not really a part of education, but superimposed upon it. Nothing could be farther from the truth, and the sooner you accept this, the better. Tests, in a formal sense, are a sampling process. They are selected tasks, picked out because they are typical. From your performance on these tasks, certain conclusions can be and are drawn as to your ability to perform similar tasks. Good performance on the sample tasks is taken as an indication that you have learned well the principles and facts on which their solution rests, and therefore as an indication that you can learn other tasks and perform them well. Poor performance casts doubt, both on the learning that has taken place and on the ability to learn in the future.

In this testing process, there is, of course, a heavy responsibility on the test maker. If he selects tasks that are not typical—either too easy or too difficult—the measurement of past performance is poor, and the prediction of future performance is poor. This is, of course, unfair to the person who takes the test. This is why the methods of making tests change very slowly, for test makers cannot consider themselves as privileged to take chances on unfair measurement. For example, tests of personality have never been widely used as college entrance devices, the reason being that we cannot assure ourselves from the evidence that we accumulate that they are, or will be, fair to all of the students that take them. These same problems apply to tests which might otherwise be used in advising students in their choice of careers. The tests we have do work in some cases, but not in others, and must therefore be used with extreme caution.

But, if there is a heavy responsibility on the test maker in the testing field, there are also heavy responsibilities on the test taker. He must first recognize the fact that during the years from age 15 to age 25 he will encounter tests in large numbers and in all forms and sizes. Some of these are formal tests, like the College Boards or the Medical Aptitude Test. Some are end-of-course examinations. But more of them are informal or even concealed tests, such as conversations with older people, performance in learning the routines of a new job, the acceptance and discharge of responsibility.

Most people react or learn to react to tests in a way that reflects their day-to-day performance. This is a happy fact upon which the entire business of testing rests, and upon which it has rested since the beginning of time. Those of you who are interested in the earliest written records of tests, and selection based upon them, might well refer to the book of Judges, Chapter 7, verses 4 through 7, which tells the story of the selection of Gideon's 300 men with whom he overcame the Midianites, a process almost identical with the one by which men were selected during the last war for dangerous or special duties. These four verses are, in fact, a model of reporting, for they state the circumstances surrounding the problem, the problem itself, the selection criteria, the testing method, and the result. No reporter has ever done it better.

But there are also individuals who do not reflect their day-to-day performance in their tests. These fall into two broad categories.

There is the individual who is, or who believes himself to be, a person who is congenitally unfortunate on tests—that is, who can never do himself full justice on a test. I, like everyone else who has ever worked as an admissions officer, have encountered my full share of these people and have struggled with charity on one side and better judgment on the other over the question of admission to college. To those who suffer from this malady, I can offer some sympathy and no comfort. Failing tests is a bad habit. It may be a symptom of maladjustment, but more often it represents a form of laziness that has to be conquered. For it is an obvious truism that a person who cannot pass the various tests which his adult life will present to him cannot control his own life, and this is the path of personal tragedy.

On the other end of the scale is the person who cannot work in a day-to-day situation, but who can perform magnificently on tests. Such people are scarcely more to be envied than the test failers, for they have shown that their obvious native ability lacks the ingredient of consistency, and that their life is likely to operate in a series of fits and starts, with magnificent successes punctuated by arid periods of mediocrity and near-failure.

You will recognize that in describing test takers I have in effect described the range of human operations as it applies to any conceivable situation. There is always the great group that reacts as it is expected to, and always individuals on either end of the scale who do not react as predicted. However, I think it important to note that the person in school has an advantage that is denied to those not in school. It is the advantage of being able to carry the problem of poor performance to people who are accustomed to dealing with it and getting help in improving the situation. This, I repeat, is a tremendous opportunity, even though it may sometimes seem difficult to approach. Taking advantage of it, or not taking advantage of it often makes the difference between good performance and poor performance.

It is now appropriate to pass from general discussion of tests to the experiences that you are about to enter upon as a result of the testing you have undergone.

Most of you who are here graduating today are going to college in the fall. Some of you are not, but, even among those, most will sooner or later follow additional formal schooling. Therefore, what I am going to say, in the form of prophecy based on probabilities which, in turn, are based on the national experience, will apply in greater or lesser degree to everyone in the graduating class.

The first set of probabilities that might interest you is that probably 75 percent of those who enter college from this graduating class next fall will finish college. This is a figure above the national average, which informs us that only 50 percent of the students who enter college in any given year may be expected to complete the course within four years. However, I think I am safe in assuming this degree of success for the company here assembled. You have had secondary schooling opportunities that are better than the average secondary school opportunities in the nation. The fact that you have been in a private school argues a certain degree of financial support, of family background, and of motivation, which will probably give you a better than average college performance, in terms of completion.

As to how you will perform in college as individuals, I cannot be quite so definite. I think that in general you may expect that your college performance will be about the same as your secondary school performance. This will be a disappointment to some of you and to some of your parents, who believe that with increasing maturity you will do better than you have done. I should therefore hasten to say that while the average group performance will be about the same as your average performance in secondary school, individuals may vary a good deal. There will be some of you, I regret to say, who will fail in college for reasons that cannot now be predicted and may perhaps never be ascertained. There will also be some of you who will succeed in college to an extent that cannot now be predicted from your school performance. These individuals are now generally called "late bloomers." There is no question that late bloomers exist, and that some individuals glory in the classification. However, I should point out that any individual who considers himself to be a late bloomer had better go immediately to get some fertilizer and put it right to work. I would point out that the century plant is, in a way, a late bloomer, but will also comment that people who have seen the bloom of the century plant have wondered if it was worth waiting for. In other words, no special virtue attaches to being a late bloomer. It is a form of hope deferred, and the deferment should not be continued.

Now, departing from academic success and going over to the reasons for going to college. Most of you who are going to college have an announced or an agreed purpose in going to college. Some of you plan to be engineers, some doctors, some of you are going to take a general or liberal arts course and make up your minds later, many of you do not have any specific plans except to go to college and follow the course the college lays out.

I am sure it will come as a shock to most of you who are graduating, and to some of your parents, that many of you are going to change your minds as to what you plan to do in and after college, and are going to change them fairly soon after entering college. Experience would indicate that about half of the students who enter college change their minds as to their plans within the first two years of work. This is because many of the goals and objectives they set up for themselves are the result of urgings and pressures coming from outside. Many of these pressures are unobtrusive and perhaps unnoticed and unintentional, but nonetheless very real pressures. For example, at the present moment, there is a considerable pressure upon students to plan on studying engineering, or medicine, or mathematics, or science in college. There can be no doubt that there are great opportunities in these areas, but these opportunities are not for all. Individuals who pursue these opportunities as they might purchase a stock which looks like a good speculation are likely to get hurt, just as they are likely to lose money in speculation. Where there is honest interest, determination, and ability, the risk is worth taking, but where there is doubt about these, the risk increases.

What I am saying is that you must not consider yourselves as committed to a life work because you now think it attractive, and that you must be prepared to change when the evidence is clear that you should change.

One thing that I think is of utmost importance for you to understand now, as you plan on entering college, is that most present goals for college students require more than four years to complete. In other words, if you are thinking of college in terms of entering in the fall of 1957 and going to work in 1961, you had better consider the fact that the strongest colleges and universities—and many of you are entering the strongest colleges and universities—generally expect that from 60 to 80 percent of their graduates will continue graduate or professional work immediately after leaving college, and will continue it for as much as four to six years. This means that, when they admit you, they expect that there is better than an even chance that you will enter professional or graduate school after you leave college. This, too, has important implications for your parents. College costs are likely to continue for more than four years, and the per year costs do not decrease in graduate or professional school.

Specifically, anybody who is planning on law must plan on a minimum of three years beyond college, plus one year of apprenticeship, before being admitted to the bar; anyone who is planning on medicine must plan on four years beyond college, plus two to four years of internship and residency before entering upon his own practice; anyone planning on teaching should plan on a minimum of one year beyond college, and, if he is thinking about college or university teaching or research, should consider that his graduate school work may extend from three to five years. Engineering is theoretically a four-year program, but most students take five years to complete it. The same could be said for a number of other programs which students are planning to follow, such as a plan to take a liberal arts course and then go into business. Here the present indications are that students who graduate from a liberal arts college and then go to a good business school for two years of graduate work leading to a further degree get much better jobs and move more rapidly in business than do students who enter business directly from college.

We have heard a good deal about the liberal arts as the best preparation for life. Speeches by corporation presidents extolling the virtues of the liberal arts blossom as verbal flowers every June at the commencement season, and many of them will be displayed before your eyes in the newspaper columns during the next few weeks. It is true that the liberal arts have been shown to be a good preparation for a successful life when success is measured by income and responsibility. Probably the reason for this truth is that the liberal arts give a full view of the background of our life and culture. They require a study of the sciences, of mathematics, of the humanities, of the social studies, and of languages. For the reason that they do require this broad sampling of studies, they also form the best selective device yet invented in picking out individuals who are likely to prove successful in technical or professional, or nontechnical or nonprofessional activities. That is to say, a student who can cope with these various disciplines can usually cope, as an adult, with the varied problems of management and of organization, as well as with the special problems involved in a profession.

The gist of this talk is that most of our education today ends up as education for a specialty. Many are impatient to get to their specialty early. This accounts for the fact that some people leave college before they have completed the course, and it accounts for the fact that others go from college directly into business or industry. But education for specialty has certain traps to it which should be reviewed. If a student begins his specialization early, he has made an early commitment, and this commitment may turn out to be not entirely the right commitment. Hence, it is just as well to delay and take the time now to try out other interests. This form of tryout is actually the form of following a general program for at least a year after entering college, and is the reason why so many colleges, including engineering schools, today emphasize a year of general preparation before going into the specialization of a profession.

So far, this discussion has been directed toward college preparation for specialty. This means that it is more directed to men in college than to women in college. There are two reasons why this is so.

First, there is a certain amount of both social and biological pressure on women to marry at an age which is earlier than the average marriage age for men. This means that some young women marry while they are still in college. In most cases, when this happens, they do so with the intention of finishing college but drop out without doing so. This cuts down on the proportion of women finishing college, which is probably lower than the percentage of men finishing college. There are also other reasons which operate to cut down this proportion, but many of these are financial, resting on the fact that the higher education of women is more of a drain on family incomes than is the higher education of men, since there are fewer scholarships for college women, fewer student employment opportunities, and more necessary expenses.

Second, there are, in fact, fewer opportunities in professions for women than for men. This means that while there are plenty of employment opportunities for women college graduates, there are relatively few such opportunities with a really enticing financial opportunity to be seen in the future. There are, in turn, two sets of reasons why this is true.

The first such reason is that until very recently the supply of men necessary to fill employment opportunities has been adequate or, as in the thirties, more than adequate. It is, in fact, only since the war that any really good professional opportunities have begun to open up for women.

The second such reason is that prospective employers and leaders of professions all know that women must have family rearing responsibilities, and that these responsibilities are bound to draw them away from employment or professional practice for some years.

However, despite all these facts which affect opportunites for women, it is also a fact that a woman who neglects a chance to complete preparation for employment or for a profession is taking a needless chance with the future, by shutting off an option which she might wish, or even need, to accept under other circumstances.

There are four general cases which apply here. The first, that young wives must often assume the role of breadwinner for the family while young husbands are completing their education; the second, that a certain percentage of marriages come to an early termination, which forces the wife back on her own resources for support; the third, that it is very often possible to work out a family life in which both husband and wife are employed, and to have a more satisfactory life than one in which the wife's concerns are chiefly with home and community affairs; the fourth, that many women find as their children grow older that employment offers an interesting change of pace.

These points are particularly addressed of course to the young women in the class, but I hope that the young men will consider them, too. We are entering upon a period in which the percentage of all adults who are employed will rise. We will never reach the point where all adults are employed, but we are much nearer to that point now than we were 30 years ago, and 30 years hence we shall be nearer still. This, therefore, is a fact to be faced in planning education. Those who fail to plan education to prepare to face this fact are failing themselves, and this ultimately is the worst failure of all.

Translated into terms that relate to you who are graduating today, it means that you will all be well advised to consider the college that you are going to enter in the fall as a form of life insurance. It is, of course, not insurance in the usual meaning of the word. Rather it is a form of insurance which consists of opening doors to the future and of keeping them open. I do not wish to moralize, but I must take the risk of seeming to do so when I remark that every failure closes a door to the future. As you sit here now, within minutes of putting a formal end to your secondary schooling, all doors are open. From now on you will begin your selection of the doors you wish to use, a selection based on the path that lies beyond each door. Your main problem will be to maintain your freedom of choice in order that you may finally make your choices wisely.

These remarks are in a sense the ending of a chapter in the life of each graduate here present. With their ending, my task for the evening has ended too. It remains only for me to wish you good fortune, and this I do with the greatest of pleasure.

This paper gave me an opportunity to explore a problem that has long fascinated me. It still does, and I hope that some day it will be attacked by someone with the time and the insight for a careful study.

"The Intangibles of Admissions"
Address to the Association of College Admissions Counselors meeting, Excelsior Springs, Missouri, on October 14, 1957.

This invitation to talk tonight, when issued to me some months ago, was, for several reasons, a welcome one. As a refugee from an admissions office, I find great pleasure and solace in telling admissions officers about their business, secure in the knowledge that I do not have to, indeed cannot, practice what I preach. But, more important than this personal pleasure is the fact that I have long felt an urge to open a discussion of those factors that control admissions but over which we ourselves have no control—the intangibles of admissions. I have hesitated to do so, knowing that such a discussion would be bound to have its moments of abstruseness and more than its share of dubious psychologizing, and would therefore require a tolerant and understanding audience. Having such an audience, I now undertake to present the paper. I know that you will recognize those places where I have taken too many liberties with theory, but I trust you will accept, for what it is, an attempt to open discussion of admissions problems from a viewpoint that has usually been left to the practitioners of the behavioral sciences.

The intangibles of admissions are for the college admissions officer those factors beyond his control which determine the behavior of individual candidates. They determine how many applications he will receive, how many scholarships he must award, how many acceptances he must issue, how many ghosts he will house in the drawers of his candidate files, and ultimately the size, quality, and distribution of his freshman class.

The intangibles are the factors that make applicants fickle and mobile, that produce swollen application lists and inexplicable disappearances from those lists. They are the factors that cause applicants to turn their backs on a local college to travel hundreds of miles to a college that may have little more to offer. Also, they are the factors that stop a promising student at the end of high school in order to make him a statistic in the roster of undeveloped talent. They are the factors that develop the mysterious pecking order of colleges in which enrollment in one group of colleges is affected by the policies of another group of colleges.

A substantial part of the present-day work of the admissions officer is created for him by intangibles. The efforts to control multiple applications, the elaborate tables for calculating the incidence of ghosts, waiting lists, discussions about clearinghouses, private treaties between schools and colleges—all of these are caused by intangibles. So, too, are enrollments below capacity, the endless hours of candidate interviewing, elaborate recruiting programs, and all the other factors that characterize the admissions programs of underpopulated colleges. All of these recognize the existence of intangibles and seek to circumvent, or at least to minimize, their effect.

Since intangibles operate directly on the candidate and only indirectly upon colleges, we have no certain knowledge of them. However, since they recur yearly with each new crop of candidates, we know that they represent factors which are inherent in the present relationships between candidate and college. Since they operate in more or less predictable fashion, we have some basis for grouping them according to their symptoms. Once grouped, we can do a rough factor analysis and move at least part way toward identification and, possibly, eventual cure. Many groupings are possible. I have not attempted to deal with all possibilities, but rather to concentrate on three groupings of these intangibles.

The first grouping has to do with candidate attitudes toward college. Here, curiously enough, the problem begins with the colleges themselves. In recent years the colleges have discovered, or rediscovered, that an economic advantage attaches to college attendance. This economic advantage gets tremendous emphasis each year at the time of the annual raid of the corporation ivory hunters on college campuses, but it is also a regular part of all college publicity. This discovery is probably the greatest catastrophe suffered by American education in this century, for it has turned attention away from the central purpose of education, which has to do with worth of the mind, and toward the results of the system which emerge in the form of selection, all-purpose training, and preparation for occupations. But this comment is beside the point. The point is that college attendance is currently being presented to the prospective students as a "good thing."

The arguments for going to college that are now in use are basically economic. They are only occasionally intellectual, or even cultural. It is true that college catalogs all have a standard paragraph which states the college aim as "preparation of the whole man for life through the establishment of social, cultural, and intellectual values," but I would doubt that anyone in this room is prepared to state precisely how this is accomplished. On the other hand, I would expect that everyone here present would be able to cite statistics of the type which prove that a college graduate earns on the average $100,000 more during his lifetime than does a noncollege graduate, or would be able to produce a file of clippings on the placement of college graduates, or would be prepared to point out that college is the only port of entry into professional life.

C. Wright Mills says, in *White Collar:* "Formal requirements for entry into different jobs and expectations of ascent tend to become fixed by educational levels. On the higher levels, college is the cradle of the professions and semi-professions, as well as a necessary status-mark for higher positions."[11] This quotation is a succinct statement of the present attitude to college.

It is true, of course, that we cannot use quite the same economic arguments in presenting women's education. This may account for the fact that there is a consistent attempt to rationalize women's colleges and women's education in intellectual terms. Nevertheless, there is a basic economic and occupational argument for women's education which rests upon the fact that college graduation is the best possible preparation for marriage to a college graduate, a truism that is now being supported by the additional fact that nearly every woman now enters the labor force at some time in her life. This, of course, turns back to the general economic argument in support of all college education.

Because the economic argument is most prominent in the presentation of college, it is naturally the most prominent part of the student image of college. But college is also presented to students in social terms through the medium of glossy, outsize view books, and not infrequently in glorious

---

11. *White Collar: The American Middle Classes.* New York: Oxford University Press, 1951, 378 pp., p. 266.

technicolor. These presentations emphasize the social opportunities of college, the attractiveness of social life in college, and suggest the after-college values of belonging to the collegiate stratum of American youth. It is also presented in intellectual terms, although the intellectual aspect, necessarily couched in abstractions and generalizations, is always difficult and too often apologetic.

Thus the student forms images of college which are economic, social, and intellectual. There are undoubtedly other images, too, which may be even more complex than these, created by factors other than the college presentation, but since we do not know how these are formed, we must omit them from our list of intangibles.

The student images of college are intangibles which have their effect on the admissions operation, but their importance is essentially indirect, as the basis for the view the student takes of himself and of his relationship to college. This set of relationships is to be considered under a second cluster of intangibles.

This cluster I should describe as being concerned essentially with student self-evaluation or self-imagery.

Self-evaluation probably begins within the large framework of the social climate. Let me illustrate this by an example. In a firmly stratified social structure, such as the English have had, it is difficult, almost to the point of impossibility, for a child of the lower middle class to conceive of himself as a university student or to look beyond student days to a career as a professional man, or an upper-level civil servant, or a barrister, army officer, or broker. His actual home life and friendships are bounded within a world of wage earners; he knows that his military service will be as a private in the ranks and that his future wife will be a wage earner whose education has ended, like his own, with the General Certificate of Education. In such a social climate, a youngster of 15 or 16 may not even know any friend or schoolmate—much less relative—who has broken out of this structure. Therefore, his self-evaluation, on which he bases his plans and his images of himself as an adult, may not even consider the possibility of aspiration beyond steady employment and a daily wage, or, at most, a small business of his own. This picture of England is, of course, overdrawn for purposes of emphasis. Actually, there are opportunities for social mobility in England, and the opportunities are increasing. But the overdrawing is not so great as to distort the contrast with our social climate.

We have—or believe we have, which amounts to the same thing—a social climate which permits of great mobility. It is easy for a youngster, regardless of his social status, to at least think of himself as a college student and to cast beyond college days to a position as a professional man, or a corporation executive, or a scientist. If he is afflicted with nightmares, he may even dream of being an admissions officer. But the point is that there is ample proof that no ambitions are closed to him and that achievements are bounded only by his own limitations.

Within such boundaries, a student's images of himself may acquire tremendous importance. If he conceives of himself as very able, he will then aspire to superior status. Since colleges are eager to supply information on the status achieved by their graduates, the student will have plenty of information to use in choosing the college that will help him to seek status. If he wants to enter a profession, he will seek a college which can assure him of entry. If he seeks a position in big business, he will seek a college which can assure him of such a position. In the pursuit of such a college, a student, driven by his self-image of success, will be ruthless with his colleges. He will make and discard applications, will dicker and dangle until the end. If scholarships are identified as a mark of status, he will seek scholarships. Need, in such a context, is unimportant, but success is of the essence. Mills has said that "The aim of college men today, especially in elite colleges, is a forward-looking job in a large corporation."[12] If such be the case, then it is a clear case of student self-imagery.

There is another variety of self-imagery which has elements of pathos and sometimes of tragedy. It occurs within the situation in which the student or his family predetermines the limit of aspiration. This is far more common than we think, for we see only a small fraction of it. The fraction that we do see is of those youngsters who turn away from a strong college where they fear the unknowns of social and intellectual climate in order to go to a lesser one where these can be known. I would suggest that much of the success of Harvard's admissions policies has been due to a frank recognition nearly 20 years ago that the existence of these unknowns of

12. *Ibid.*, p. 267.

social, financial, and intellectual climate at Harvard had kept many able students away. Once this was recognized, there followed an intelligent, careful, and successful campaign to dispel them, and Harvard today is the most successful admissions operation in the country. But Harvard's willingness to change its ways has not been copied, as it might be, by other institutions, and many colleges do not understand or attack these unknowns. The loss, unfortunately, is their own.

I have said we see in college—any college—only a fraction of those who fear unknowns, for most of these never go beyond high school. Those among them who have high ability are characterized as lost talent. The others are statistical additions to the labor force and pass unnoticed in the hue and cry of the talent search, yet their motivations are the same as those of the able ones whose absence is noticed, recorded, and deplored, and the loss to them as individuals may be just as great.

Happily, we have always a modicum of youngsters whose self-images correspond with what the college catalogs and educators say they should be. They conceive of themselves as learners, seekers, experimenters, sometimes as creators, and they ask only the opportunity to fulfill their conception. Not all of these are of equal ability, but, at any rate, they all come as students. For them, college is a foretaste of heaven, and, if there are enough of them in a freshman class, even the English department will speak kindly to the admissions officer.

There are other self-images to consider. It is alleged that girls sometimes enter college propelled by the image of themselves as married to college men, and it is certain that some boys enter college in pursuit of the image of themselves in the guise of athletic heroes.

It would be silly to fail to recognize that many student self-images are almost totally unformed in any sense that is classifiable by adults. We do not know how many students apply to college, enter, and even graduate without any clear vision of their own identity or purpose. Some of these carry through on a kind of rote ability without ever being noticed. Some disappear when their rote ability is not enough to carry them through. Others suddenly awaken, enter the adult world, earn the title of late bloomers, and become the darlings of their discoverers.

I realize that in this catalog of student self-images I have not said anything about parent-imposed images. I wish I did not have to, for they introduce great complexities, but I must, because they carry great importance. The best way to attack them is by dividing them into several groups.

The first group we can call "fully imposed." In such cases the only image the student has of himself is the one that his parents have conveyed to him. Perhaps a better way of saying this would be to say that the student's self-image in this case agrees fully with his parents' plans for him and evaluation of him. It would be a mistake to assume that all fully imposed images are those which lead to a ruthless drive to success. There are many such, but success has many faces and not all seek the same face. Sometimes limited aspirations are created by parent-imposed images. If the aspirations are too limited, the student is never seen by any college but disappears into the labor force. Still another and very common form of parent-imposed image is the one which dictates that the child must go to the parent's college—what might be called the hereditary college syndrome. Still another is the type which holds the child away from any college which may change him—perhaps a tremendous factor in motivation.

A second group of parent-imposed images is what we might call "partially imposed." These may frequently be traced in students who have not matured to the point of developing their own self-images and accept instead the positive proposals of their parents. Such partial acceptance of parent-images is, of course, common. It accounts for many college choices and for many occupational choices. Often the student becomes reconciled to full acceptance of parent suggestions. At least as often he changes plans and directions. The bewildering shifts and veerings of college students cannot be altogether explained by this concept of partially imposed images, but certainly many of them are related to the student's struggle to build his own conception of himself out of the blurred conception that must result from a partially imposed parent-image. It is dangerous to even attempt generalization on the ultimate resolution of most of the choice problems arising from such images, but there is some reason to think that parents are more ambitious, or at least more specifically ambitious, than their children and that many of the choices away from professions and away from family-chosen colleges may be the result of this resolution. This is probably as it should be, for, in our culture, we believe that parents should carry weight and authority but should not overuse either.

Finally, in this group of self-images, we come to "fully opposed parent–student self-images," in which the student refuses to accept parental evaluations, parental plans, or, in some cases, parental money. We see very few of such students, since very few of them get to college. In this respect they are like the students whose aspirations are limited by fully imposed parental control, but, as individuals, they are likely to be completely different. The limited-aspiration student tends to be docile, easily defeated, predictable; the fully opposed student is familiar to us, when we do occasionally see him, as rebellious, determined, but often inconstant, carrying his parental opposition into a self-image of permanent opposition until such time as he can justify himself through success.

Still another result of student–parent relationship may be the "college-is-college-is-college attitude," in which the parent decides only that his child may go to college but takes no responsibility beyond this decision, leaving all choices to the student.

This is not the full catalog of self-images. It is rather a suggestion that these images, which we know exist, are of tremendous importance in their effect upon the student—his choice of college, the manner in which he pursues his choice, the manner of his behavior.

I wish that I had the time and the personal self-image of knowledge to trace these developments into the home, the community, and the social structure. But I would not wish to try to summarize in one page what has been written by Reisman, in *The Lonely Crowd* and in *Faces in the Crowd*, or by Mills, in *White Collar*, or by Hollingshead in *Elmtown's Youth*.[13] I can only recommend these as important reading for any admissions officer who undertakes to delve into the underlying complexities of his task.

These attitudes of the individual toward himself are quickly convertible into attitudes toward college. I have already made clear my own belief that the student whose self-image is one of success will be ruthless in his search for a college which will support success, and I have commented that

---

13. David Reisman, with Nathan Glazer and Reuel Denney, *The Lonely Crowd: A Study of the Changing American Character*. New Haven: Yale University Press, 1950, 386 pp. Reisman, in collaboration with Nathan Glazer, *Faces in the Crowd: Individual Studies in Character and Politics*. New Haven: Yale University Press, 1952, 751 pp. C. Wright Mills, *White Collar: The American Middle Classes*. New York: Oxford University Press, 1951, 378 pp. August de Belmont Hollingshead, *Elmtown's Youth: The Impact of Social Classes on Adolescents*. New York: J. Wiley, 1949, 480 pp.

other types of student self-images produce different levels of aspiration and different expressions of them, including some which operate to close the doors to college. Now I want to examine these self-images in their relation to choice of college and to attitudes toward college.

The student whose self-image is one of success will wish to choose a college which, *within his experience*, will guarantee success. He may seek success in medicine or scientific research, or he may direct himself to a corporation job. But, whatever his goal to success, he will head straight for the college that will give him the best prediction of future success. Again, to quote Mills: "In the white-collar life and its patterns of success, the educational segment of the individual's career becomes a key to his entire occupational fate."[14] If the college is beyond his means, he will seek for a scholarship to bring it within his means. It will not matter that a college near at hand which is within his means can offer comparable preparation. It may well be—and, if he is a scholarship applicant, it will often be—that he will apply to several colleges of the type he has identified with future success. In that case, he begins to get ready for a ghostly career as an applicant, since he will have applied for scholarships to several different colleges and to at least one standby college, thereby insuring that he will, in September, be one student and several ghosts.

It is worth speculating on the types of colleges that are left out completely in the planning patterns of the success-bound student.

Private colleges which maintain low-cost patterns do so in order to make it possible for students of all income levels to attend. But it is very notable that their goal is not achieved. A low-cost pattern in fact acts as a negative selector in that students who can afford higher costs will not enter them if they have their choice of attending a higher-cost institution. Low-cost colleges are also associated with low prestige. Therefore, they fail to attract those who fit the college's cost patterns but who prefer to attend higher-prestige institutions with scholarship aid. The statement that low-cost institutions are associated with low prestige may be disturbing to some. Yet it cannot be otherwise. Except for a handful of colleges where large endowment is used to keep cost down or, as in the case of Rice University and Cooper Union, to provide free tuition, costs are

---

14. C. Wright Mills, *White Collar: The American Middle Classes.* New York: Oxford University Press, 1951, 378 pp., p. 266.

held down at the expense of faculty salaries and instructional facilities. Such institutions must be educationally stodgy because they cannot afford to change. They are likely to be educationally sterile because they can offer no hope or incentive to their faculty. Such institutions can hardly hope to attract their fair share of able students, and their deficiency in this respect adds to their lack of appeal. Low-cost public institutions are, of course, another case, but the differences are not so great as one might expect. State universities, and particularly their graduate and professional schools, spend more per student than do the state colleges, teachers' colleges, and junior colleges. Ordinarily they cost their students more, and ordinarily they draw a larger proportion of superior students than do the other state units.

The factors that operate with respect to costs also operate with respect to admissions requirements and college standards. Colleges with low entrance standards offer no extra appeal to strong students. If they enter such colleges, it will be for other reasons. And colleges which retain poor students who have entered on low standards do not thereby increase their appeal to good students, but rather diminish it. Of course, a case can be made for state institutions which may admit on low entrance standards but enforce rigorously high standards for remaining in school. However, even these colleges, by their method of operation, introduce an element of risk for some youngsters who will prefer to avoid the chance of being caught in a mass elimination before they have had a chance to get their bearings.

These factors of low cost and low admissions standards may thus operate in a fashion precisely opposite to the one intended. On the tangible level, their standards and costs can certainly be rationalized and perhaps even justified. But the operation of the intangibles—the unknowns of student attitudes and ambitions—may work against the very goals they seek to achieve.

These same factors may well operate in the area of program. Many small and medium-size colleges undertake to operate a wide variety of programs. These will include the traditional liberal arts program, often rather skimpily supported in the upper years, so that the challenge of rigorous advanced courses based on research and seminar-type instruction is either missing or is present only in a pallid form. In addition, they will ordinarily have a business administration major, a laboratory technology curriculum concealed in the science department, plus a secondary education and an elementary education program offered by a one- or two-man teacher-training department. If the college has a department of music or of speech or home economics, it will, in addition to majors in each of these fields, offer the corresponding teacher-training majors. A year's course offered by the librarian will add a school librarian option. A teacher of stenography, typing, and office practice will add a secretarial program. Thus, what is advertised as a small liberal arts college—one of the vertebrae in the so-called backbone of American higher education—becomes on closer inspection a combination of meager liberal arts, preprofessional, professional, semiprofessional, and vocational—more like a slipped disk than one of the functioning vertebrae.

It is, of course, easy enough to rationalize such a program on the basis of broad educational opportunity, but the fact is that when opportunity is added at the bottom of the education scale it has no attraction for those who seek the top of the scale. Consequently, when student attitudes come into play, the college ends by drawing only those students whose attitudes are undefined or negative, plus, at best, a group of students for whom such a college does represent a step upward in the scale of opportunity.

Such colleges with low costs, low standards, or diffuse programs run a further risk when they are put into the role of being alternative choices for students who have aimed higher. In such cases the student who fails in his higher choice may enter as a disappointed and disgruntled person, uninterested in what the college may have to offer and eager to leave at the first good opportunity.

One last consideration of attitudes is in order: this time the result of a parent-imposed attitude rather than a student self-image. We have already mentioned the hereditary college attitude on the part of some parents. There is an antithesis to this attitude in the determination of some parents not to send their children to the college they attended. This attitude will most often be found in individuals who have moved beyond what they deem to be the level of the college they attended. This attitude, a very real one and important both in student recruiting and alumni relations, is not often considered, perhaps not often even realized, in listing the intangibles that affect admissions.

This list of intangibles is, of course, incomplete. No man can make a complete list, and if he could we would not believe it. The list of suggested effects of these intangibles on admissions is even less complete and speculative to boot. We do not know that these intangibles, assuming their existence, produce the effects that are here discussed. But we do know that the effects are produced, that admissions has become a sort of large-scale guessing game, and that no tangible cause can be adduced why this is so. Therefore, there is basis for discussing intangibles. The question of what to do about them is another matter.

I believe that there has been a tendency to lose sight of candidates as individuals even as we intensify our interest in them as statistics. If we knew more about them—who they are, whence they come, why they come to us—perhaps some of the intangibles could become tangibles and admissions officers could abandon their guessing games to the actuaries, returning gratefully to the practice of simple arithmetic in their calculations on their entering classes.

5. The Sputnik Era: 1958-1960

The three years from the beginning of 1958 to the end of 1960 were a period in which the pressures for change that had been accumulating within American education ever since the war were released, to work with bewildering speed on every part of the system.

Sputnik was the visible trigger that set off this change, but it would have come about under any conditions, perhaps delayed until 1960 and the new national administration.

The consciousness of change and the dislocation brought about by new conditions set interesting tasks for the Board's officers. We had to spend a great deal of our time at meetings explaining the causes, and speculating on the effects, of things that were happening, such as the high school physics course developed by the Physical Science Study Group, or the development of programs provided for in the National Defense Education Act.

We also had other things to do. The changing conditions in our field— steadily increasing numbers of candidates, growing membership, the tremendous developments in financial aid for students—put a whole set of operational demands on us. The need for direct communication with schools and colleges newly entering the Board's work area had to be met through the establishment of regional offices. The training of admissions officers and financial aid officers was developed through seminars, organized and paid for by the Board, utilizing as faculty the few overworked experts in the field, including at one time or another all of the Board's staff.

As is evident from the papers that follow, the period was fascinating in its opportunities and demands.

In September of 1960 I took a leave of absence for two years to go to Paris as the director of an undertaking entitled "The International Study of University Admissions." This was an enterprise jointly supported by Unesco and the International Association of Universities and supported by a grant of $250,000 made to the College Board, which was to act as fiscal agent, by the Carnegie Corporation of New York. The results of that study will be dealt with in the next and final chapter of this book.

---

*The following paper was in a sense a think piece that became exposed to pub-
lic hearing. I had been puzzled for many years about why colleges and
universities behaved so differently and had such different relations to each other
in different parts of the country. A generous, "hunting-license" invitation to
speak before the Association for Higher Education supplied the incentive for my
attempting to think out this problem.*

*The answer to the question is probably no longer valid. Conditions have
changed, and the whole area of institutional relationships should be examined
again. Let us hope that it will be.*

"Patterns of Dominance and Choice"
Address at the third General Session of the fourteenth
National Conference on Higher Education, sponsored by the
Association for Higher Education, Chicago, on March 3, 1959.
Published in the *College Board Review* No. 38,
Spring 1959, pp. 5–10.

All educators, and this phrase must, by courtesy, include administrators,
believe that their work has value for the future. This paper is a series of
speculations based upon that belief. These speculations postulate that we
have a very large measure of control over future forms of higher education,
hence, a series of choices to be made, but that the choices we have before
us are not necessarily the ones we think we have.

In order to discuss these areas of choice in the future, it is necessary first
to describe the base on which the future rests. I therefore offer a present
view of higher education. This view is not statistical, but is rather couched
in terms of attitudes and purposes. I suspect that some of the generalizations will be found overly broad and will concede in advance that some
identifications and interpretations are open to question. But these risks
have been accepted in order to identify trends, groupings, and patterns.
Some of these I found to be uncomfortable as I set them down, but I did
not then and do not now find that such discomfort is any reason for avoid-
ance.

Before I set about descriptions I have certain terms of reference to establish. My first one is that the American secondary school as of today has

been deprived of its mobility. By mobility I mean the freedom to set new goals, plan new programs, accept new responsibilities—in other words, the freedom to develop diverse forms within the broad framework of secondary education. I read and hear my evidence in reports, articles, books, speeches, and public documents, all of which now define the purposes of secondary education within terms essentially traditional. These terms acknowledge only two forms of secondary education—one which prepares for higher education and one which fails to do so and is too often, for this reason and this reason only, denounced.

This definition of the secondary school's role is important for three reasons: first, because it gives to secondary schools as their major task a fixed task; second, because it does not accept any but traditional methods of carrying out that task; third, because it represents or appears to represent public opinion, and public opinion operating through the peculiar political heritage of local control of primary and secondary education has, at least for the time being, established this point of view.

My second term of reference is that although secondary education has lost its capacity to meet new needs with new programs, the need for diversity is increasing, not diminishing. For nearly 30 years each age group, as it has approached the age for entry into the labor force, has been given a choice between employment (which for a time emphasized and still includes military employment) and more schooling. For a time an expanding system of secondary education supplied the schooling, but as the age of employment rises, the burden of supply is shifted to higher education. As the age groups increase in size, the burden may become tremendous and may assume forms that cannot now be foreseen.

My third term of reference is to the effect that within higher education the creation of diversity has become a task for the universities. Undergraduate colleges have found as a practical matter that they cannot retain form and status as colleges and offer a diverse program, for, if they try, they face the choice of moving toward university status, which many of them have done, or of scattering and enfeebling their programs and moving toward a kind of vocational junior college status, which others have done. On the other hand, universities have been able to develop new programs, to change old ones, and even to experiment in defining new tasks for education.

My fourth term of reference is that the university, responding to new problems, has expanded its influence along with its size and has now replaced the undergraduate college as the dominant unit in higher education. This statement is probably provable statistically, but such proof is not really germane to the point. Dominance in this case means domination of educational thought, the setting of academic patterns, determination of intellectual goals, the capacity to create an atmosphere of stability or of change. Numerical dominance is unimportant. I offer two observations as illustrations of my meaning. The first one has to do with a program now operated by the College Entrance Examination Board called the Advanced Placement Program, which is a program of examinations for giving college credit for advanced work done in secondary school. This program was begun about six years ago as an idea of Gordon Chalmers of Kenyon College. It was supported by a number of undergraduate colleges and for the first two years of operation was often called the "Kenyon Program." The larger university colleges were not consulted in planning and were excluded from having anything to do with operations. The program has been a tremendous success. It is operating in over 400 secondary schools and is supported by faculty action in at least 200 colleges. Twelve thousand students are expected to take the examinations this May. If it had worked out as planned, it would have solved the enrollment problems of the colleges that established the program and of dozens of others. But that is not what has happened. It has become essentially a program for students entering the undergraduate colleges of the major universities and is apparently continuing to develop in that pattern.

The second observation came out of a recent return to the selection committee of a national fellowship program after an absence of eight years. Here I was immediately struck by the extent to which the proportion of superior candidates from the smaller colleges had shrunk while the candidates from the university colleges had increased in both number and quality. It must be observed that this was, in one interpretation, a purchased dominance because of the number of these superior candidates who had been on scholarships all through college, but it was no less real because it was purchased. This dominance may explain some of the difficulties that the American undergraduate college, particularly the small college, is encountering today.

My fifth term of reference is investment. The rate of investment in education, taken as a function of national wealth in any given year, has probably remained fairly constant for most of this century, but it has gone through several phases. In its first phase, the investment was largely private philanthropy which went to the support of private higher education, particularly to that segment of it which we now think of as the prestige institutions. This meant for the most part universities in being, or colleges with the advantage of location and leadership which would enable them to develop into universities. This phase of support began before the turn of the century and continued until halted abruptly by the depression.

During the depression the source of funds for investment in education shifted from private to public. The incidence of investment shifted also from higher education to secondary education to make possible the near approach to the goal of universal secondary education. This investment period continued through the thirties and closed with the outbreak of the war. Had it not been for that tragedy, we might well have seen still further developments in that area and we might be dealing today with a completely different set of patterns.

Since the war, the investment has shifted again. Tax-supported higher education, which for years received only a meager share of the annual new investment, is enjoying a larger share; secondary education is limping at a subsistence level. Private philanthropy, on the other hand, no longer gives direct support to private higher education at the rate it once did. But a new form of investment for both private and public funds has appeared in the area of research. Here, in effect, there is more money available than can be absorbed by universities, with the result that we are witnessing the creating of great research activities very like those attached to universities, but under corporate control.

This research investment is in a sense an indirect investment in education, but it is having a profound effect upon universities, even to the extent of shaping their programs and of contributing to, perhaps even producing, the position of dominance already referred to.

In addition to these terms of reference, I have a point of nomenclature. We have always recognized these forms of support of higher education by using the terms "endowed," "church-related," or "tax-supported." But in the light of present circumstances, these identifications have lost meaning. Neither endowment nor church relationship now takes the place of tuition support. If we wish to identify in terms of present status and future problems we must identify our colleges and universities as either tuition-supported or tax-supported.

With these preliminary comments out of the way, I now offer an impressionistic description of our existing organization of higher education. In this view, our higher education is divided into three major university groupings plus one embryonic grouping. By a university grouping, I mean a number of dominant universities within a geographical region operating with generally similar programs and standards, drawing students in part directly from secondary school and in part from undergraduate colleges which are really feeder colleges. Feeder colleges are independent of universities as to their finance and control but follow their lead as to programs and standards.

The oldest of such university groupings is to be found on the Eastern seaboard. It is dominated by universities which are tuition-supported. These universities represent a very heavy concentration of professional and graduate schools, accounting between them for more than half of all the professional and graduate work enrollment in the United States. About half of the enrollment in these advanced programs comes from the undergraduate colleges of these universities, the remaining half from feeder colleges. In this grouping, the feeder colleges are predominantly tuition-supported. They compete for their students on much the same terms as the universities they feed, and it is one of the marks of this grouping that their ability to attract students is directly related to their ability to prepare for later university entrance. Colleges that are not successful in this respect are having serious problems in getting students, which, of course, means that their tuition support is minimal.

There are, of course, numerous tax-supported institutions in this Eastern grouping, but it is a notable fact that their operations, programs, and standards follow the pattern set by the dominating universities.

These tax-supported institutions have developed relatively slowly. The state universities, with only one major exception, have been slow in their development of graduate and professional programs; the teachers colleges have been held rigorously to their original function and have not been permitted to expand into regional colleges; and the junior colleges and community colleges have barely begun to make their appearance.

Enrollments in the Eastern region are on the whole stabilized. Very few institutions are operating far below capacity, and there is not a large number of unfilled vacancies. There is pressure for expansion on a few institutions, but in general it is being resisted. Most of the plans for expansion are being made by tax-supported institutions. Perhaps because of this stability, it is one of the characteristics of the Eastern region that relationships between the secondary schools and the universities are under heavy strain. In general within this grouping the universities and their feeder colleges operate on a basis of selective admissions. This is conducted on several different standards, but always by methods which emphasize quality of preparation and results of objective tests. In this, as in other respects, the tax-supported institutions of the region follow the procedure established by the tuition-supported institutions.

Much of the current criticism of secondary education is centered in this region. Most of the efforts to redraw the secondary school curriculum in terms of specific college entrance programs are taking place here. And, on the other hand, although the secondary schools are attempting to meet university requirements, they are having serious problems in getting the necessary guarantees with respect to the acceptance of their graduates.

The second large grouping of universities, the Midwestern, has characteristics markedly different from those of the East. In the first place, despite the fact that there are important tuition-supported universities in the area, the dominant university pattern is that of tax support. In the second place, while the Midwestern universities have sizable and excellent graduate and professional programs, it is probably true that they derive a great deal of their stature from their large and diverse undergraduate offerings. In the third place, within this grouping of dominant tax-supported universities there is a numerically large group of tuition-supported undergraduate colleges. And, finally, in this region neither capacity nor enrollments have been stabilized. The tax-supported institutions have been increasing their capacity steadily and are continuing to do so, even to the extent of creating new universities out of institutions that were formerly specialized schools or teachers colleges. Thus each year there are vacancies within tax-supported higher education, but each year as the former year's vacancies are filled new ones are created. But, while this development is going on, the tuition-supported colleges, which, by reason of capital shortages, have increased their capacity very little, are operating at a fairly steady vacancy rate. Because there are vacancies available each year in the Midwest, there have been no serious problems in pupil placement for the high schools, and very little disposition on the part of the colleges and universities to complain about student preparation. As a result, the school–college relationships are much less difficult than they are in the East, and the schools have something very near to equal partnership in the admissions process.

It is within this pattern that the tuition-supported colleges have their problems. They must compete with tax-supported universities, which up until now have offered fairly easy access to college, and they must also compete with their sister tuition-supported colleges and universities in the East, which make a strong appeal to those interested in graduate and professional admission and which on occasion have generous scholarships to offer as an additional lure. As a result, college admission in the Midwest has taken on the form of a compromise in which many of the forms and rituals of selective admissions are observed, while within the forms the actual practices often follow the tax-supported pattern of relatively easy access.

The West Coast grouping is perhaps best described as composed of two unequal parts. One part is a relatively small group of tuition-supported and tax-supported universities and colleges oriented toward graduate and professional work, conducting a rigorous system of selective admissions, or, to be exact, two distinct rigorous systems of selective admissions, one of which depends partly on firm control of the secondary school curriculum while the other is essentially the Eastern system. In many ways this group resembles the Eastern grouping in its academic strength, conservatism, and stability. The other part, larger but less influential, is composed of a large group of universities and colleges, mostly tax-supported but including a considerable number of tuition-supported institutions in their lessened emphasis on graduate and professional work, their constant expansion (with its concomitant of the continued filling of existing vacancies and the creation of new ones), their vigorous recruiting and easy access, often within the form of an apparent pattern of selective admissions. Combined with these unusual features is the fact that the West Coast probably represents the heaviest investment of capital in research to be found in the country when university, corporate, and government facilities are considered. On the West Coast we also have the only large-scale program yet devised for drawing pressure away from existing colleges and universities by creating a parallel system of higher education which offers tremendous flexibility on a very large scale in a relatively simple operational pattern. The West Coast grouping, finally, is almost completely self-contained. There is some, but not much, migration of students and faculty members in both directions to and from other parts of the country, but the pattern on the whole seems to be set in West Coast terms.

The fourth university grouping is Southern. It is hard to describe this grouping, for it is still in a forming stage in which the dominant unit of higher education remains the undergraduate college. In this pattern a true grouping of a number of universities oriented toward graduate and professional studies and dominant enough to impose their patterns of organization and their standards upon the remainder of the Southern structure of higher education remains a development that can be foreseen but that still falls short of full achievement. In the light of this generalization several comments are pertinent. First, the Southern states produce annually a sizable crop of excellent students of university caliber, many of whom are attracted to the Eastern university grouping for their undergraduate and graduate work. Second, the South has a sizable nucleus of excellent secondary schools, colleges, and universities, which, if they were concentrated in a smaller geographical region, would form a university grouping of real stature. Third, the capital shortages which in other parts of the country bear heavily on tuition-supported colleges affect, in the South, both tuition-supported and tax-supported institutions, or, to put it another way, the basic problem which has yet to be overcome in the South is the cost of enlarging the total enterprise of education to form a base strong enough to support a university grouping. Fourth, the problem of development has been masked and hindered over the years, in part by the fact that Southern students have been accommodated in other regions for their college and university work. This masking effect will diminish as university groupings in other sections of the country tend to fill with students and to force the South back upon its own resources. Viewed in this light, segregation is a matter of some importance, not as a moral or ethical issue but as a self-perpetuating economic drain which slows educational development at all levels by diffusing the capital available for educational growth.

Having offered a view of our educational structure, I should like to consider now what changes may be produced by events of the foreseeable years ahead and what choices we may have within these changes.

With respect to secondary education we have the fact of the present emphasis on the major role of college preparation. If we add to that the fact of strong community controls which will tend to hold it within that role, then we can predict that there will be few curricular changes.

There will be changes within secondary education, but they will be changes to consolidate and strengthen it for its task. These changes will fall into two major groups.

First we can expect a major movement toward intensified counseling and guidance which will assume two separate forms. In one form there will be more attention paid to the factors outside of school which affect the individual as a student and as a person. In the experimental project now being carried on in New York City's Junior High School 43, it already seems clear that a social service program which extends into the home and the community can produce an important change in academic motivations and interests, and reveal abilities and talents which would otherwise have lain dormant, perhaps throughout the student's whole life. This experiment, of course, represents a maximum effort to set up a counseling situation which approaches the ideal. Perhaps we cannot hope to expend this much effort in all of our schools, but if present plans are carried out we will see, and very soon, an attempt to try out the idea on a large scale. Parenthetically, the project has produced a marked decrease in the juvenile delinquency rate in one of New York's problem areas, and this of itself may bring additional support to this idea.

The other area in which counseling and guidance will move will be toward early, careful analysis of individual strengths and weaknesses as a guide to long-range planning. For this it may be necessary to develop new guidance instruments and techniques, and it will certainly be necessary to make better use of the ones we have. But these things can be done, and if they are done they will produce another great increase in the holding power of the schools and will simultaneously involve the schools much more deeply in the actual process of the selection of students for college entrance.

The second change will be the development of programs of advanced and accelerated courses offered in secondary schools, probably developing in some communities into separate honors schools. These programs and schools will rely upon long-range counseling and guidance for the selection of their students and will represent fairly homogeneous groupings of high-ability students. In general they will cover full college preparation by the end of the present eleventh grade, and a full year of college-level work by the end of the twelfth grade. The development of such programs would presuppose college willingness to allow credit for the college-level work, but this now seems attainable although it would not have been acceptable 10 years ago.

Neither of these predictions is a new idea, and both of them are now operating on a limited scale. They have proved merits, and they will certainly be extended. Both will go far to ease the relations between secondary schools and colleges.

With respect to higher education we can expect that the developments in secondary schools will have two direct effects and one indirect effect. In one direct effect, the number of students entering college will increase because of improved preparation. That is, better counseling and guidance will help a larger percentage of high school students to prepare for college, and this effect will be quite unrelated to population increase. In its second effect, better prepared students will do better work in college and will tend to remain through completion of the course. This will mean that colleges will have larger enrollments, in part because they will increase their holding power and have a larger percentage of juniors and seniors, which means making better use of existing facilities in the junior and senior years of college. Curiously enough this use need not produce much additional expense. These are now our most expensive programs, but this is largely because they are not used to capacity. At capacity use their costs per student will come down, and we will find that we actually have more resources than we thought we had.

I mentioned also an indirect effect. It is that as students bring better preparation, remain in college longer, and make fuller use of facilities standards go up.

Rising standards in any educational system tend to cut two ways. They select and hold strong students, creating an increasingly homogeneous ability grouping within the student body. In turn the capacity of these students creates a demand for opportunities to go farther and deeper in studies. This demand is met initially by crowding existing programs, then ultimately by lengthening the time necessary for completion. This has happened long since in the professional fields related to health, has happened recently in the sciences, and appears to be happening with respect to training in the field of management. The process in time produces a group of institutions specialized in the offering of programs of great depth and solidity with advanced study and research as announced institutional goals —in other words, universities or strong supporting colleges.

On the other side of the coin, rising standards in a system tend to force weaker students toward educational levels where they can work more comfortably. For such students the fact that their educational goals are limited by their capacity is not as important as the fact that they must have educational goals. At present our system falls short of providing adequate goals for its marginal students with the result that a tragically large number drop out without having reached any goal. It may be that many who drop out would remain had they been better prepared, emotionally and intellectually, to use their opportunities. But this is beside the point. The point is that when, in a single system, standards are forced so high and goals are so restricted that only the ablest students can meet them, the system itself is on the way to intellectual stratification and the formation of an elite.

The alternative to eventual stratification is to form a dual system, and this actually is what we have. Our higher education is composed of two parallel divisions, each four years in length, very similar in program, in outward appearance, and in announced purpose. In one segment of the system, the students ordinarily continue through all four years, and over half of them continue on for further formal study. This segment is tied to our dominant universities and to the colleges which send students to them. It is the segment which prepares for our professions, for management, for teaching, for scholarship and research, and for the higher reaches of government service. In the other segment, only about one-fourth of the students stay all the way through the four years, and few of them go beyond. It is this segment which prepares trained men and women with technical skill and the capacity to work as specialists within a society which has an almost unlimited need for specialists. Most junior colleges and community colleges are part of this enterprise, and this is generally recognized. But also many four-year colleges, including some that are very large and complex, are in this category.

Until now the differences between these two parallel segments of our system have been masked by their similarities. However, we may now expect that the two segments will begin to pull apart into separate systems marked by differences in methods, programs, and purposes.

In this pull apart, the dominant universities and their feeder colleges, both tuition-supported and tax-supported, will become more difficult of access than they now are. They will require rigorous and firmly patterned preparation, probably somewhat beyond the present mean preparation now required for college entrance. Some form of entrance examination will be required by all. Admission of students will be a selective process, and the secondary schools will have a large share of the responsibility for the final decision. Emphasis will be on proved intellectual capacity and interest in advanced study. Programs will be planned as combinations of undergraduate and graduate or professional study averaging six years in length, and students who are not interested in such programs will be discouraged from entering. Because of the care used in admissions, plus the high requirements, student mortality will be low. This will represent a marked change from the present situation of some tax-supported universities. Instruction will move in the direction of aiding the student to use the institution's resources to teach himself. Independent study in the form of a series of learning contracts will form a part of the curriculum as early as the first or second year of college. Auxiliary methods of instruction in the form of taped lectures, films, and closed-circuit television may be used as instructional resources but will not replace student–teacher contacts. Costs will probably be high, but student aid in the form of loans and scholarships will be available and carefully administered in relation to need. These institutions will, in short, be even more oriented toward advanced study, professional preparation, and research than they now are.

The institutions concerned primarily with general education, with provision of opportunity in a variety of fields, and with specialized training particularly in semiprofessional and subprofessional areas will by contrast be relatively easy of access and will handle their admissions in terms of minimum entrance requirements. Schools will work with these colleges on student admissions but will not be required to accept responsibility for the student's success in his studies. Programs will be of varying length, but none of less than one year nor more than four, and some of the four-year programs leading to degrees may be almost completely elective with little or no concentration or specific preparation for any occupation or further study. Instruction may take a variety of forms and may include, particularly where the learning of skills and techniques is involved, considerable direct instruction through films, tapes, and television circuits. Some classes may be conducted entirely through use of recorded materials, with teachers' aides taking care of the routines of attendance and assignments. Student mortality will tend to be high, and this will be expected. Student personnel programs will emphasize guidance and counseling and remedial instruction. Costs to the students will be low, and the principal forms of student aid will be through short-term loans and work opportunities.

In this pattern of higher education it will be necessary to provide opportunities to move between the two systems. This will always be possible, but transfer may be more difficult than it now is and will probably require some testing with respect to interests, achievements, and motivation.

Some institutions, particularly those in large cities, will conduct work on both levels. Some institutions will themselves move from one grouping to the other, depending on their resources, the students available, and the type of program they are best fitted to offer.

It is interesting to speculate on how students may be divided between these groupings. If we assume that standards for entrance to the university grouping will remain where they are, which taking the whole country is about at the seventy-fifth percentile of ability within the age group, then that group in from 10 to 15 years will be about as large as the total enrollment in higher education today, and in 20 years will be larger. The terminal education group will, in any given year, be as large as this university group, starting in 10 years or perhaps less. This balance in enrollments will represent a relative decrease for the size of the university grouping, which with its feeder colleges today accounts for about 60 percent of enrollments, and correspondingly a relative increase for the terminal group.

The prediction of balance in enrollment as between two divergent forms of higher education is in effect a prediction of the results of choices that are being made now, by us. These choices are in the resolution of the clash between the totally new concept of mass higher education and the traditional concept of university dominance over higher education which has been so recently established in our system.

In trying to estimate the probable results of this clash, we have some of our own recent educational history as a guide, for it is now about 40 years since the idea of mass secondary education—then totally new—encountered the entrenched concept of secondary education as college preparation. In the end, both have won. Mass education is numerically stronger with its own curricular arrangements, but it has lost in a bid to control the curriculum. College preparation, numerically weaker, has been established as the primary task and is in the intellectual ascendancy.

Over a long time, which in this case is defined as a time beyond our own probable life span, the history of our secondary schools may well be repeated in our colleges and universities. Over the shorter term—10 to 20 years—we may expect the balance already suggested. Over a longer term, the mass education function will probably become numerically dominant. The question of intellectual control is a different matter which cannot now be predicted, but eventually it will be the central factor in the shaping of our educational future. The appeals of mass education are powerful, and they have a quick political value which has been noted by our politicians. The pressure to support its expansion at the cost of graduate study and research will be strong—is already strong. Yet the values which mass education brings are not the same values we seek in our graduate schools and our research enterprises. Herein, finally, are the principal choices to be accepted or rejected. They are choices in values.

Much depends on the choices we make, and the wrong set of choices could easily damage much that we have achieved. We have come, almost unknowingly, to a position where we depend on the ultimate worth of knowledge. This means that our choices are not economic, or industrial, or political. They are choices with respect to human values. If we invest in them wisely we cannot be wrong.

U*ntil I went through the files to make the first tentative selection for this book, I had not realized how many different lines of Board activity came into form and focus in 1959.*

The efforts to develop an inexpensive preliminary test, linked to the Board's Scholastic Aptitude Test; to bring secondary schools into voting membership;

and to have score reports made available to candidates, had been going on for five years or more. To be able to report that each of these ideas was now transformed into a working part of the program was the achievement of a goal that had been considered impossible in 1950, when they were first—and very tentatively— suggested in committee meetings.

In this, as in other talks made from 1955 on, there is the suggestion that American colleges must carefully consider two things with respect to their freshman classes.

First, there are their admissions methods, which encourage multiple applications, overadmission, pressure tactics on candidates, and other forms of gamesmanship. These can be cured only by a genuinely cooperative effort on the part of the colleges, and probably by the use of genuine data processing equipment. However, any serious discussion on this point has been stopped by the "have" colleges on the grounds that they may no longer get the pick of the candidates, and by the "have-nots" on the grounds that the "haves" will get even more pick than they now enjoy.

Second, the colleges should make efforts to find out what is actually being taught in secondary school and use their new knowledge in the revision of their freshman programs.

There is ample evidence that many freshmen are overprepared for college, and more than a suggestion that some of them leave college because of the disappointing quality of their studies.

As this is written, early in 1967, no real progress has been made on either problem.

"The Year in Review"
Address at the annual meeting of the College Entrance Examination Board, October 28, 1959. Published in *Fall Meeting Proceedings*, 1959, 42 pp., pp. 1–11.

The program this morning represents a major change from the past programs for College Board meetings in that it is a direct report and commentary on the work of the College Board with some preview of ideas and plans for next year. This year the report will be a joint effort by S. A. Kendrick, vice president for examinations and research, and myself, and we expect to report and then to answer questions.

Before I go into any details with respect to Board activities, let me first point out that this is the first meeting in the history of the College Entrance Examination Board which has included representatives of secondary schools as Board members. There have been many secondary school men and women who have been regular attendants at meetings and who have served the Board long and well, but they have always come either as representatives of associations or as representatives-at-large elected by the Board. On behalf of the Board here assembled, I extend a welcome to all who come to this meeting for the first time in the new status of representatives of a Board member school.

My report can begin logically with some figures on growth and development. During the past year more than a million of the Board's tests were taken; 473,210 candidates took the Scholastic Aptitude Test, and 137,060 the Achievement Tests. Without troubling you with comparative figures, I can say that the regular program figures showed an increase of 37 percent over the preceding year. The College Scholarship Service handled a total of 40,000 original Parents' Confidential Statements as against 34,500 the preceding year.

In addition to these figures on what might be called our basic program, a total of 388,649 candidates took the Scholarship Qualifying Test in October 1958. This test, as you know, has now been replaced by the Preliminary Scholastic Aptitude Test, which was administered last week to a number of candidates which, so far as we can determine from the incomplete returns, was in the vicinity of 700,000. As still another statistic, we distributed approximately 100,000 copies of *The College Handbook* at $1.50 each.

Having, I hope, established the fact that this has been a busy year, I am glad I can also say that it has been a prosperous one. Our total income for the year was $6,290,067; the expenses $5,120,935, leaving a net income from operations of $1,169,132. This surplus is not unexpected, since a year ago at this meeting our budget estimates indicated a probable surplus in the amount of $336,200. The fact that we have exceeded this estimate by some $832,931 is due almost entirely to operating economies both in the Board's offices and at Educational Testing Service.

The figures for the current year reflect the decrease of $1 in the SAT fee which you authorized a year ago. As you will note, they are also favorable figures, so much so that the staff has recommended to the trustees, and the trustees will recommend to you, two actions relating to finance:

1. A fee reduction effective June 30, 1960, lowering the cost of the SAT from $6 to $5 and the Achievement Tests from $9 to $7.

2. Prepayment to ETS of the capital grant scheduled for payment in 1960–61 in the amount of $400,000 to make possible the early development of additional facilities, specifically sufficient additional space at Rosedale to make possible the consolidation of the entire ETS operation at that location.

We believe there is a possibility that we may be able to recommend still another fee reduction effective in 1961, but in the light of past experience, we also believe that it is best to wait a while before committing ourselves to a recommendation.

We feel that the financial report is rendered all the more impressive by the fact that it is only three years since we were forced to report to you an unexpected and very sizable deficit for the year 1955–56, then just completed, and an anticipated deficit for the then current fiscal year, 1956–57. In order to meet this deficit you authorized a fee increase, effective in 1957. At that time we looked upon such an increase as inevitable and felt that we must expect still further increases not later than this year. This being one of the few times when I have been pleased at having been proved a bad prophet, I think it worth our while to examine the reasons for our changed situation.

One reason which is not to be neglected is that we have added a good many safeguards to our budgeting and expenditure control procedures. For example, we have no contingency items hidden in our individual estimates of income and expense. We do have one sizable contingency item, but there are no other cushions in our budget. These controls account for substantial savings, but it is hard to be precise as to amounts.

Another reason is our insistence that programs should always be planned in terms of self-support even when, as in the case of the Advanced Placement Program, such a goal may be some distance off. By taking this view, we avoid the pitfall of tolerating poor financial practices merely because they are in a good cause.

Third, we have moved slowly in filling positions. Sometimes I think we have been too slow, but, at any rate, we have each year spent less for staff personnel than we had anticipated at the outset.

Fourth, and I think most important, ETS has consolidated most of its test handling operations in new and efficient quarters just at a time when candidate volume was reaching a level at which machine operations would become truly efficient.

Thus, I can report that our financial situation is good and that the outlook is good.

Before leaving the subject of finance, I should mention that Educational Testing Service has a new test-scoring machine under construction which is expected to produce additional economies in both time and money. Since Henry Chauncey, president of ETS, is to report to us later, I will leave to him the further discussions of this interesting item.

The College Board's program during the past year has undergone a good many changes. Perhaps the most important has been the discontinuance of the Scholarship Qualifying Test and the inauguration of the Preliminary Scholastic Aptitude Test. This is actually a change much more important than the mere substitution of one test for another. Its importance lies first in the shift of emphasis from scholarship competition—inherent in the title SQT—to guidance, inherent in the new title of PSAT. But another point of major importance is the availability of this guidance test at the beginning of the eleventh-grade year, a time late enough in a pupil's career to permit a valid and reliable measurement of ability, but early enough to allow room for changes of plan and direction. I believe that this test within three years will attract more candidates than the SAT and Achievement Tests combined.

In the regular program our only program change has been to take first steps toward adding an Achievement Test in Russian. The matter will not come before you for action until next fall, by which time a test will have been developed and readied for use in the 1961 Achievement Test series.

The CSS program has been changed in several respects. Parents' Confidential Statement forms are to be distributed through schools, and computations are to be made on all cases. The fee increases of a year ago have made it possible to balance the budget, thus achieving a financial goal that has been sought for some time. Our work of the year has included the conduct of a number of computation workshops which have really been training programs for student aid officers. These workshops are to be continued this year, and we hope will include a number of interested secondary school representatives.

Another activity in which we have acted as an agent has been in the distribution of a booklet on administrative aspects of student aid programs, prepared by William C. Fels, president of Bennington College and John F. Morse, vice president of Rensselaer Polytechnic Institute at the suggestion of the Fund for the Advancement of Education.

In the area of test interpretation and guidance, John M. Duggan, director of test interpretation, has produced another important pair of publications for general circulation in the form of a booklet for candidates who have taken the PSAT, with a companion booklet for advisers. Another publication still in preparation is to be directed to the guidance problem in small schools where professionally trained guidance personnel are not available —a situation which, as we know, holds true in thousands of American high schools.

Mr. Duggan has also during the year, with the help of other staff members, conducted a series of prediction seminars dealing with methods of using College Board test scores, school records, and other variables to predict college success. These seminars have turned out to be far more than a statistical exercise, have in fact been a form of training for admissions officers that has in several cases produced unexpected dividends in the form of changes in existing operations. As in the case of the CSS computation workshops, we expect to continue the seminars this year and to draw to them a good sampling of interested college guidance officers from secondary schools.

The Advanced Placement Program has continued its remarkable growth: 5,862 candidates took 8,265 examinations last May as against 3,715 candidates and 6,800 examinations in 1958. Our consolidation of the separate examinations in English Literature and Composition seems to have been accomplished without disaster. The very substantial fee increase from $10 per candidate to $5 registration and $8 per test apparently affected the number of candidates only by discouraging those who might have taken tests on the long chance of success, and this, needless to say, was a welcome effect so far as we were concerned, since we still had a deficit of $21 per candidate. This year we plan a further step of handing over to the schools direct responsibility for administration and supervision of the Advanced Placement Examinations, but contemplate no other major changes in the Program.

In reporting on the Advanced Placement Program, I do not wish to give the impression that the Board's staff is concerned solely with numbers of candidates or numbers of dollars. Actually, we find that our principal concern with the Program is that it should be understood and given its true value. It is now unimportant that the Program was originally conceived as a counter to a threat which never materialized—the threat that early admission would strip the schools of their ablest students. What is important is that schools and colleges should recognize in it the opportunity to identify and encourage able students and coincidentally to produce curriculum changes in secondary school and to avoid repetition in college of work already covered in school. It is, we think, one of the three really new ideas to come into American education in this decade, and our concern is that it be understood and used. (The other two ideas are, for the record, large-scale student aid, and talent identification and utilization, both of which are matters of close concern to the Board.)

The expansion of the Board's activities has resulted, as was forecast a year ago, in some staff enlargement. Charles M. Holloway has come to us from the post of Assistant to the Commissioner of Education to assume the new post of Director of Information Services. John A. Valentine, formerly head of the Department of Psychology at Middlebury College and more recently at ETS with responsibilities for the Graduate Record Examination and other important programs, has joined us as Director of Examinations. Lois D. Irish has come to us from the National Scholarship Service and Fund for Negro Students to be Rexford G. Moon Jr.'s associate in the management of the CSS, and Paul Hazlett Jr. has joined us to carry out a carefully designed project for the evaluation of the Advanced Placement Program. Julius H. Hlavaty, on leave from DeWitt Clinton High School, where he is head of the mathematics department, is serving as Director of the Commission on Mathematics program, completing distribution of its report—of which we have, incidentally, distributed some 35,000 copies—and performing other necessary duties in conducting the active phase of the Commission's work.

While we are on the topic of the Commission on Mathematics, I report with pleasure that its program has become the basis of the ongoing activities of a major project for the preparation of mathematics teaching materials, which, supported by the National Science Foundation, is located at Yale University under the chairmanship of Edward Begle.

Our regional offices, announced last year as plans, have now been opened, with G. Leslie MacMitchell, long a member of our staff here in New York, as our Pacific Coast representative; Hollace G. Roberts, formerly Director of Admissions at Western Reserve University, as our Midwest representative with an office in Evanston; and Ben F. Cameron, formerly Director of Admissions at the University of the South, as our Southern representative.

As a further note on both program and staff, I am glad to report that the Commission on English, which has been a topic of discussion for nearly two years has now come into being, with Floyd W. Rinker, on leave from his post as chairman of the English department of Newton High School, Newtonville, Massachusetts, as its executive director, and Harold C. Martin, chairman of the Committee on General Education at Harvard University, as its chairman. In broad terms, the task of this Commission is to determine the difference between what is achieved in secondary school and what is expected in college in the way of competence in English, and to suggest how the difference is to be reduced to agreement. They will have their first meeting in November.

Another item to report to the Board is the fact that in January 1959 we held a two-day newswriters' conference in which members of the staff of the Board and of ETS and representatives of schools and colleges discussed a wide variety of admissions problems with a group of 22 professional journalists, all of whom were engaged in reporting education news. The conference was judged a success, so much so that a similar affair is to be held this December at Arden House.

I should also report that the American Association of School Administrators and the National Association of Secondary-School Principals are jointly supporting an investigation of burdens placed upon schools by expanding testing programs. This has already been a matter of some concern to the College Board's staff, so that we are now completing a preliminary study on this very point and will hope shortly to publish our findings.[1]

As my final item in this section of my report, I am pleased to state that the *57th Report of the President* (which is one of the most mysterious of all College Board activities) has begun to assume tangible form as an ambitious and fairly long review of the Board's work since the formation of

---

1. This was subsequently done in May 1960 with the publication by the College Board of *A Survey of the Use of Tests in the 11th and 12th Grades*.

Educational Testing Service and the reorganization of the Board. The report is now two-thirds completed and has been since September 8. To be entitled, *Admission to College: A Perspective for the 1960s*, the report will be published by early May 1960.

Having now completed discussion of events of the year, I think it is appropriate to go on to some commentary.

The increase in the volume of Board activities has naturally been an item of much interest to its officers. Superficially, it is easy to ascribe the increase to the rising tide of students, but this is a reason which does not stand up on examination since, in fact, there has been no significant increase in the size of the college-going age group for some years. There has, of course, been a considerable increase in the percentage of the age group going to college, but the actual numerical increase in the number of college candidates has not been so large as to call for a tripling of the Board's volume of testing activities over a five-year period, which is what has, in fact, taken place.

I am inclined to feel that the increase is a product of several other more or less independent factors. First, there has been considerably more prosperity in the land, and it has been possible for a larger number of youths to plan on going to college. Second, there has been very full employment and a shortage of trained people to take on responsible positions. This has tended to increase the interest of business and industry in the younger trained people, and hence there has been a constantly improving market for college graduates. Third, a good deal of national pressure has been directed toward urging students to go to college; and fourth, and to my mind perhaps one of the most important factors of all, there has been a good deal of criticism of educational standards, which, I believe, has tended to force educators toward an interest in tests as an easy device for determining what standards are being applied and for maintaining control of numbers. It is this last factor which has, I think, been particularly important in the drawing into the Board of a number of tax-supported institutions, and I think we must regard these institutions as merely being the forerunners of a much larger group which may be expected to join the Board within a relatively short period of time.

The trends in the direction of even more use of tests by colleges seem to me to be unmistakable, so much so that I feel quite safe in prophesying that within five years virtually every four-year college in the country will be requiring a program of entrance examinations. I do not believe that all these tests will necessarily be those offered by the College Entrance Examination Board, and, in fact, would prefer that the Board would not have a complete monopoly on testing. At the moment it does not have such a monopoly, and this leads me to a comment upon the appearance last spring of the American College Testing Program. This program, as we all know, rests very heavily upon the technical skills and equipment of E. F. Lindquist, director of Iowa Testing Programs at the State University of Iowa. Mr. Lindquist has been a leader in the testing field for a good many years, and his tests have a deserved reputation for excellence. It is in no sense derogatory to these tests and to the ACT Program to note that the existence of this program actually depends upon the existence of the College Board's program.

This statement may seem a little startling, so I had better enlarge upon it. The whole idea of a national program of college entrance examinations originated with the College Entrance Examination Board. The Board has established the method of handling entrance examinations from a central agency, the concepts of security and validity upon which examinations rest, and the methods for using results. It has, in effect, gained acceptance for the idea through its publications, its meetings, its programs, and the work of its members and its staff. If this had not been done, particularly over the last 10 years, with an expenditure of some millions of dollars, neither ACT nor any other new testing venture could hope to succeed.

I would also note that one of the main differences between ACT and the Board's activities lies in the fact that it does not support such developmental activities as the College Scholarship Service and Advanced Placement Program, an ongoing research program, or such training and information activities as are implicit in the Colloquium on College Admissions, the prediction workshops, the Advanced Placement Program conferences, and the CSS computation workshops.

Now to continue the commentary with a shift of subject. We have all noted with interest that for a good many colleges this year the admissions pattern was one of receiving fewer but on the whole stronger applications and of admitting in an expectation of an acceptance rate of 55 percent but actually encountering an acceptance rate of 65 percent. The result was, of course, a certain amount of confusion and a number of oversize freshman classes.

There has been a good deal of speculation as to what happened to produce such a change in one year. My guess is no better than anyone else's, but I would like to point out two things. In the first place, this last year 81 Board member colleges released class characteristics reports as against 35 the preceding year. Even more important in my view was the fact that last year College Board scores were for the first time released to final candidates along with information on interpretation. I do not wish to claim that these two items alone produced the results noted above, but I do think that better-informed students and better-informed advisers were bound to produce better results.

I am well aware, of course, of the strong opposition in many quarters toward the idea of score release, and I still feel that the action taken in approving the release was a calculated risk in the sense that we were all unable to predict exactly what the patterns of school and of candidate behavior would be. Nevertheless, I think the action has not only turned out well, but actually better than we expected, for a reason which none of us foresaw. This was that the candidates' knowledge of the scores has added to the candidates' own responsibility for a proper choice of college and at the same time has added to the school's responsibility for proper guidance. I believe, too, that the recognition of the fact that most candidates knew their scores operated as a moderating counsel in some admissions offices. These comments on changes in attitude are, of course, assumptions on my part. If they are correct, then we are making some progress in this admissions business.

Another line of comment has to do with application pressures. We are reasonably certain that there will be a buildup of pressures, and we are puzzled as to how we are going to deal with them. As we know, a good many colleges have already reached the point where they must now say that they find no rational basis for discrimination between candidates. If this reaches the point where it holds true generally for Board member colleges, and I think the trends are in this direction, it will be necessary to realign the admissions process in terms of new standards and new tests. I happen to believe that the signs of this are now at hand—that, for example, the Advanced Placement Program is a special form of response to rising admissions pressures. This being my belief, it leads logically to the observation that the solution for admissions pressures lies in raising admissions standards, and I will go on to predict that over the next quarter century the average requirements for admission to American colleges will rise by the equivalent of one full academic year, or, in other words, colleges will, a generation hence, hold as their requirements for admission the requirements that they now apply to admission to the sophomore year of college. This can be done without lengthening the secondary school course, and I am reasonably certain that it will be done.

This may be a long-term solution, but it is not easily applicable to the class of 1964, which must be dealt with next spring. Here there are problems of real difficulty for which no solution can be found even though they are now and have been under constant study.

I resist, with great struggle, the opportunity to offer my interpretation of the causes of these immediate problems, but will merely say that it appears that the competition for students tends to force the admissions operation earlier in the year. It would appear that it has now been forced so early that there is a question as to whether the performance of the twelfth-grade year can be measured well enough to be considered in the admissions process. This begins to bring up a serious question of what I call academic morality, at least with respect to certain kinds of admissions information. For example, there has been some move to use the December Achievement Tests, originally offered for the convenience of several institutions that admitted February classes, for testing of final candidates. In what might be called the continuing studies, foreign languages and English, this is all right, but when students take examinations covering such studies as advanced mathematics or science or even social studies, which has such a large American history content, the measurement, regardless of the score, lacks real authority. In effect, as the admissions process is pushed toward the early part of the final year, the base for the prediction becomes smaller and less stable. So long as only the very best students are selected this way, the method works fairly well, but the flaws are obvious.

An alternative method has been to leap all the way back to the eleventh-grade year, collect the best available information and make admissions decisions then. This is a long-range prediction but can be expected to work well, so long as it is confined to superior students.

Rising applicant pressures may well tend to force most admissions procedures earlier in the year and, if they do, may produce a larger number of poor predictions because of necessarily limited evidence available. Under the circumstances, it seems reasonable to suggest that colleges might consider a two-stage admissions procedure which would begin in the eleventh-grade year with a simple preliminary operation, which would establish eligibility for admission, and then go on to the second stage of final admission in the twelfth grade.

I am moved to make this suggestion because I think there is cause for real concern over the divergence between admissions operations and admissions philosophy on the one hand, and academic standards and purposes on the other. Academic programs, content, achievement, are the foundations of the admissions operation, but at an admissions meeting a casual observer would have difficulty discovering this fact. Instead, he would find that the procedures involved in college admissions have become increasingly a matter of prediction, and that prediction is projected over longer and longer periods of time.

What I am suggesting is that it is getting very near to the time when the colleges must make a new affirmation of their academic standards in their contact with secondary schools and that it is very difficult to establish contact on this point when the college's admissions operations disregard most of the work of the final secondary school year. The problem is to retain the administrative ease of our present operations without losing sight of the importance of the academic contact.

This talk was made some time after, and to some extent as a result of, a talk called "The Nature of Guidance," which had been delivered at Washington University in October 1958. The publication of that talk in the Personnel and Guidance Journal *of October 1959 was something of an event, for I as the author had no professional standing in the guidance field and, in addition, I had set forth in the speech a thesis on guidance that did not accord with the prevailing professional doctrine.*

A professional guidance group at Teachers College, Columbia University, asked me to elaborate on my ideas, after the talk referred to above was published. The paper that I prepared for this second exposition was really a set of expanded notes, at once simpler and more comprehensive than the earlier speech. With the same ground covered by two papers it was obvious that only one of them should be included in this collection, and it has seemed to me that the second of the two in point of time of delivery is to be preferred.

To me, the most telling paragraphs of this paper are those that refer to the counseling of students in terms of their College Board scores. As the paper indicates, the decision of the Board to authorize schools to release scores to their candidates for college had been made only recently, and it was still considered a controversial matter. Actually, admitting its controversial nature, I nevertheless consider it to have been the most important single action taken by the Board during my years as its chief officer.

Its significance lay in the fact that it broke a taboo of silence that the schools and colleges had joined to create, which excluded the candidate from highly significant information as to his chances of success in college and the reasons for his admission to or rejection by a given college. The taboo had no genuine educational justification—it was a mechanism for protecting the interests of the institutions. It did not—could not—benefit the candidate. At best it did not harm him; at worst it damaged his aspirations for college and denied him basic information that he required for his own guidance.

The opposition to the idea of releasing scores came from many quarters, and it was based on a great many reasons. The support for the idea was limited and at first unenthusiastic, for every guidance counselor and every admissions officer knew that score release meant more work for them. Nevertheless, after years of discussion and more years of formulation of plans, it finally won a quick and surprising victory. I like to think that it was a triumph of morality. At any rate, no better explanation of the triumph has ever appeared.

"Observations on Guidance"
Speech before Teachers College guidance group,
January 11, 1960.

It has been suggested to me, gently but clearly, that I talk about guidance concepts for today's needs. This is a clean-cut and altogether admirable suggestion which I accept in principle. For purposes of application I translate it into my own areas of concern as: "Why does everybody want to go to college, and what should we do about it?"

This represents some change in the topic, but I think the change is more apparent than real, for actually most of today's needs and most of the newest guidance concepts are bound up with problems of college going.

Of course, not everybody does want to go to college—but it does seem that way to those on the receiving end. In a few years I think it will seem that way on the sending end. Just to establish a frame of reference let me suggest that in about ten years every student who enters high school with an IQ in the range 100–110 may be expected to go on to six years of schooling, of which the last two will be called college; every student in high school in the IQ range 110–120 may be expected to have four years of education beyond high school; and in general those above 120 will go beyond college to graduate or professional school. In other words, half—perhaps a little more than half—of the college age group will be in an institution defined as college.

In making these generalizations attached to IQ levels, I am not advocating a return to the IQ test as a college admissions test or its use as the kind of deterministic guidance instrument it was in the twenties. I am merely saying that students who have ability levels now regarded as too low for college will, by the 1970s, be regularly in what will be defined as college; that those who have ability levels now regarded as minimal for college success will be finishing college; that those who have high ability levels will on the average go far beyond the point they now reach.

Now, there are several comments to be made about these suggestions.

The first is that this forecast is not based on any large accumulation of figures. It is partly trend, partly hunch, and one set of very interesting figures from a study done in April 1959 by Elmo Roper.

As to trend—even the most rigorous calculations today indicate that 30 percent of the college-going age group are in college, and some free-wheeling calculations call the figure higher. Recent enrollment figures show the percentage of women high school graduates to be going up—this being the problem area in which we have been suffering the most of our widely publicized talent loss. Male enrollments have gone up, too, as a percentage, but in a different pattern with some drop in full-time enrollments and a sharp increase in part-time enrollments.

The hunch is based on observations and conversations and cannot be otherwise detailed.

The Roper study was done last spring for The Ford Foundation. It was a study typical of this type of research, done on a single day all over the United States using a carefully planned questionnaire with a total of 5,000 families as the sample. All parents were asked about college plans for their children, and out of the question came the result that 69 percent of the children of all parents questioned were being directed toward college, as far as the parents were concerned.

One striking feature of this percentage figure was that only 18 percent of the parents interviewed were themselves college products. Another striking feature was the extent of uncertainty within this 69 percent figure. The total population of 100 percent of the children of these parents interviewed was, according to the parents' aspirations, divided, with 31 percent of the group not destined for college; 29 percent certainly destined for college; and 40 percent probably destined for college. The 40 percent is a large marginal group, and the marginality was further emphasized by the fact that, of the total group of parents who were questioned, fewer than half had any idea of the real cost of college and were not only underestimating those costs by $1,000 or more, but had no plans of consequence for supporting the child in college and had apparently no idea how they were going to accomplish it.

My second set of comments on the suggestions about coming patterns of college attendance has to do with the definition of college.

You will recall that in making the prediction, I emphasized the phrase "defined as college." I should now explain this. Very few colleges today are planned in terms of an entire student body of truly average ability. That phrase as we now use it for college purposes means something like an IQ of 115.

I am proposing that there will be brought into existence a group of colleges which will be geared to student groups with ability levels from IQ 100 to IQ 115.

Some of these will be two-year, some four-year institutions. They will deal with many of the materials presented in college today and with other materials not now considered as of college level, as for example, subjects now taught in vocational high schools, and more elaborate versions of the courses which lead to the general, or noncollege high school diploma. Entrance to these colleges will be on the basis of high school diplomas, and it will be easily accomplished. Their standards will be no lower than low standards today, but no higher.

My third set of comments is that the stronger colleges, by the 1970s will be admitting on a standard distinctly higher than high standards today and will be quite set apart as a group from the rest of the colleges. In other words, as more people go to college, low standards will be more widespread; high standards, higher.

It is now reasonable to ask, "Why this pressure?" The basic reason, I should suppose, is that unskilled labor as a commodity has been forced off the market. This is a fact which can be dressed up in a great many ways and discussed at great length, but I think the simple statement is best when reinforced with the observation that the best way to avoid being in the unskilled labor market is to go to college. It used to be, of course, that it was possible to avoid being in this market by going to high school. I think it can be said that this is no longer the case. A high school education no longer carries a person deep enough either into the understanding of the culture or into occupational preparation to qualify him as skilled labor.

There are, of course, other factors which can be adduced. It may be pointed out that young people now preparing for college or in college are themselves children of individuals born during and shortly after World War I. These individuals knew, as young men and women, both the boom of the 1920s and the terrible depression years, and might therefore be expected to have a built-in aspiration for security as far as their children are concerned. Education certainly represents security. Indeed, I sometimes think that this is the main aspect of it that our college-bound students focus on.

There is also the aspect of status as acquired through college attendance. I am sure it has some importance, but I suspect that it is more important to parents than to children. I mention it, but I do not know how to value it.

Then there is the fact that going to college is economically feasible for many, many students who would never have had access to college before. This is because real wages have been going up for a portion of our population more rapidly than the cost of education, which has tended to go up slowly, and therefore higher education has been brought within reach of new income groups. The effect of changing real wage income has, of course, been the reverse for a good many of the white-collar classes, and it is having a disastrous effect upon the college plans of their children, but this does not have numerical effect on college attendance.

The consequences of changing college-going habits as far as students are concerned begin with the well-known effect of college overcrowding. As we know, this is selective overcrowding. The selectivity is regional as well as institutional, so that here in the northeastern part of the United States very nearly all institutions may be defined as overcrowded—at least by comparison with institutions in other regions. This overcrowding has had a definite effect upon college admission standards and the intricacy of college admissions operations, and is making a great many colleges hard to get into. This is a very elementary and obvious fact, which does not really need repeating, except that it is necessary as part of the logical sequence that I want to establish.

This fact of overcrowding indicates that the old method of deciding to go to college along about the middle of the twelfth-grade year is now badly outmoded. The question is, when *is* a good date to make a decision with respect to going to college? A few years ago, college admissions officers and, for that matter, the College Board staff were advising whoever would listen that students should begin their college choice-making in the eleventh grade. This was good advice for the time, but I think the best advice I could now offer would be that the student should really have made his basic decision to go to college by the time he enters the ninth grade, and should, by the time he finishes the tenth grade, be in a position to discuss with his adviser, in terms of his performance to date, what kind of college he might aim for.

This decision must be made not later than the end of the tenth grade, because it must then be decided how much mathematics, how much foreign language, and how much science the student is going to take. As we know, this is controlled by the choice of the eleventh-grade program, and the wrong choice at this point may knock a student completely out of the running as far as quite a number of colleges are concerned. This point about courses and requirements is a new one, destined to become more important. It is the forerunner of the rise in requirements I mentioned earlier. I think it will not stop until the colleges which can do so have increased their requirements by the equivalent of one full year beyond the twelfth grade.

Furthermore, the end of the tenth-grade year is perhaps the last chance that the student has to begin to turn over a new leaf academically in case he has been operating at a low-quality level. Colleges are disposed to forgive two years of mediocre work, but very few will forgive three years of mediocre preparation, and none will forgive four.

While on the subject of mediocrity of performance by students and poor choice of courses, I will comment that the second chance, as far as college admission is concerned, has virtually disappeared. By "second chance," I mean the custom that was established and prevailed many years ago of sending a student to private school for a fifth, or even a sixth, year of college preparation after finishing high school. The fact is that almost no private schools now exist which do this kind of work, and those which do exist no longer feed the first-rate colleges.

The consequence for students, as far as present college-going trends are concerned, is that college is becoming an even more elongated experience, by which I mean that the stronger colleges are holding up to 80 percent of their students from the freshman year all the way through graduation, and, further, sending on to graduate and professional school 50, 60, and even 70 percent of their graduates.

This means, in effect, that the mean length of attendance in institutions of higher education for a student entering any of the most sought-after colleges in the nation would probably be in the neighborhood of six years. I am not at all sure that this is understood by a great many students or parents, and I am not certain even that all college guidance counselors understand that the student who enters one of these colleges must, to all intents and purposes, be prepared to spend at least six years before he is ready to go out and begin earning a living.

A major consequence of this change as far as guidance is concerned is the creation within the last 10 years of the totally new branch of guidance which has slowly come to be named "college guidance." A few years ago the only branch of guidance that was recognized in a great many high schools was vocational guidance. Indeed, about seven or eight years ago, when I attended a national meeting in the guidance field and got up to talk about problems of college guidance, I found myself in a distinctly hostile atmosphere, in which the emphasis was on the obligation of the school to help those who were going to work—with the implication that those who were going to college were bright enough and well-heeled enough to take care of themselves.

I think it would be fair to say that college guidance is the Cinderella branch of the profession, for its rise from the ashes of the chimney corner in which it was forced to sit a few years ago has been spectacular, and the authority and stature of successful guidance counselors is a little short of remarkable. This is, of course, a difficult and intricate field. A college guidance counselor, to be effective, has to be willing to accept the necessity of starting his guidance at least on a nondirective basis during the ninth or tenth grade. He has to go on from there to sort out and divert those students who are headed in too ambitious directions, and he may also wish to accept the responsibility for sorting out and steering in the proper direction those students of exceptional ability who appear to be bypassed within the school. Carrying the problem further, as the student gets up toward the eleventh grade the guidance counselor must be very familiar with college entrance requirements and must be a master of timing in knowing which students to begin encouraging at the eleventh-grade level to make first contacts with colleges in the hope of getting early assurances, and in beginning to make plans with respect to college finance.

There are instruments at the disposal of the college guidance counselor today that he did not have a few years ago. For example, upward of a hundred colleges are now issuing what we call "characteristics leaflets"—that is, a description of their freshman class, giving the kind of information which would enable a guidance counselor to judge whether or not a student might be able to meet the requirements. As recently as two years years ago only about 25 of such leaflets were published, so that the development of interest has been great. However, this is no more than a beginning. The only colleges which now issue leaflets are the strong and self-assured. And noticeably, only a few of them distribute their leaflets to candidates. In time, all colleges will publish the pertinent facts about their freshman class, but this may take several years.

While I am on this topic let me suggest the reverse type of publication—a school characteristics leaflet discussing last year's twelfth-grade class: how they performed as students, how they did on tests, where they went to college and in what number, what else they did. Such leaflets help colleges to know the schools with which they are dealing and help this year's seniors and their parents to know what to expect.

The guidance counselor also has the freedom to discuss a student's scores with the student, and to point out to him what qualifications he does and does not have. It is curious now to realize that only two years ago there was very bitter opposition within the College Entrance Examination Board to the very idea of releasing scores to schools so that they could, in turn, release them to students. There was great fear that students would have their values warped by learning their own scores, but I learned from hearing my own children's conversation that SAT scores have now become one of the peer group measuring devices. One unfortunate may be dismissed with the phrase, "That jerk—he only made 420!" The bright, steady student is appreciated with his high 600, and the unsuspected genius with his 700 is held in awe. This is not exactly the use of College Board scores we had in mind when we decided to authorize their distribution, but it's possible to think of many worse, so perhaps we had better not complain.

The college guidance counselor must face the fact that he is really the person who makes the college choice. He makes it both negatively and positively. There are many parents who, as we know, overaspire as far as their children's choice of college is concerned and have to be detoured gently and patiently in other directions.

A great many parents and a great many students are also honestly puzzled as to how to go about making a college selection. When, as is often the case, neither the parent nor the student really knows where—or, for that matter, why—the student is going to college, the choice of college can become extraordinarily difficult. I can testify to this because the number of letters that come into the College Board office asking for direct advice as to colleges is considerably larger than one might suspect, and we always make it a point to try to answer them. In so doing, we often get ourselves into some extraordinarily difficult and complicated situations, and almost always because the student or counselor had started with inadequate foundations for his plans or his structure of advice.

While I am on the subject of college choice, perhaps it would be well to give some examples of poor college choice. Last year the admissions officer at Harvard reported that a student had just graduated from Harvard College magna cum laude, who had been advised four years before by his school guidance counselor that he would not be permitted to file a Harvard application, since Harvard would not admit a student with his type of record. The student actually had a good record, but it happened that he was not the top student in his class, and his College Board scores were not up in the high 700s; therefore, the guidance counselor was unwilling to risk the reputation of the school in supporting such a student. The student had enough ambition and nerve to disregard his counselor, but obviously not all students do so.

One of the College Board staff has been having a similar experience this year. A relative of his in a small city high school on the eastern seaboard was doing well and aspiring to something beyond the mediocrities of a local institution but was virtually prohibited by a guidance counselor from applying to Columbia College—mainly on the grounds that no student from that high school had ever entered Columbia. Again, due to favoring circumstances, the application was made, and the student is now in Columbia College.

I know of another case. A student in a girls' school, who had been doing brilliant work in all subjects and who had a particular interest in mathematics and science (and this, incidentally, was a school which did not teach physics), discussed with her headmistress the procedure for applying to M.I.T. The headmistress, horrified at the very idea, referred the student to the school's consulting psychologist, who, by intensive therapy at the expense of the parents, has been able to direct the girl's interests into more ladylike channels.

These all seem to me to be rather shocking cases of breach of trust. The fact that they come from ignorance rather than malice almost makes them worse, for a person set up in business as a guidance counselor is not entitled to be this ignorant about the problems of college going.

Another level of activity with which the college guidance counselor must concern himself is that of a student's finance. A few years ago our high schools were engaged in a bitter competition to see which could get the most scholarships for its graduating class. Scholarships have not been increasing in quantity in recent years and on the whole—as tuitions have risen—have become rather less effective in covering total college costs. As a consequence, loans are now making their appearance as a major method of student finance and will probably become even more important in the future.

The guidance counselor owes it to himself over the next few years to become thoroughly conversant with problems of student finance, to understand the costs of college, how a student can meet them, the amount of loan that can safely be taken, the importance for the student of knowing the different kinds of loan funds available to him, and other such factors.

The College Board, through its College Scholarship Service, has been undertaking to the greatest extent that it can the orientation of college guidance counselors to the student financial problem, but there are a great many schools and the process is, of course, a lengthy one.

The college guidance counselor, having elbowed his way into parity with the vocational guidance counselor in the secondary school, is destined over the next few years to take on still another level of activity. This is the level of activity which takes place at the junior college, or community college, level. For this is the institution which is going to assume the terminal function the American high school had up until, let us say, 1940 or even as late as 1950.

Until now, most colleges have done very little about guiding and advising their students with respect to occupation. But, except for California, we have had very little contact with the junior college students, and I think it is valid to point out that in California the guidance function of a junior college is an important one. This level of guidance actually is one which is going to require a good deal of exploration and probably a good deal of training so far as personnel is concerned. I would not be at all sure that there are many provisions—at least in this part of the country— for offering training at this level.

A topic that falls only marginally within the area covered by this talk is that of advanced placement. I am going to mention it only because I think it is the most important new academic activity in the entire school–college relationship. The idea is not particularly new, nor is there anything out of the ordinary about the fact that secondary schools can teach advanced courses. But there is a new idea in the closeness of the relationship between schools and colleges involved in the program, and this idea may in time produce a change in our entire approach to secondary education.

Certainly we must recognize that if secondary schools can offer advanced mathematics, or chemistry, or any other college subject to a few students they can offer it to many, but only if the preliminary courses are rearranged and reorganized. I believe it is quite obvious that secondary schools that will, as ours will, send 50 percent or more of their graduates to college must be different schools from those we now have. I believe, too, that secondary schools can decide what changes must be made. But I also believe that the kind of close relationship with colleges which the Advanced Placement Program exemplifies will go a long way in helping to build a better secondary school curriculum for the future.

There is a good deal more that could be said about educational consequences of the rush for college, but I would like to go on from this topic to the suggestion of some ideas which I think are of importance to us who are concerned with problems of guidance.

The first suggestion—which is in part a guidance problem and in part a problem created by the guidance officers and in part a product of other forces—is that which we have now identified as multiple testing, defined as excessive demands for school support and time with respect to the administration of testing programs. The College Board has recently done a not-very-formal study of this problem, using questionnaires sent to some 200 schools, and has concluded that there is indeed a serious problem of multiple testing. However, we discovered that some schools are themselves among the worst offenders, and I would like, therefore, to argue for what I might call an "economy of means."

For example, we know of a number of schools giving three different scholastic aptitude tests to their students in the first semester of the senior year. Thus, a student may be required to take the California Mental Maturity test, the old American Council on Education (Thurstone) test or the new Sequential Tests of Educational Progress, and also advised to take the College Board's PSAT.

From this he goes on to the next step of taking the College Board's SAT in December, January, or some later date, so that the school has now acquired four different ability measurements, which is three more than it needs. One wonders in such a case if better scheduling would not have put the school's tests earlier in the student's school career and left the externally administered tests for the later years.

While talking on the subject of multiple testing, it might also be germane to comment on the amount of testing done in secondary schools which is not reflected in the advice given by counselors or in the information the students have about themselves. In other words, without for one moment defending the amount of requests for aid that descended upon the secondary schools with respect to testing, I would also point out that schools have themselves still got a certain amount of homework to do with learning how to use effectively the tests that they themselves give.

I suggested not long since to another group the possibility that the problem of multiple testing might be dealt with by setting aside two periods of several days each during the academic year when all testing programs would be administered. This would be practicable as far as the College Board is concerned, though a good many of our members would require a good deal of persuasion. But I think colleges would accept the idea. I wonder if the schools would. This is a topic I'd like to hear some more about, and I hope we will have time to discuss it.

Actually, the multiple testing problem is bound to get worse rather than better, for what we are seeing is the second stage of the movement which will eventually require all college applicants to take some form of entrance examination. The College Board now deals with 80 percent of the candidates for independent institutions and 20 percent of the candidates for tax-supported institutions. The ACT program probably will deal with another 20 percent of candidates for tax-supported institutions. This means that more than half, perhaps three-fifths, of college candidates are now being tested. Any increase in this number will almost certainly bring added burdens to the schools, not only in assisting in testing programs but in nearly every other point of relationship to guidance and application.

The next topic I'd like to suggest is that of what I call "two-stage admission." This is the idea that schools and colleges could by agreement actually begin the admissions process on a preliminary or screening level at the eleventh-grade year. My idea, which is only one way of phrasing the problem, is that students might apply for admission to what we call a "guarantee group"; that is, by applying early in the eleventh-grade year and submitting all credentials, including examinations, they would be told by the end of the eleventh-grade year that they would or would not be admitted to a group which would be guaranteed admission within a sizable group of colleges, although no guarantees would be offered as to admission to any one college within the group.

Here I should comment that the development of the data-processing art has come to the point where electronic memories could store all forms of information about students beginning as early as the ninth-grade year, and in very short order produce all this data on one or more cards—not only condensed and transcribed, but also scored in terms of its indications for college admission, financial stability in college, field of major interest, probable success, and various other factors germane to his admission.

The second stage of the two-stage admissions plan would of course be for those students who had passed through the first stage to make their formal application to particular institutions. Those students who had not received their guarantee through the first stage—and I would assume that their number might be considerable—could pass their applications on to other institutions. I believe that such a two-stage admissions process could be operated with dignity, humanity, and great usefulness. I believe also that it could be operated economically, so far as students or schools are concerned.

Another set of admissions ideas I would like to suggest is that it would be entirely feasible for a group of colleges to make guarantees to students who needed financial aid—guarantees to the general effect that students admitted to a given institution would receive financial aid up to the full level determined by the computation process recommended by the College Board's College Scholarship Service.

Financial aid, of course, would not be a guarantee of scholarship aid, and the student would have to be told explicitly that some of the aid would be scholarship, some loan, and some guaranteed employment. I believe a guarantee could be forthcoming, and with the guarantee the student could make his own choice of college without having to wait for the final scholarship action. It would, of course, increase the amount of risk to the student, but, if a number of colleges agreed upon this as a procedure, it would eliminate the troublesome waiting and decision period when admissions notices are out, but scholarship actions—which always lag behind admissions action— are not known. I have already suggested earlier in this talk that the problem of student finance is to become very important in the future. My suggestion seems to me the direction in which the field will almost certainly move. In other words, I do not expect sizable increases in scholarship programs, and I do expect increases in loan programs.

The College Board not long ago released the returns on a research study which it had been financing for several years. This was a study on the question of whether or not it is possible to establish a nonacademic criterion of college success. The answer to the question is that at least in one institution this was done by a method of faculty polling which was based, in broad terms, on three types of statements by the faculty.

1. We are glad to have this student here. He has been a superior contributor to the institution, both personally and academically.

2. We are content to have this student here. His contributions have not been great, but he is certainly not an unsatisfactory individual.

3. We, on the whole, would prefer not to have this student here, but since we have him we will make the best of it and graduate him.

Having established these three broad categories by which students' success might be measured in a nonintellective sense, the research study has now produced indicators that success according to these criteria can be predicted. This has been a problem with which the Board and many admissions officers have been struggling for many years, and it is very heartening to be able to report that we finally have some evidence indicating that a prediction instrument dealing with personality, motivation, and attitudes can be devised. We don't know, of course, whether this instrument will work in other institutions and localities, but at least we have gotten this far and the prognosis is a happy one.

This has been, despite the length of the talk, a sort of once-over-lightly, so far as the problems of guidance—as reviewed in terms of a future in which the majority of students will go to college—are concerned.

These are some of the other topics I would have liked to discuss.

1. Talent loss: it has been overdone, but there is more to be said.

2. Submerged talent: the Junior High School 43 project.

3. College curriculum reform: to match the reform being imposed on secondary schools.

4. The consequences of overcompetition.

5. The loss of the spirit of intellectual adventure.

This paper was delivered at a time when there was a good deal of discussion about standards and changing programs. It was an attempt to gather and discuss what we knew and what could then be forecast about the reasons for observed changes and the nature of changes to come.

As a speech, reread some years later, it stands up reasonably well. The comments were useful short-term predictions at the time, and some of them have proved to be quite accurate. They should have been, for they were essentially extrapolations from trends and from data, both of which were already under observation.

"Our Changing Colleges"
A speech delivered separately during the month of April 1960, to a meeting of the National Council of Deans of Women, Philadelphia; to the California Association of Independent Schools meeting, Santa Monica; and to the Columbia-Barnard Alumni Conference, Detroit. Published in the *National Association of Women Deans and Counselors Journal* No. 23, July 1960, pp. 158–165.

My remarks today are essentially an inquiry into change in education; that is, they begin with a review of major changes that are today affecting education, consider some of the most important and most obvious changes now in progress, and go on to a projection of the consequences of current trends.

Much of the recent history of education has been a resistance to change, followed often by a yielding and then a complete adoption of a new pattern. I think this is particularly obvious when we review changes that have taken place over the last 30 years. I trace six of such changes as having occurred within the span of my own working years.

First, during the period of the late 1930s, the completion of the revolution in secondary education which brought a high school diploma within the reach of all—and in the process destroyed the college preparatory program as the dominant secondary school course, swept away the old formalities of college entrance, and overturned the established relationship between school and college. This was perhaps the most important change of all, for it was the one which has made necessary our present efforts to establish a new relationship between school and college.

Second, the war, with its emphasis on pre-selection and training which was to set the stage for patterns of college entrance that are still gaining in popularity, and with its emphasis on total use of human resources. One consequence of this emphasis was to speed the discovery that women can be trained to do—and do well—tasks that men ordinarily do. This fact had remained out of the common wisdom for some centuries, perhaps because the common wisdom is controlled by men, and men, having discovered that they could not be trained to do tasks that women ordinarily do, had left the converse of the proposition unexplored.

Third, there came the postwar readjustment, during which we observed, but did not learn, that the educational revolution of the twenties and thirties which changed the American secondary school was being transferred and was to be the revolution of the forties, fifties, and sixties, changing higher education. We finally learned this about 1955 and have been trying to adjust to it ever since.

In the process of postwar readjustment we also learned what federal government support for higher education could accomplish, and subsequently we applied this to the areas of mathematics and science when we felt that we were not getting sufficient results from our education in these areas.

Fourth, we have learned, very slowly, the reasons why students come to college in such numbers. We began our learning by noting that the colleges which were most popular were those which offered prestige. This produced a considerable effort on the part of some colleges to obtain the chemical formula for prestige, but this effort has died down as it has been discovered that prestige is simply a combination of bright students and, if possible, bright faculty, with decent surroundings and access on graduation to good jobs or good professional schools.

However, prestige is not enough to explain the rush to college. Ultimately, the cause traces back to the labor market, to the fact that every man *and* every woman must now expect to enter the labor market, and to the fact that a high school diploma, once a passport to a preferred job, now entitles the holder to little more than the status of unskilled labor. This fact therefore makes college attendance, or at least postsecondary education, necessary for anyone who aspires beyond unskilled labor.

Another aspect of this same development of necessity for advanced education is to be found in the steady lengthening of the college experience. It is a curious, interesting, and overlooked fact that while we continue to speak of and advertise college as a four-year experience, it is often, for students entering the selective and competitive colleges, a five-, six-, seven-, or even eight-year experience. Further, it may be noted that graduate and professional schools are beginning to make strong efforts to attract more and better students. This suggests that in a few years the admissions problems at this level may be very similar to the more crowded undergraduate admissions problems.

Fifth, as a necessary corollary to the general discovery of need for college, we have seen the discovery of student aid. The word "discovery" is used advisedly. A generation ago student aid was rarely a major concern of educational policy. A few scholarships for high-standing students, some grudging aid for students in desperate need, other scholarships for the purchase of geographical distribution, or athletes, or oboe players (and these are rarest of all), and a tiny, dormant loan fund, were characteristic provisions for most colleges. Today, scholarships compete with faculty salaries when it comes to apportioning the proceeds from tuition increases; loan funds are augmented by federal funds and even by commercial bank funds; and the apportionment of student aid is a full-time task for a trained professional. In short, the development of the concept of student aid ranks as the most important educational change of the last decade and, in all probability, the one most likely to influence educational development during the coming decade.

Finally, very recent and only beginning to appear above the surface, there are signs of curriculum modernization and even of new curricular ideas. Modernization has certainly appeared in the secondary schools. The effort to reestablish the relationship between secondary school and college has already begun to change secondary school programs in physics, mathematics, and foreign language. Within a few years, there will be changes in other sciences, in English, and in the social studies. But this, although a first step, is no more than that. The real problem of college preparation in recent years has been to challenge the able student, and this is now being done for the first time in our generation with the development of the Advanced Placement Program. This program has added a dimension to secondary education that did not exist before. It offers the opportunity to give advanced courses to students who have covered required elementary work. But it also offers the opportunity to add courses to the secondary school curriculum that have never been there before—anthropology, sociology, psychology, analysis and design, history of art, language and area studies —to mention some, but by no means all, of the possibilities.

This has been a hasty summary of what I call "changes" and what others might call "trends." It does not matter what they are called. What does matter is the changes wrought through them in our colleges, and, beyond those, changes we may anticipate.

Changes which have taken place that strike me as of particular importance are perhaps less numerous than might be expected. The first one is the consequences of candidate pressure. Not long ago I saw a faculty committee report on the desirable size for a particular college. After an able summary of present facts it noted the excellence of the college's reputation, the need for maintaining it, and the damage that would be done if enrollments were increased in response to candidate pressure, concluding by pointing out that it would be far better for the college if there were better admissions policies, if more classrooms were available, if class sizes were reduced and faculty salaries increased—in other words, no recognition that any change had taken place in the college's circumstances or was likely to.

This, of course, is nonsense. A college that admits 250 out of 275 applicants is not the same college when it admits 250 out of 2,000 candidates. It has changed the size of the community on which it draws, its reputation, the academic and the social quality of its students, increased the percentage of students it graduates, and expanded its relationship to graduate and professional schools. In short, even if it has the same president, faculty, and curriculum, it is a different college. And a neighboring college which continues to admit 250 students out of 275 candidates is not the same college either. It has lost relatively in reputation; it has lost absolutely in its ability to draw students, in the quality of its students, in the success of its graduates in graduate school or in professions. Its community has shrunk rather than expanded, its intellectual capital is being expended, and it is heading for intellectual bankruptcy.

A major change toward sharply increased selectivity in a sizable group of colleges—and by this I mean that there are now more than 100 colleges in the selective-competitive group, while 10 years ago it numbered only 25, and 5 years ago only 50—appears to be on its way to producing a new sub rosa, or de facto, series of entrance requirements.

The new requirements begin, properly, with English. Here it is now expected (or coming to be expected) that a candidate will be able to demonstrate reasonable facility in writing. The requirement of ability to write actually represents an internal raising of standards within colleges, and this has been going on ever since rising candidate pressures commenced to change the composition of freshman classes. In general I would say that this requirement as to ability to write may replace the present implied requirement that a student should be well read.

In modern languages two changes are taking place. First, more language is certainly to be required. Thirty years ago the high entrance requirement colleges required three years of a language. Then that requirement was enfeebled and finally disappeared. It is now returning. Furthermore, two years of a second language will be urged. But, in addition to this quantitative change, it will be expected that students will be able to use the language in conversation. This development has been foreshadowed by the success of the Board's oral-aural tests. It is quite predictable that what is now a suggestion or an emphasis will be a requirement in a few years.

In mathematics it is certain that a full four-year secondary school course is now, in many colleges and certainly in all engineering schools, being viewed as desirable for all students, and that the program may well reach into either modern mathematics or calculus, depending on the direction of the student's interests. This requirement may not be extended to girls, but it is nevertheless certain that their mathematics requirement will also go up.

Finally, in the sciences there has already been developed a physics program which after further modification will probably displace traditional high school physics and, in fact, may acquire such appeal as to crowd out chemistry as the dominant high school science. History and social studies courses will probably rest fairly undisturbed, since they have been considerably altered during recent years.

The program as sketched is, of course, a stiffened traditional course and therefore no more than the obvious response of colleges to increased pressure. There are other possibilities to be discussed under this heading, but they are still in the future and must be set aside for a few minutes.

Perhaps the other important change that I note today in our colleges is a negative one. I call it "the end of experiment." I am talking about the fact that there has been no real educational experiment in the sense of programs such as the General Education and the Great Books programs of Columbia and Chicago during the twenties and thirties or the examination program at Chicago, or the early development of the use of aptitude tests for college admissions at Columbia and Stanford, or new approaches to curriculum building and to teaching as at Bard, Sarah Lawrence, Reed, Bennington, Black Mountain, St. John's, and the Experimental College at Wisconsin, or the development of institutions to meet new social purposes as at the General College at Minnesota or the junior colleges in California. Then there was the entire series of experiments in secondary education beginning, in effect, with one at the Lincoln School in the twenties and ending with the Eight-Year Study in the late thirties.

This by no means completes the list of experiments that could be named, but it is notable that all have in common that they came into being during the thirties. The fact that there has been no major new experiment for many years may well prove that there is a relationship between the urge to explore and the need to explore. Certainly, during the thirties there was tremendous urgency to explore and to experiment. We felt then that all our values and beliefs had come down about our ears, and we experimented in the hope that we might find new ones. Today we are, despite our complaints, comfortable; and there is little need to experiment. In fact, the only two experiments I can cite as being of possible significance for the years ahead are the College Board's Advanced Placement Program, already mentioned, and the remarkable undertaking in guidance at Junior High School 43 in New York City.

Another characteristic of the current educational scene has been the emergence of state universities in a distinctively new role with respect to admissions policies. I think it is not unfair to say that for many years it has been customary to think of state universities as the principal proponents and practitioners of what is best termed "deferred selection"—that is, selection through the elimination of students who have failed to do well in college. Because they had carried this type of selection to general acceptance, it has been a matter of interest to note that during the past several years a number of state universities have announced stiffened entrance requirements and the use of preadmission tests as instruments to be used in a selective admissions operation. This is actually a decision of considerable significance in that these state universities, which already have graduate and professional schools that are in every way comparable to the same schools in private institutions as to selectivity and standards, are now moving toward selective admission on the undergraduate level.

The effects that these changes and present conditions may have upon colleges in the future is partially a matter of projection, partly of surmise, and partly of hope; and it is important to know which is which. For example, as a matter of projection of present trends, the following may be assumed.

First, all four-year colleges will within 10 years or less require entrance examinations which will be used for some degree of selective admission.

Second, much of the bulge of enrollment that is anticipated will be taken care of by expanding existing four-year institutions. Those in urban locations will probably expand their part-time enrollments to equal their full-time enrollments. Standards for part-time enrollment will continue lenient as compared with standards for full-time enrollment.

Third, the amount of scholarships and of loans, and particularly of loans, will go to levels far beyond anything now envisioned. As college enrollments draw in increasing numbers of students from the penumbra where the middle class and lower class overlap, the percentage of students who must borrow to obtain higher education will increase. Loans must come increasingly from commercial sources, even though federal and state loan funds will be greatly increased.

Fourth, the amount of testing required for college entrance will be going up. It has already gone up in every possible way, shape, and form during the past 10 years. As one example, because of increased numbers of colleges using Board tests, the Board is testing 750,000 candidates this year as against less than 100,000 eight years ago. As another, the American College Testing Program is dealing with sizable numbers of candidates and will certainly deal with more. And as a third indicator, schools everywhere have expanded their own testing programs. The net result has been to double or treble within a space of a few years the amount of testing to which an individual, college-bound student may be subjected.

Beyond the area of projection lies that of surmise—that area wherein we know that there must be developments, but beyond that are uncertain as to what the developments will be. So far as our colleges are concerned, several surmises may be offered.

First, the development of new colleges to take care of part of the enrollment bulge will probably move slowly. Here in the East we are unlikely to see any major developments within the next decade. This is partly because there is considerable room for expansion in existing institutions. In particular, a number of small colleges have a good deal of room for growth, and, as suggested a moment ago, the urban institutions can still enlarge their part-time programs.

Second, when new colleges are built they will be planned for students who in present-day terms are not thought of as prepared for or interested in college. This may mean that the new colleges will be essentially institutions of general education, though it would be a pity if this were so, since one of the great weaknesses of our present education is that students on the lower end of the college ability distribution already get so little that is concrete and so much that is general.

Third, admissions procedures will probably begin earlier than they do now. Recognizing the time already required to process long files of applicants, it seems reasonable to expect that processing will have to begin for most colleges during the eleventh grade. For many it already begins there; about half of the candidates who now take the Board's tests are juniors. In fact, the colleges must recognize the dilemma. Either they begin their selection process with the eleventh graders, or the schools will take over completely the first stage of the admissions process. There is evidence that this is already happening on a wide scale, with schools giving advice and even making decisions with respect to college plans and college choices.

Fourth, as a product of advancing application dates, new tests will certainly be needed. As matters now stand, there are well-established needs for a test of scientific and a test of mathematical aptitudes, a test measuring motivation, and a test dealing with ability to adjust to college environment. Beyond these, new subject-matter tests could well be developed which would test for the possession of the combination of abilities at analysis and synthesis which we call problem solving.

Fifth, as entrance requirements go up and as admissions pressures accumulate around some colleges, other colleges will lose in relative stature and appeal. The end result will be two or three distinctive groupings of colleges, one of which will have, de facto, higher requirements than others. It is probable that there already exists a gap of a full year's achievement between the highest and lowest standards for admission to accredited four-year liberal arts colleges. In 10 years the gap may not widen, but it may be better known and more freely acknowledged than it is now. As the gap develops it will be learned that the institutions at the top end of the scale are in preferred positions in respect to jobs for graduates and access to graduate and professional schools.

Sixth, we may expect that graduate and professional schools, heretofore somewhat aloof in their dealings with students, will become active in recruiting and will at the same time begin to complain about overcrowding and candidate pressures. It is not generally understood that the number of outstanding graduate schools is considerably smaller than the number of strong colleges. Hence, when graduate schools begin to select their students using college records plus test scores (probably on tests yet to be developed), the premium on the quality and status of the undergraduate college will go up even higher than it now is.

Finally, there is the area of approaching change about which we know little, but hope much. Over the next decade, our most important change, which will be at once our greatest trouble and our greatest opportunity, will be in finding a new working relationship between school and college.

We know from our figures that we may reasonably expect 50 percent of the age group to go to college. We know that this may mean as much as 75 percent of high school graduates will go to college. We know that present numbers of students are overloading our admissions operation and our guidance officers. Obviously, present methods cannot handle these new numbers. More to the point, our present *ideas* cannot handle them. Colleges cannot prescribe preparation and guidance from on high, criticize at will, demand change at will, and at some point in time calmly step in, take over the individuals involved and their destinies, and sort them out as the colleges please. Yet this is exactly what too many colleges are doing and what too many recent pronouncements by admissions officers and presidents have stated as policy for the future.

. . . .

With these several and assorted comments covering, Heaven knows, a broad spectrum of opinion mixed with considerable hindsight and some dubious prophecy, this paper is ended. There are some points I would have liked to have made and others that I know I neglected; but the main point which I hope I have established is that values are not to be maintained merely by clinging to an unvarying formula. Education is changing constantly in every imaginable respect. If we wish the values we cherish to endure, we must test them constantly, preserve them from moth and rust, strengthen them with new ideas, and, above all, see that they are used.

This was a perfect example of a programed speech, prepared to meet rigid conditions. It was to be the only formal speech (and the speaker was to be the only one wearing academic costume) on the occasion of a convocation of St. Peter's College, a Jesuit college in Jersey City, New Jersey, held for the purpose of awarding honorary degrees to Francis Cardinal Spellman and General George Henry Decker (then vice chief of staff, United States Army).

The problem was to state a common theme that could get a churchman and a soldier into the same academic framework. The interesting thing in the writing was the fact that as soon as the problem was stated, the speech practically wrote itself, and, wonderfully, was completed in time to send a copy to the college.

The occasion was also my closest approach to public disaster. I drove to Jersey City from my home in northern New Jersey, took my speech out of my brief case, got my academic robe and cap, and went in to lunch.

No sign of disaster appeared until I was on the platform. I took my speech out of my pocket for a last check, and found an eight-page essay that I had written on "The Principles of Guidance."

The situation was desperate, for the speech was complex and depended on precision of phrase. I simply could not ad lib it.

A helpful monsignor, who had been sitting behind me on the platform, slowly paced the long length of the auditorium bearing my car keys and a description of the car.

The ceremony went on: Father Loughlin, the president, made a few remarks; Cardinal Spellman received his degree and made a terribly brief acknowledgment.

General Decker received his degree—and my monsignor friend had had time to make three round trips to the parking lot. General Decker acknowledged his degree, I am happy to say, at some length. Then the chorus stood up to give a musical postlude to the honors, and the monsignor appeared at the distant end of the hall. The dignity of his pace was almost unbearable, and he had no paper in his hands.

But he made it to the platform, midway in the second verse. "I couldn't find your car," he said, "but I ran into our public relations officer. He had a mimeographed copy. Here it is."

There may have been some typos in the copy I had, but I do not remember. In my relief, I reached oratorical heights never since attained.

The speech was a huge success and was printed and reprinted in half a dozen publications.

When I told my story, General Decker quoted a couplet:
The hall was still, the speaker mute—
His speech was in his other suit.

"The Three Great Callings"
Speech at convocation at St. Peter's College, Jersey City.
Published in *The Educational Record*, Vol. 41, No. 3, July 1960, pp. 203–217.

The three great dedicated callings of our time—the religious, the military, and the educational—we have come to take for granted, for they are part of the fabric of our life. Because we take them for granted we have, almost absentmindedly, classified them as three among the many professions which manage our institutions. These include such old and honored professions as medicine, law, engineering, and the skilled practice of the arts; also such newly recognized professions as management, social work, journalism, public administration, and, perhaps, the newest of all—that of the management of opinion with all of its subdivisions, such as the direction of the great mass communications media, radio and television, and the controversial areas of advertising, public relations, and opinion analysis.

In a technical sense this is a proper classification, for all professions have in common the characteristic of being based on a body of specific knowledge and doctrine, the selection and training of practitioners through a long apprenticeship, and the final attainment—professional skill and the assumption of responsibility for specialized judgment and decision. Yet these are distinctions which override technical similarities. The professions that I have just enumerated are, in a sense, the product of an organized society. They are related immediately to the needs and problems of individuals. They have the purpose of easing our lives, though sometimes they trouble them too. They supply services that are available at need, and they supply comfort and personal opportunity to those who practice them. But valuable, even necessary, as they are to a smoothly functioning society, they do not control the stability or the nature of a society, nor do they touch the fundamental needs of individuals for security. Nor are they necessary for understanding man and his temporal environment or for attaining the spiritual understanding that we call for. These functions are reserved for the three great callings that support our society.

It is certainly neither chance nor imitativeness that has molded these callings into similar structures. They are hierarchical in form. This means that the growth of the professional skill and knowledge of any individual who enters these callings is denoted by a grade, a title that we call a rank, and that these ranks have a universal meaning not only within a given society or culture, but within any society or culture, for these professions have similar characteristics in all societies and cultures.

Each is controlled by a rigid and traditional discipline that includes the subordination of the individual to the requirements of his profession as a whole. And the profession vests judgment concerning the requirements of its practitioners in those of senior rank. This, in turn, involves the acceptance of limits on personal reward and, in effect, allows rewards to the individual only in terms of increasing responsibilities and ever deepening dedication.

In return for placing himself under discipline, the individual is granted security within a life that is necessarily modest and often supported on a level that is perilously close to subsistence. But he is also granted the priceless assurance of accomplishment in service, and, if he is unusually fortunate, he may come to know the tremendous satisfaction of being an instrument for the introduction of some new idea or element into the social structure. Thus, the religious calling has introduced such great concepts as the stability of the family, the responsibility of the individual for social behavior, and the community of man in the sight of God; the military calling has introduced the idea of group responsibility for security and, as a product of military art, has developed the great profession of engineering on which so much of our contemporary society depends; the teacher has, over generations, worked unceasingly to affirm man's insight into knowledge and the free use thereof, and, if he has not succeeded totally, he has, at least, established literacy and the idea of cultural heritage as basic concepts that are acknowledged and accepted even in the most illiberal societies.

Because the three callings are at the same time hierarchical and disciplined, they are also conservative. Dealing as they do with the foundations of society, they move slowly in response to pressures for change. And it is right that they should do so, for many such pressures have appeared for relatively brief moments in the long span of human history, expressed their urgencies, and then disappeared. Alfred North Whitehead has pointed out that true change is a slow process and that it may take a thousand years for any truly new idea to be accepted within large social structures. Thus, such ideas as universal literacy, or that men should have voice in their temporal governance, or that men should live in peace and love their neighbors are not yet accepted throughout our world, even though they have been a part of the common currency of thought for more than a thousand years.

These are callings that have their roots deep in history and, indeed, are historically oriented to an extent that is true of no other professions. They are today essentially dedicated to the service of society, and yet their histories are longer than the history of any other organized segment of society as we know it. Indeed, each of these callings has been indispensable to the development of nations as we know them and has, out of its own organization, discipline, and concept of service, contributed the basic elements of stability on which nations have built the idea of the state as the servant of its people.

These callings have been responsible for the basic ideas of professional training and service on which all our professions now rest. They are, even now, unique among professions in that they are self-sufficient in the management of their own selections of new individuals to enter their service and in the control of their own institutions for education and training.

It is worthy of note that these three callings alone, of all the contemporary groupings of society, have retained their own special symbols of vocation in uniforms, vestments, and badges which set them apart from all other groups. These symbols are, in a sense, affirmations of continuity, for they may be traced in a direct line to the earliest emergence of the professions and are affirmations of the dignity and respect which are the strength of enduring values.

The definable characteristics that these callings have in common are matched by definable methods of approach to problems. All three professions have long since established that the proper method of approach to any problem, large or small, is orderly, logical, and calculated. But within their method lies the paradox that they are simultaneously affirmative and pessimistic. They are affirmative in that they always stand for positive purposes and goals: the religious in seeking to make man conform to the great designs of our Creator; the military in seeking the strength that guarantees peace, and with peace, stability and security; the teacher in his dual mission of searching out and explaining the ultimate secrets of our life and environment. But they are also eternally pessimistic about their own a-chievements, alert to their failures, and always convinced that their resources are insufficient and their personal competencies and dedications are inadequate for the tasks at hand. Thus, the military can never be assured that they have the strength required for their mission; the teacher never has enough of knowledge, nor of the resources required to transmit knowledge; the religious strive always for greater faith and for greater works to affirm their faith.

Finally, in this catalog of the characteristics of the three callings, are the characteristics of evangelism and idealism. Their evangelism is an eternal expectation that the great truths on which the callings rest must be understood and can be understood if only they can be truly communicated.

From this it follows that the tasks of leadership in each of these callings have a continuing duality: on the one hand, they have the task of maintaining and strengthening the disciplined organization as a force in being, addressed to the tangible tasks and current problems; on the other hand, they have the task of gathering new strength by applying the skills that are inherent in what we call prosaically the behavioral sciences to the motivation and disciplining of new groups who will carry the greater responsibilities that lie ahead.

And these callings are idealistic in that each looks forward to a time beyond the present when all goals will be reached, all negations overcome, and all doubters converted—a time when men will achieve peace, unity, security, understanding, and salvation.

This view of these three great callings is, in effect, a form of inquiry into the human needs that brought them into being, that have maintained them through uncounted generations and have brought them to our time, still vital, still dynamic, still the solid foundation of our social order.

Now, to cast forward for a view of these callings in time to come, to find the only true certainty in the future of uncertainty. We do not know the shape of tomorrow's world. Indeed, we do not really know the shape of our present world, for there are few minds, perhaps none, that can grasp the enormity of the idea that we can now destroy in a day all that our race has built through all time past, and if we cannot understand this idea, we cannot truly know our world. We can be certain only that if there is a world of tomorrow, it will be built, as it has always been built in the past, on the foundations supplied by the three callings, which are here joined in one purpose. But even within this certainty we face uncertainty as to the challenges that these callings must face, the forms that they will adopt, and the new purposes that they must serve.

The religious calling is confronted with problems that arise from the paradox that we now have available and at hand the means to assure all men of the basic decencies of human life, including reasonable chance of being able to attain adult status, sufficient food, and a measure of social freedom. We are a long way from realization of each of these decencies, but we have seen them evolve from impossible hopes into evident realities in many regions. And even in whole countries we can see signs of still further changes to come, and we know that only political organization, or lack of it, prevents the general enjoyment of these basic decencies. The paradox lies in the fact that the tasks of the religious calling become more complex, but in a sense less direct, as a culture moves from the terrible stability of subsistence to the mobility of affluence.

In a simple society, man's unity with God is a simple idea to be simply presented and simply accepted. In a mobile and affluent society simple ideas become obscured and overlaid in the action and turmoil of daily living, and the religious calling is required to penetrate into every stratum of the complex structure in order to continue to communicate the continuing simplicity of its basic premise. Thus the calling itself becomes ramified and complex as it adapts to its changed environment. Its unity and its purpose remain unchanged, but its tasks are subdivided into a range of undertakings that spans the tremendous distance from the devotional to the secular. In such a future it is impossible to overestimate the requirements for the discipline, wisdom, administrative skill, and understanding of the human heart that its chosen leaders must bring to their appointed tasks.

The military calling has before it tasks of comparable magnitude but of a different order. Military leadership has been defined as the management of violence, which is indeed a paradoxical definition, for violence always carries a connotation of unmanageability. Yet, until this time in human development it has been a valid definition. Now we are faced with the certainty that violence, if it is again released on a large scale, will be unmanageable; and so the military calling faces the need to reduce the amount of potential violence at its disposal through the complex arrangements that we call "negotiated disarmament." Yet, the hazards of total disarmament are unacceptable, and so the military calling continues, and must continue, in being.

In this strange situation military organization must become increasingly compact, increasingly skilled, increasingly disciplined in order to avoid tragic error, and also must become increasingly dedicated to its basic purposes. We begin now to see the new form that this honored calling must accept. It is the form of compact force, equipped with the finest products of our technology and skilled in the use of those products in that truest of all forms of defense of security, the advancement of human welfare.

This is no new role for our military calling. Military engineers opened our nation for settling and exploring and for building bridges, dams, railroads, and canals, including the tremendous achievement, the Panama Canal. Military medicine conquered the worst of tropical diseases and opened the tropics to comfortable human habitation. Military administrators controlled the greatest scientific achievement of the century in the opening of the atomic age, and military engineers and scientists are now exploring the edges of outer space, even as they explore the depths of oceans and the polar boundaries of our known world. These facts are not new to any of us, but taken together they are a magnificent proof that the military calling, as we know it, serves greatly, whether in peace or in war.

It may well be that for the military calling of the future, arms and armaments will become secondary, and the primary task will be the undertaking of enterprises so great as to be beyond the reach of ordinary means. The exploration of space may be the most glamorous of these tasks, but the pioneering of new methods of communication and new vehicles for transportation, the testing of new materials, and even the guidance and supervision of major engineering projects in underdeveloped countries may have more immediate importance for our time. But whatever the assignments and challenges of the period may be, we have the certainty that the military calling, under its dedicated leadership, will hold to its skills, its purposes, and its disciplines.

Finally, we come to the calling of the teacher. The forces, social, scientific, and technological, that are changing the religious and the military callings are changing our education almost before our eyes. The average child born in 1900 in America could hardly have expected to finish grammar school. The average child to be born in 2000 may expect to finish college. The eight years of schooling that lie between these two averages represent social, financial, and psychological changes such as the world has never seen before. The change we know, intense and dramatic, is in some measure reflected in every part of the globe. It is a change that will place heavy strains on the structure and the discipline of the teacher's calling. There will be knowledge to be sought, gained, verified, arranged, and presented. There will be new programs to be created. There will be new aspirations to be met and some old and tragic oversights and failures to be remedied. There are abilities and talents that lie buried deep beneath layers of prejudice, poverty, and neglect, as well as faults and problems of which we have common knowledge. There will assuredly be no shortage of tasks for the teacher's calling, but unless we can in the future practice our evangelism with more skill and fervor than we have ever practiced it, there may be a shortage of manpower.

Of these three great callings, the future offers the least tangible task to the religious, the most difficult task of readjustment to the military, and the largest task to the teacher. But, in a sense, the terms of reference to their future tasks do not affect these callings either in their own views of themselves or in such detached views of them as we are able to achieve. The importance lies rather in their purposes, for these are purposes by which our lives, our beliefs, and our faith are held secure.

6. The New Task—International Education: 1960-1963

Three of the five papers that make up this chapter reflect my work from October 1960 to October 1962 as director of the International Study of University Admissions. Of the others the first is a prediction, written not long before my leave began in 1960, and the fourth is an attempt to look squarely at education in the South.

After my return, most of the first year went to the task of trying to develop a program for the next 5 to 10 years of Board development. And, just as certain elements of such a program began to fall into place, my own decision to resign my position left all forward planning in the capable hands of my colleague, Richard Pearson.

The short memorandum on probable developments in higher education in 1960-70 was done in the early fall of 1960 to suggest some guidelines to the College Board staff for the coming decade.

This was a time when virtually all forward planning by individuals or organizations was being seriously inhibited by political uncertainty. The Eisenhower administration was drawing to its end, but its laissez-faire policy with respect to education would not necessarily end with the administration. Indeed, in terms of established federal postures, the Eisenhower administration had not been any more standoffish with respect to support for education than most other administrations, regardless of party. It may be argued that the National Defense Education Act had been forced on the administration by public opinion, and that it represented the least that could have been done. But it could also be remarked that the NDEA represented more than any other administration had undertaken, and that it had been done.

The question of what a new administration—Republican or Democratic— might do was difficult to answer, for not many people had any very clear ideas as to what needed to be done. The memorandum was an attempt to predict direc-

tion of movement for education, saying in effect that certain things were likely to happen no matter who was in charge of the federal government.

"Probable Developments in Higher Education: 1960–1970" Memorandum written in September 1960.

Some thoughts come to mind in contemplating the probable course of development of higher education over the next 10 years.

1. By 1970 three quarters of high school graduates will enter college. At the present rate of increase in demand for higher education this is a reasonable projection. It depends only on our ability to build facilities and create programs to accommodate high school graduates in the IQ range of 100 to 110. Unless this is done, the alternative will probably be severe underemployment.

2. Acceptable formulas will be found to permit substantial capital support from public funds for both public *and* private higher education. Capital in the form of loans or grants is needed if private education is to continue to expand to meet demands upon it. Such funds need not compromise the integrity of private institutions, and even loans from government sources, if properly handled need not be a burden. Public funds are the only possible source.

3. The United States will accept as a matter of governmental policy and support the large-scale use of our system of higher education as an instrument of technical assistance for underdeveloped countries. This will be nothing more than a formalizing and extending of present policies with, it is to be hoped, better arrangements for control of the quality of education.

4. There will be no sizable increases in scholarship funds, but more than half of college students will need financial assistance and will be aided through loan funds. There is no apparent source for further scholarship funds. Alumni giving and additional income from tuition increases are needed to support daily operations, corporations have not shown real interest in support of scholarships, and public funds will probably go into loan programs. Need for student aid will go up sharply as the 100–110 IQ group moves into postsecondary programs of the community college type.

5. Secondary education will move generally to a multitrack organization of the curriculum featuring two—or in some cases three—parallel pro-

grams of college preparation, one of which will be at an advanced level. This is merely a continuation and extension of present trends. The advanced level of college preparation and admission has not been formalized, but that process is well under way, and also under way is the development of the large-scale guidance apparatus that is necessary to make such a program effective.

6. Increasing sophistication in the use of tests will reduce the amount of testing undergone by secondary school students and at the same time improve effectiveness in the use of tests. The large-scale use of tests for college guidance and college entrance is so new that the programs have not yet been adjusted to other types of testing programs. As a result there is a good deal of duplication in testing and also a great deal of unused information available and going to waste. In time there will be some consolidation of existing programs and, it is hoped, the development of new programs that will get at the problems of the marginal student who is nevertheless college bound—problems that existing college entrance tests do not reach effectively.

7. Schools and colleges will agree on some form of multistage system for the admission of students, thus eliminating most of the abuses and discomforts of present methods. There are no serious technical difficulties in the way of such arrangements, and indications are that efforts will be made in this direction—particularly after the difficult admissions problems that were uncovered in the spring of 1960. This should be accomplished within a year or two, at least in tryout form.

8. There will be evolved a program for the award of degrees by examination with little or no requirement of formal instruction. Such a program is the logical outcome of present developments in the offering of leisure-time education in suburban communities, of television instruction, of do-it-yourself instruction kits for home learning of languages, and various other devices for learning. There is no great difficulty in the devising of examinations, but there are difficulties in obtaining the recognition of degrees awarded on this basis. Also, the undertaking is likely to be costly, so that it is possible that it will not be undertaken until there is more information about the actual demand for such a program.

9. There will be relatively little expansion of the present professional sector of higher education, but very decided expansion in technical educa-

tion. The professional sector of education, represented by the small nucleus of major graduate and professional schools with their feeder colleges, has in recent years expanded mainly through the addition of service programs supporting its professional programs. Given the close control that the senior professions exercise with respect to professional education, it is unlikely that this pattern will be changed. The expansion of technical and technological education will be very great indeed, particularly for the group of students referred to above who will be in the 100–110 IQ range.

10. The handling of foreign students will be done through an interuniversity agency. Present arrangements for handling foreign students are scarcely better than arrangements 25 years ago, and the numbers have gone up tremendously. Establishing a cooperative organization that would support overseas representatives to arrange for guidance and testing of applicants before they come to this country, and also support one or more gateway institutions or programs, would improve the entire situation at relatively small additional cost per student.

Six years later several comments on the preceding memorandum are allowable.

1. The prediction that three quarters of the high school graduates would enter college by 1970 seems reasonably certain to be realized. Certainly, what we now call universal higher education is an accepted fact.

2. Capital support from public funds for both public and private higher education admittedly seemed pretty remote in September 1960 and during the last days of the Eisenhower administration. However, it came about with astonishing ease under the Johnson administration, and it will probably continue.

3. The use of our system of higher education as an instrument of technical assistance for underdeveloped countries has enlarged considerably since 1960. (This was not a difficult prediction, since the idea was already established.)

4. The prediction that there would be no substantial increase in scholarship funds but that there would be very large increases in loan funds has proved only about half correct. There have been large increases in loan funds, and there has also been a substantial increase in scholarship funds. What happened, of course, was the movement of the federal government into both fields, which was not part of the 1960 prediction.

5. The prediction that secondary education would move to a multitrack organi-

zation of the curriculum featuring two or three parallel programs of college preparation seems to be evolving, but it has not yet proved demonstrably correct. However, it is correct that the large-scale guidance apparatus necessary to make a multitrack college preparation program effective is being developed. Actually the multitrack problem is working out to be more complicated than it seemed in 1960, with the development of universal higher education as, in many cases, a continuation of high school. What we may well see in the future is essentially a six-year high school program for students, carrying through to a fourteenth grade, rather than the present four-year program.

6. Seen in retrospect, the prediction of increasing sophistication in the use of tests must now be considered as an expression of wishful thinking with respect to the general overhaul of the measurement of the problem. Actually, there has been very little change in the form and utilization of tests, and the number of test types available for use seems to have increased rather than decreased. The present rapid expansion of the entire education system will probably discourage any new developments in the testing field for at least another decade. Conclusion: no foreseeable new developments in testing.

7. The idea that schools and colleges will agree on some form of multistage system for the admission of students has also proved to be wishful thinking. What seems to have happened is that everyone seems to have become accustomed to the present methods and to have learned to accommodate to them with all their inherent creakiness of operation.

8. Prediction looking toward the awarding of degrees by examination, with little or no requirement of formal instruction, is progressing more slowly than anticipated, but it is progressing.[1] As matters now stand, genuine support is available for the idea from foundations and perhaps even from government sources, but the institutional willingness to take the plunge is still lagging. The problem is more complicated than it appears to be on the surface, for the fact is that the awarding of credits and degrees by examination is perfectly simple for any institution, but there is no present way of guaranteeing acceptance of the award by any other institution or agency. My own idea for handling this problem would be to imitate the external examination and degree program of the University of London and set up a degree-granting institution whose statements and diplomas and degrees would be, like those of the University of London, accepted at full face

---

1. In 1965 the Council on College-Level Examinations was established by the College Board.

value. (The Russian correspondence program is also relevant in this context.) This would be quite an undertaking, for it would in effect involve setting up a national university that would have no resident student body, but I see no reason why this could not be done.

9. The prediction of very decided expansion in technical education has proved accurate. Part of this is traceable to the arrival of universal higher education a good deal sooner than it was expected.

10. The handling of foreign students through an interuniversity agency continues to be hoped for by many individuals in American education. The problem, of course, is that college and university faculties, particularly at the professional and graduate levels, have such a fear of usurpation of their authority by some shadowy and uncontrollable agency, that they will not agree to any delegation of authority to discuss terms of admission, financial aid, programs, or degrees with any foreign applicant for admission. Actually, what would be involved would be the development of an organization analogous to the College Board, which has proved quite manageable over the years insofar as institutional authority has been concerned.

On the whole, it remains true that, as suggested in the memorandum, "Present arrangements for handling foreign students are scarcely better than arrangements 25 years ago . . . ." The only difference is that "25 years ago" can be changed to "32 years ago."

The following speech, presented at Brighton, England, in July 1961, was part of a historic occasion of sorts. It was the first attempt that had ever been made to give a group of prospective candidates for English universities some broad ideas about choosing a university and a career. This fact is, of course, a product of another fact: that until recently the method of selection for the English sixth form pretty much took care of the questions of later educational choices by excluding all those who had not made up their minds about their futures. The system was not, of course, planned to work that way, but that was one of its consequences. However, the enlargement of opportunity in England brought in students who had problems in reaching decisions or who could not find the opportunities they were seeking.

*Veterans of that dread American institution, The College Day (or Night),
will recognize this as a bigger and better version of their old acquaintance. It
went on for three days. All participants were housed at the Training College
(teachers' college) in Brighton. A number of vice chancellors, headmasters, and
officials from the Ministry spoke.*

*My own talk was intended to supply some interest by offering an external
view of the problems. My interpretation of its reception was that the audience of
English school boys (and a few girls) reacted just as an American student audience would have to a foreigner: they could not have cared less, and they sat
through it only out of politeness. Perhaps a different speech, or a different speaker,
or both would have done better. The speech itself seems to me to be interesting,
and that is why I have included it.*

"Contrasts in Education: Europe and the U.S." Speech at Brighton, Sussex, in July 1961. Published in somewhat altered form in the *College Board Review* No. 46, Winter 1962, pp. 13–18.

My assignment this evening is to present a comparative sketch of higher
education in the United States and Europe. Since this is a large subject
which may produce a good deal of rambling, I want it to be a matter of
record that I have fulfilled my assignment. Therefore, I offer the following
facts.

Europe, if I limit myself to Western Europe, which I must if I am to get
anywhere with this comparison, has a total area of 2,280,000 square kilometers and a population of about 245 million, and its people use some 14 languages. At international conferences these languages may all be used at once,
but otherwise they are more or less confined to given localities and become
part of what sociologists call "regional differences" or "regional characteristics." I mention this because American regional characteristics are
discussed often by visiting observers and I would not wish it thought that
Americans claim a monopoly on them. There are 280 institutions of higher
education in Western Europe and approximately 900,000 students in them.
If the American definition of higher education as "any instruction that
takes place after finishing secondary school" were used in Europe, the
number of institutions would probably be doubled—say 550—and the num-

ber of students would probably be increased by about 50 percent, to 1,400,000.

In the United States there is a population of 179 million and only one language. We have a land area of 3,600,000 square miles (equal to 5,800,-000 square kilometers). We have about 2,000 institutions of higher education and a student population of 3,300,000. If European definitions were applied to our higher education, we would have about one-third the number of institutions and half the number of students.

As is the case with all fact-packed statements, a good many items can be mined out of this one, and more questions are raised than are answered. However, I think it is clear that the central question is: Why are there so many more institutions and students in the United States than there are in Europe? The usual answer is that it is because American standards are low, but this is not, as a generalization, true, and it is in any event an argument on quite another point. It is a point worth considering, but it must wait its turn.

It is, I think, clear that such differences in numbers must come as a consequence of different attitudes toward education. The best way to trace these is to examine the reasons for the formation of higher education.

In the most primitive societies, three groups have first claim on education—priests, chiefs, and witch doctors. In the history of higher education in Europe these same claims can be traced in the foundation of the universities. In fact, for 500 years after their foundation they concentrated on their traditional faculties of theology, law, and medicine. Other faculties were, in time, added, but these basic three remained supreme. In time they extended themselves formally or informally to include preliminary learning—the classics, humanities, mathematics, a smattering of science. When this had been done, the universities comprised a system of education which began at about age 12 and went on for 10 years or more. It was a standard system in all countries, based on the same languages, the classics, the same learning, and the same methods. It was also a closed system, for it could be entered only by someone who was literate, adequately supported financially, and willing to enter one of the professions for which the system would prepare him.

The point of literacy is important here. Five hundred years after the first European universities were founded the majority of Europeans were still illiterate. This suggests that universities were not much concerned with literacy or lack of it, and I think this was so and probably still is so. A. N. Whitehead has remarked that it takes 1,000 years for a new idea to be accepted. Universal literacy had been a new idea for a long time before it finally emerged into the general view toward the end of the eighteenth century. When it emerged, it did so partly because it was equated with political and personal opportunity, partly because commerce and industry were beginning to develop complexities that required more trained people than the apprentice system could produce. However, when it emerged it could be implemented only by the foundation of a totally new system of common schools, quite unconnected with the university system which already existed. Indeed, as soon as this system emerged, the universities fenced themselves off with examinations and requirements to avoid contacts with the common school. Many of these requirements, be it noted, still exist.

This fencing-off achieved two important things. First, it protected the integrity of the universities. It protected it so effectively that the universities became the base of a subculture with great strength, its own method of self-perpetuation, and its own mystique. Second, it forced the common school onto its own resources, the training of its own teachers, the making of its own decisions as to what it would teach. When it, as a separate system, was in turn forced into expansion by population growth and, more important, by the unfolding of the Industrial Revolution, it had to expand in its own channels, and these inevitably led in the direction of immediate needs and practical skills. Thus the common school trained the children of workers to become in their turn workers, and in time did it so successfully that an elaborate structure of technical and even subprofessional training was set up, along with a teacher-training establishment to support the structure. And as this happened, a curious phenomenon appeared. This common school structure came to overlap the university structure. It was extended first to parallel the preparatory part of the university, though not, of course, with the same subjects or emphasis, and then, as educational requirements continued to go up, it came to overlap the university itself.

As it grew, still fenced off from the university, unable to have its teachers trained in universities, unable to have even its best products enter universities without ridiculous loss of time, it developed its own resources and pride—and, incidentally, became finally an acceptable alternative to university education.

The matter of timing becomes of importance here in explaining differences between Europe and the United States in their treatment of these alternative programs.

Higher education in the United States was established on the European pattern as already modified by Cambridge and Oxford. It was not further modified in the United States for some time, except that after the Revolution certain of the new states set up their own universities. Virginia, North Carolina, and Georgia were among the first, and others followed. But these American colleges, state or private, were no new institutions but an exact copy of models already imported from England. There were not many of them, and they provided the same level of opportunity that was then provided in England. Had they remained dominant, American education would hardly have differed from the European.

The first break in the pattern came when the United States established its first engineering school—the military academy at West Point—on the model of St. Cyr, and this in turn became the parent institution for all of our engineering education.

The next break was more important. It was the establishment, beginning in the 1820s, of small regional offshoots of the colonial, English-modeled colleges. Wave upon wave of these colleges were born into small red-brick buildings over the entire Midwest and South, and the explosion of Methodism in the early nineteenth century multiplied them almost unbelievably. The majority of them are long dead—perhaps one-third of them survive—but it is not their number that is important. What was important was that their products formed a base for the expansion of the common school, and it was during the years of their formation that the idea of the public high school began to develop in America.

The third break was even more important. It was the formation, with support from public funds, of colleges of agriculture and mechanical arts. These land grant colleges were a part of the decision to give the public lands to the people—a necessary part, because they provided the opportunity for training along with the opportunity to acquire land. They were called "land grant" because public lands were given by the federal government to support them, and they became, as a matter of interest, the instrument whereby agriculture in the United States became a profession rather than a vocation.

The importance of these establishments—both the small denominational colleges and the small land grant colleges—was that they represented the extension of the opportunity that the common school offered. As this extension developed, it came in time to full parallelism with the system that had been built on the colonial colleges of the East.

The time required to accomplish these changes was, for the United States, a long one. The first systematic attempt to establish the public high school as a true extension of the common school came in the 1840s. After this beginning came normal schools; local colleges; then, just 100 years ago, the land grant colleges; and, in the seventies and eighties, a group of special technical institutes and the beginnings of adult education. These were all encouraged and acclaimed, and benign legislatures granted them funds and charters. The standards were not necessarily high. The Pennsylvania legislature, in a moment of truth, chartered the Central High School in Philadelphia and gave it the right to confer degrees, which it still does, on the grounds that its standards were not inferior to those maintained by the colleges of the time. But, high or not, they were the standards of a system of education that paralleled but did not touch the system that had come with the colonists from Europe. It was 75 more years before there was parity between the two systems. One was neat and tidy—built on the English model, supported by special preparatory schools, tied to a small and select group of professions and to an upper-class clientele. The other was built on the common school, a rambling, uneven, often shabby education structure open to all who cared to come, treating the older learning with scant attention, and the new subjects with a lighthearted disdain for the classical method. New programs and new professions were created blithely, and, when they finally came together, it was because the new professions had to be acknowledged and the older colleges could no longer stand aloof from the pressures of the new system. But to show what the merger of the two concepts meant, be it noted that if the 1900 definition of higher education were applied in the United States today, we would have only 40 percent of our present enrollment. If the 1960 European definition were applied, it would cut present enrollments almost exactly in half.

I have supplied detail and editorial comment here in order to establish my basic point. The difference between the structure of higher education in Europe and the United States turns largely on the channeling of the development of the common school. In Europe this has been elaborated on the technical level beyond what is ordinarily done in the United States, and this elaboration has been accompanied by a series of sanctions, so that these technical programs are filled with students who have only a limited choice of movement among programs. The development has been predominantly lateral, and the ceiling has not been high. It is clear that all over Europe the ceiling is being raised, that there will be increasing freedom to move from the technical line to the university line, and even (as already in England with the Colleges of Advanced Technology) to a paralleling of the university line. But this is only the first step in a long process. New forms and definitions of education emerging from this process must yet gain acceptance, and until they do some of the limitations will remain.

In the United States, the public high school, which is the extension of the common school, has not been elaborated on the technical level. Instead, it has been developed with the intent of providing an opportunity for every child to graduate, in itself not a dissimilar concept to the General Certificate of Education in England. The distinctive fact is that any student, and I repeat, any student, who can manage to secure a high school diploma in the United States—and this is not difficult—can gain entry into an institution that at least in name is identified as offering higher education.

This statement suggests that the next topic to be discussed should be that of standards.

The great difficulty about comparing standards lies in the realm of proof. Assertions are easy, but establishing facts is difficult and time consuming. I shall beg lack of time and avoid claiming proof, relying instead upon a series of limited assertions.

First, I must make the point that in Europe and the United States there is agreement on one point with respect to standards. That is, that it is possible to maintain standards only by the selection of individuals who can meet them, and that selection is possible only when there is a reasonable alternative to offer to the individual who is selected out. This is provided for in each system, but in different ways. In the European system, where the selection of students for higher education is accomplished before—and usually well before—the completion of secondary school, the alternative offered is another form of secondary education: technical, administrative, professional, or, in some cases, teacher training. In such a system all goes well until either the students selected out are not satisfied with the alternative offered them, or the students selected for the university line in secondary school find another selection hurdle at the end of the line, which, if you will permit an observation, is what appears to be happening in England. In the American system, by contrast, where selection takes place toward the end of secondary school, the alternative offered is another form of higher education. This may be either of the same type on a lower standard, or of a different type, but the point is that it is available as a palatable alternative.

Second, the great American universities, numbering perhaps 50 (and their feeder colleges, such as Amherst, Reed, Oberlin, Swarthmore), operate on high standards, and their products stand with the products of any European university. These institutions are made up of the nation's best undergraduate colleges, the strongest graduate schools (which produce almost all the nation's Ph.D.s), the leading medical and law schools, the leading research enterprises. They also produce other professionals and specialists, including a great many in the fields that support medical practice, and another large number in areas related to management. The total enrollment in these institutions is about the same as the total enrollment in European institutions of higher education.

Third, much American higher education, some of it of high quality, would not be defined as higher education in Europe but would be considered as subprofessional or technical. By American standards nearly all European education in these areas would be considered deficient, both as to the general education on which it is based and as to the content and duration of the technical instruction.

Fourth, a substantial section of what is offered as higher education in the United States is below European standards. Much of it is designedly low in standards to provide further education for high school graduates who need additional skills in order to get jobs. Much, too, is provided as a form of guidance program, and this is particularly true in junior colleges and community colleges. Much is provided at this level because the alternative is no provision and no opportunity to raise group levels. Nearly all of the tax-supported Negro education in the South is of this type.

Fifth, no sensible American could possibly deny that the standard of preparation for the university line in Europe—that is, the line of the grammar school, the lycée, the *gymnasium*—is higher than the standard of the comparable program in the United States. However, the major American institutions exercise their right of selection and pick students from the preparatory program who as individuals could probably be matched against their European counterparts.

Sixth, requirements for admission as stated in the United States are deceptively simple and very nearly uniform. The requirements for William Jennings Bryan University, in Dayton, Tennessee, a remarkably fundamentalist Baptist institution, are not different from those stated by Harvard. The difference is in the enforcement, but the enforcement will always be on standards, not subjects. The elaborate requirements set up by many institutions in England and on the Continent may or may not produce higher standards of entrance. My own theory is that they are mostly nuisances and should be treated as such.

The next point of importance is the nature of control over institutions of higher education. This may be defined as the power to decide who will teach, what will be taught, what the standards will be, who will be admitted and how many, what its rules will be, and other such matters.

In the United States, control is usually very near to the institution. The trustees are related to the institution, often graduates of it. They and the president make policies and give it direction. They determine its size, its program, its faculty, its discipline—everything about it as an institution. The faculty may enjoy great freedom of individual action, but they do not have a major role in control.

This extremely close and direct control, with each institution exercising decision concerning its own destiny, accounts for the fact that American institutions vary so greatly in programs and in standards, and that they even oppose money from government for their support, on the grounds that to accept it would be to surrender their freedom.

In Europe, control is more central, more linked to government, more divorced from details. This makes for more stability of policy, even more homogeneity in educational processes and aims. It also leaves faculty free to run the institution locally, which means that European faculties become very powerful in those functions that they do control, such as appointments, programs, admissions requirements, and standards. This means that change is not just a matter of institutional decision, as it may be in the United States, but often it must pass through both faculty and the central policy-making group in the ministry. Change, under such circumstances, tends to be slow, and decisions to be conservative.

The point of control is linked closely to that of financial support. In Europe clearly a great deal of support comes from government, some from churches, relatively little, apparently, from private philanthropy or foundations, and (outside of England, where most universities indicate that 12 percent of their income is from fees) relatively little from tuition charges.

In the United States this pattern is almost reversed. The greatest single source of financial support, taking the country as a whole, is from student fees; the next probably from philanthropy, including income from endowment, yearly fund-raising campaigns, and foundations. Support from tax funds for a total of about 400 state-supported institutions is probably next, and funds from churches next.

The pattern of support determines the philosophy and facts of costs to students. Control and support through government channels, as in Europe, means government assumption of responsibility for students and their welfare, which includes charges to students. This brings these matters into the sphere of politics. Thus it is not coincidence that in every European country costs to students are held down by direct subsidy, sometimes to the point where charges are nominal. I would predict, incidentally, that these subsidies will eventually go down, but my only basis for prediction is that charges to students have been going up very rapidly in the United States, and that a repetition of this pattern in Europe seems to be not unlikely.

In the United States where there is no control through central government and no fixed policy of government support, there is no government assumption of responsibility for student costs. The principle is that the student pays part, ordinarily at least one-third, of the cost of instruction. Thus charges to students are high in the high-quality institutions where costs of instruction are high—and this is true even in tax-supported institutions. Where quality and costs are low, charges are low. The guide is not infallible. There are excellent institutions that charge very little to students, and poor ones that charge high fees. Provision for financial aid to students who cannot pay high fees is generous. Some of the money for such provision comes from gifts, some from tuition, almost none from government sources, save in certain states. On the other hand, government sources have been generous with loan funds.

The point of student employment is also of interest, and here I think we should recognize two varieties—the first in which the student studies full time and is employed part time, the second in which he studies part time and is employed full time.

In the United States the employed full-time student is not only very common, he is also encouraged. Students very often work even when there is no need for them to, simply because it is a custom, like wearing shoes, and to have worked one's way through college is a point of such pride that the number of claimants for this honor is considerably larger than the number who achieve it. So far as I know all universities and colleges aid and abet this custom. The employed part-time student is also very common. About one-fourth of all enrollments in higher education are of part-time students, most of them attending in the evening hours. The colleges and universities that offer these evening courses are not always our best, and they do not put their best teachers into these classrooms, but the effort that goes into these programs is impressive. These programs are in a sense the last resort. If all else fails, a student can always matriculate in an evening program. There are no scholarships, no amenities, no student life, but it is a path to education, and it is taken by hundreds of thousands.

In Europe the working student is becoming more and more common. The part-time student, taking evening classes for a degree, is almost unknown, and this I think is an instance of faculty opposition, rather than lack of demand or inability to provide the necessary programs at a respectable standard.

Another point of comparison between European and American education lies in the note I made at the beginning that there are 14 languages in Europe and one in the United States. This means that uncrowded colleges and universities in the West and South may draw off pressure from crowded colleges in the North and East. The results are on the whole good, even though there are problems of standards and sometimes of recognition of work completed. But, although there is an uncrowded university just across the channel at Caen, and others in Austria, I have heard no discussion of migration of English students to those institutions. The languages are only one form of regional difference tending to erect intellectual boundaries that are the same as regional boundaries. These differences, whatever they may be, do compartmentalize Europe. They cut up Europe's educational problems into a host of small problems, and they probably contribute to the free-floating anxiety about educational matters that one encounters in most Europeans.

Having now gone over some of the major generalities, it may be of interest to make some comparisons between a well-known American university, large and complex, but not one of the largest or most complex, and a well-known English university, also large and complex, but not the largest or most complex that might be chosen.

Michigan State University was founded in 1855 as Michigan Agricultural College. Its College of Engineering was added in 1885, the College of Home Economics in 1896, the College of Veterinary Medicine in 1909, and the College of Applied Science in 1921. The first break with its technical tradition came in 1924, with the formation of a liberal arts college. A graduate school was formed in 1930. In 1944 came the School of Business and Public Service; in 1952, the College of Education; and in 1955, the College of Communication Arts. Within this structure of schools there are programs in fine arts, nursing education, hotel and restaurant and institutional management, conservation, police administration, and the merchandising of lumber and building materials. There is also a graduate program in social work. There are officer-training units of the Army and the Air Force, in either of which male students may enroll for two years. There is a major electronic digital computer laboratory. A division of engineering research deals with fundamental engineering problems and conducts contract research when it can be integrated into the objectives of the university. The agricultural experiment station conducts research in agriculture with particular reference to Michigan problems and through the agricultural extension service is in constant touch with farmers all over the state. There is a university press, which publishes both trade and text books. The university has advisory missions in a number of countries in Asia, Africa, and South America.

Michigan State has more than 25,000 students, 20,000 of them undergraduates; 850 of them come from foreign countries. Four thousand degrees of various kinds were conferred in 1959. Between 1956 and 1961 the university conferred just over 800 doctoral degrees.

There are six trustees, each elected by the voters of Michigan for a six-year term. Tuition fees are $279 a year (three terms) for Michigan students, $750 for out-of-state students. Admission is based on graduation from an approved high school. Out-of-state students are required to take the College Board Scholastic Aptitude Test. About 80 percent of each entering class come from the top quarter of their class.

Subjects studied in high school must include three years of English and a total of seven years of study chosen from the fields of foreign languages, mathematics, science, and social studies. A typical pattern would be four years of language, two of mathematics, two of science, and two of social studies. In addition, a total of five high school years or units of study may be offered from agriculture, home economics, commercial or industrial studies, art, or music. In other words, entrance for a Michigan resident is not a particularly difficult problem.

The University of Manchester was founded in 1851 as Owen College, named after a Manchester merchant who bequeathed £96,000 for its founding. A medical college was united with it in 1852, and a faculty of technology in 1902. In 1958–59 it awarded degrees in arts, architecture, theology, music, economics, social studies, commerce, education, law, medicine, dentistry, pharmacy, and technology. It offers a diploma in nursing. Engineering includes paper technology and textile technology. In 1959, 114 doctoral degrees were awarded.

There are nearly 7,000 students, of whom just under 1,000 are graduate students and 511 from other countries. Fees are £56 a year for undergraduates. There is a university press. There are Army and Air Force officer-training programs.

Admission to the University of Manchester is based on a carefully administered program of examinations, which in turn follows completion of a secondary school program specifically directed toward university entrance.

The capsule description of these two universities underlines, I think, the similarities and differences of the two systems. It would be possible to fit the University of Manchester directly and comfortably into the American scene. Only part of Michigan State would be admissible to the European scene. The one is neat, careful, and precise, the other sprawling and untidy, offering services and opportunities that would be beyond the scope of any European university. Yet each represents a concept and the effort to fulfill it; neither can be dismissed because it fails to meet the differing concept.

---

*T*his paper was delivered to the Board in October 1962, a week after I returned from my two years in Europe. It is too long and too detailed for comment, except to say that it undertook to be a one-hour course in comparative education.

In terms essentially of what it undertook to teach, the paper was, and I think remains, of some importance to American universities. Our nation is involved in educational activities all over the world, and we must understand other systems and other philosophies if we are to hope for any valuable result from that involvement.

There is another problem. We have been belabored by eminent men extolling the virtues of the Russian, the German, and the English systems—men who have told us only one side of the story. They have pointed out the rigor, and the high standards, and the intellectual depth, and the educational polish those systems achieve. But they have not told us (if indeed they ever found it out themselves) that four out of five children never get any real chance to harvest these advantages. As Americans we have a right to these facts in making our judgment on the excellence of these systems.

The College Board's own movement toward active participation in international education has been under way for some years. I like to look forward to the day when the Board will itself extend such studies as this into other areas of international education, and will play an important role in developing those forms of international student movement which will open the best resources of all countries to the best students from all countries.

"Access to Education—A Global View"

A report of the International Study of University Admissions, delivered at the annual meeting of the College Entrance Examination Board, October 31, 1962. Published in somewhat altered form in the *College Board Review* No. 48, Fall 1962, pp. 7–15.

For the last two years a small staff, collaborating with a commission of experts from nine countries,[2] has been concerned with the problem of access to higher education—the broad question of who does or does not get into higher education, and how and why.

It was our hope that the International Study of University Admissions could identify the process by which admission and rejection take place, pick out the problems incidental to the operation of the process, trace the causes of these problems, and consider the elements of solutions to them. In this way we would be taking an important step toward helping the countries of the world meet the tremendous demand for educational opportunities which obviously looms in the immediate future.

The final report of this broad study in comparative education will deal with the admissions process, its operation, and its results in terms of the flow of students between the different segments of educational systems.

Supporting documents include detailed studies of admissions in 12 countries, plus a study of the effects upon enrollment in higher education of direct financial aid to students. The report is now undergoing its final revision and should go to press before the end of the year. It will appear as early as possible in 1963.[3]

In this study we have not tried to compare admissions standards from one country to another, nor have we tried to determine the equivalences between an Austrian *Abitur*, a French *Bachot*, an English General Certificate of Education, a Spanish *Bachillerato*, and graduation from a Brazilian

---

2. Brazil, Chile, France, Great Britain, India, Japan, Lebanon, the Soviet Union, and the United States.

3. Frank Bowles, *Access to Higher Education*. Two volumes. Paris: Unesco and the International Association of Universities, 1963, Vol. I, 212 pp.

ginásio. Such determinations make interesting exercises, but they are valuable only with respect to the students who cross national boundaries for their undergraduate or professional education. They are also a form of educational quicksand in which the study would have sunk without a trace if it had ventured onto it.

Nor were we concerned with trying to introduce the objective method of testing, the aptitude type of test, the procedures of early admissions or advanced placement, or the idea of associations like the College Board. On the whole, we encountered little interest in these American devices and confined ourselves to answering questions. Sometimes conversations shifted to such subjects as the use of admissions officers and guidance counselors, the encouragement of talented students, and the assessment of the abilities of individuals. These are new ideas in most countries, and we rarely had the opportunity to discuss them at length simply because there was no basis for common understanding. School and university men in most countries are not opposed to such ideas—they simply have no way of accommodating them within their educational frames of reference. I mention these things only to emphasize that this was an international study of admissions problems and not an effort to establish the American admissions pattern as a world standard. With respect to the work of the study, I can report as follows.

First, we agreed that an admissions process existed, and we identified its workings. Broadly speaking, the process begins when students complete primary school and enter upon a program of study which offers the possibility of admission to higher education. It ends with enrollment in higher education. I think, myself, that it does not end until the student has completed the first year of higher education, which means that this is really a prolonged test of a student's preparation and motivation. However, such a conclusion, even if valid, could not be established for more than a few countries, so it was dropped.

Two kinds of educational organizations

We actually found two forms of the admissions process, each implicit in a form of educational organization. In what may be termed the European system, secondary education proceeds in three parallel lines from the end of primary education. One line leads to the university and may be entered only by means of an examination taken some time between the ages of 10 and 12. The selection at this point is rigorous, its effect severe. In no country which follows this form of organization do as many as 20 percent of the age group pass the examination for the university line; in some it is as low as 2 percent. This select group is further reduced in the course of six or seven years of secondary school, with the result that about half drop out. There is then a final examination at the end of secondary school that is customarily passed by about two-thirds of those who still remain. These survivors are automatically eligible for university admission, and at least 80 percent of them actually enter a university. Certain faculties—usually medicine, science, and engineering—may require students to take additional examinations; but those who fail such examinations may still join the faculties of law, philosophy, and economics, which almost never require entrance examinations of applicants.

Under this system, from 1 to 8 percent of each age group enters higher education. Those who fail to enter the restricted secondary schools have lost their chance to enter any form of higher education. If they enter one of the other two lines of secondary education, they may go into technical schools or train to be primary school teachers. However, though the technical and teacher-training programs parallel the university preparatory program, they are not subject to the same requirements or standards. They do not prepare for university entrance or, indeed, for any form of higher education, since neither technical training nor the teaching of pedagogy is defined in the European system as higher education. One result of this is that the educational background and professional skills of primary school teachers and of technicians are much inferior to that of univeristy graduates, and their status is determined accordingly.

The European system of organization prevails in most of Europe, Africa, and Asia, and in all of South America.

The other kind of educational organization may conveniently be called the American one, though it happens that at least one example of it may be found on every continent except, paradoxically, South America.

In this system there is no examination for entrance to secondary schools, and all primary school graduates can move into a general secondary program. Students may be drawn out of this program into specialized courses —technical training and teacher training—or continue to the end. If, after finishing secondary school, they wish to enter higher education, they usually must take an entrance examination, since admission to a college or university is not automatic. In this system, from 70 to 90 percent of the students in each age group enter secondary school, and perhaps half of them drop out before completing it. About half of the secondary school graduates—that is, from 10 to 35 percent of those in the age group—continue on into higher education. The countries other than the United States which follow this form send between 15 and 20 percent of their students on to higher education, about twice the percentage that occurs under the European system.

Countries that follow the American system—though with marked differences in detail—are Australia, Canada, Japan, New Zealand, the Philippines, the Soviet Union, the Union of South Africa (with respect to the white population), and, of course, the United States. In most of these countries, teacher training and technical training are offered as higher education, and graduation from the general secondary course may be accepted as meeting the requirements for admission to any program of higher education, provided the student shows evidence of the requisite ability and preparation.

The two systems are so different in both organization and purpose that they almost demand comparison and discussion. But this is a report, not a dissertation, so I will limit the comparison to pointing out that the real difference between the systems lies not in the nature of the education they provide, for both systems deal with the common body of the world's knowledge, and both teach in the way men have always taught. The difference lies in the fact that one system eliminates most of its students and fully educates only those who survive, while the other retains all of its students as long as possible to give each one the opportunity to develop at the highest level possible for him. This is a very fundamental difference, and I would propose, in passing, that the College Board consider exploring it at more length in one of its colloquiums. But the subject must be left there for the moment.

World demand for education

Having established the existence of an admissions process and the fact that most of it takes place within secondary education, the study then went on to explore the nature and causes of admissions problems.

Fundamentally, these problems are caused by the fact that the present world demand for education is outstripping the present world supply of education. This applies not only to higher education, but to all levels and varieties of education. There is a great, unsatisfied demand for primary education in Asia, Africa, and South America. There is also a tremendous demand for open access to secondary and higher education in every continent of the world.

There are demands which are being met in some fashion in each region and in each country. But the very act of meeting these demands produces new demands. As primary education has been extended, and it is being extended rapidly, the demand for secondary education goes up, probably in a ratio of one place required in secondary education for every three places provided in primary school. And, as the demand for secondary education is met, there is an increased demand for higher education, in a ratio of not less than 1 place for every 10 places in secondary school. In other words, a change anywhere in an educational system produces change everywhere. And the changes are cumulative, having their ultimate effect on higher education. It is this fact, too often overlooked in educational planning, that underlies the present problems of admission to higher education and gives urgency to the search for solutions to them.

The causes of these demands need to be stated. In vastly oversimplified terms, the two principal causes are as follows. One is popular. Our ongoing world industrial revolution has in some manner touched nearly everyone in the world, and with that touch has established in each individual the conviction that education—any education—will better his or his family's lot. Hence, children are urged to acquire education beyond that which their fathers achieved; the pressure builds imperceptibly but steadily. The second cause is governmental. All governments, though some more than others, have realized the role that trained manpower plays in national development and have regarded education as something very like a form of civic duty that assures high rewards to those who are most dutiful. The need for education as a developmental tool coincides with the popular demand for education as a path to personal opportunity. Together they form a powerful force; therefore the demands are met. The result, as has been noted, is eventually to create other demands that will begin a new cycle in the future.

These demands are independent of population increases, but such increases guarantee even heavier pressures in the future. This is a particularly serious problem when, as in most South American and many African countries, the rate of increase in population is higher than the rate of increase in national income. A serious question then arises as to how educational expansion is to be paid for.

The reasons why there is not enough provision for education also need to be stated. Again resorting to oversimplification, they can be reduced to three: faulty estimates of requirements, delays for administrative and financial reasons, and direct opposition.

The first two are familiar enough to us all and need not be belabored further. The third—direct opposition to the expansion of education—is outside the experience of most of us. It is not, however, uncommon in many regions, particularly on the level of higher education. It takes one of two forms. The first is a refusal to bring new programs, such as teacher training and advanced technician training, into the established structure of higher education. A perfect example of this has been provided by the English universities, which refused categorically some years ago to assume responsibility for developing advanced technical training. When the colleges of advanced technology were founded outside the university structure, the universities agreed to recognize the colleges' diplomas as equivalent to university degrees, but would not extend degree-granting privileges to the new institutions. It now appears that the colleges of advanced technology will shortly be granting degrees, nearly a decade after the original discussions took place. But it will be a government, not a university, decision.

The second form is resistance to enlarging existing university programs. In part, this may be traced to the tradition that the professor alone has authority over the teaching of his subject. If an expanding enrollment means that the subject-matter area which he controls will be reduced by redefining the scope of his subject or that he will have to share his authority with a new appointee, the professor will resist. The strength of this opposition may be estimated from the fact that while university enrollments in Western Europe have risen by nearly 50 percent over the last decade, only eight university institutions have been founded in that region. Four of these are in England, with two only on paper at the end of the decade. The increase obviously has been taken care of by the existing institutions.

In part, too, the opposition may be traced to a desire to safeguard professional status. Examples of this may be cited from South America, where there are virtually no full-time university professors, since all faculty members are also practicing professionals. The very low rate of increase in South American university enrollments is strong testimony to the care with which these faculties guard against any uncontrolled influx of practitioners into the professions they represent. University enrollments, incidentally, are increasing more slowly in South America than they are anywhere else in the world.

Restrictions in numbers of students

The problems that have developed within the admissions process as a result of the imbalance between supply and demand can best be illustrated by three sets of examples. The first deals with restrictions in numbers of students. Such restrictions are, in fact, eliminations. There is nothing selective about them, except that they are accomplished through a series of examinations based on much the same subject matter; the examinations are usually taken a year apart for two or three years. The survivors continue on to complete higher education, but the rate of elimination is high. In France, where about one-fourth of the primary school graduates enter the lycée to prepare for university entrance, 60 percent of the students fail the first *baccalaureat*, which comes after six years of schooling. Of the survivors, only about 25 percent fail the second, which comes a year later. Of those survivors, 80 percent enter the university or one of the *grandes écoles*; but of this 80 percent more than half fail to complete any academic credential, even after surmounting all the barriers to the universities. It is presumed that these figures are typical of most European countries, although the statistics on examination failures are not known.

Parenthetically, it may be noted that European university enrollments continue to grow, despite these eliminations, because more students are completing secondary school and thereby becoming eligible for higher education. A still larger enrollment increase is expected in France as a result of eliminating the entrance examination for secondary school.

Another form of elimination is apparent in Brazil, Chile, and Japan. In these countries, over half the students who apply for admission to higher education in any particular year have already applied at least once before;

it is commonplace for students to apply annually for as many as five or six years. In fact, careful studies in Chile have shown that a student may expect to be admitted if he keeps trying regularly for six years. In all three countries a regular industry of coaching for examinations has grown up within what is, in effect, an unrecognized system of private coaching schools. Students are drilled on past examinations and probable questions on the new ones, with the objective of improving their grades enough to get them over the passing line. But the competition is so severe that successful students often find themselves overprepared for the work of their first university year and pay little or no attention to it.

The eliminations are interesting to an observer because no one pretends that the students who survive are any better than those who were eliminated, nor that the passing of the examinations means that they will succeed in university work, nor even that the repeated examinations serve any important educational purpose. But they continue, nevertheless, for a combination of reasons. For one thing, facilities are inadequate to accommodate all the candidates for higher education and many of them *must* be eliminated. For another, the failure rate has remained constant for many years in most European countries and is now maintained in the name of "standards." And finally, the students have no alternatives.

There are no alternatives because the university line leads to the only higher education there is; if it is not entered, there is nothing else. There is no range of institutions to enter, no diversity which provides a wide variety of programs at several different entrance standards, as in the United States or the Soviet Union. Nor are there evening programs or junior colleges to provide a way of improving a mediocre record.

Those who succeed in the European system become members of a privileged elite. Those who fail at any point have nothing to show for their pains. And those who pursue the other types of opportunity available will find that these opportunities are illusory and that they can hardly achieve more than a rudimentary qualification.

Problems in underdeveloped lands

Another, very different, problem of elimination exists in underdeveloped countries. Senegal is offered as an example, since it has the characteristics of an underdeveloped country in almost every respect, except that it possesses a coherently organized school system and produces good statistics. In Senegal, about 25 percent of the school-age children are in school. The drop-out rate is high—one student completes six years of primary school for every three who begin it—and, furthermore, each child will probably have taken at least seven years to complete the six-year program. Ministry of Education studies show that out of every 1,000 students who enter primary school, 620 fail the leaving examination at the end of it, 60 more fail but are permitted to repeat the last year, and 320 pass. After these survivors take still another examination, 263 of them may be admitted either to the lycée for university preparation or to a teacher-training school to prepare for primary school teaching. Not more than 2 percent of each age group enters secondary school.

Of the 263, 50 will finish the lycée, and of these finishers 25, or about .2 percent of the age group, will receive a university qualification. Another group of 28 will earn diplomas within secondary education as either teachers or technicians. This latter figure will be higher within a few years, for development of teacher training and technical training at the secondary level is being pressed.

The situation in Senegal is, if anything, better than in most underdeveloped countries, where illiteracy rates are high and opportunity is limited. An observer's attention is drawn to the low rate of entry into secondary school, but this is not the important point. What matters more is the attrition among those students who do manage to enter secondary school. The eliminations up to that point have been so severe that the remaining students should be capable of doing work of good quality. In fact, only about one-fourth of them finish secondary school, and only one-tenth complete university work.

The same pattern can be seen in the other African countries, in India, and in South America. They mean simply that the standards of secondary education and of university education are too high for 90 percent of the primary school pupils. This is a point to be pondered well by those who interest themselves in the expansion of higher education in underdeveloped countries without examining the substructure on which it rests. It means not only that the cost of educating each university graduate in such countries is astronomical, but that the human effort wasted in the process is truly wasted. Those who fail have nothing—or almost nothing—to show for their time, since in these programs there is no alternative to the university line. Those who have shown themselves capable of meeting only a modest standard have been eliminated, because no modest standard has been set. There is not even the alternative of seeking teacher training or basic technical training, for the development of these programs has barely begun. The problem is that attention has been focused on the development of an educated class, which will view itself as an elite, without any provision for the development of supporting cadres. One of my reactions was regret at the failure on the part of every agency—national and international—to plan education for underdeveloped countries in terms of the needs and resources of the countries, rather than in terms of European or American patterns.

Choice of program

The second set of problems is posed by program choices. These are difficult problems, for most countries need scientists, engineers, doctors, teachers, and technicians, yet find that their output in these fields is far below their requirements.

An examination of the way career choices are determined in Egypt offers an unusually clear view of the problems involved. Under the present regime, a determined and, on the whole, successful effort has been made to expand education at all levels. Universal primary education has been practically achieved, there is substantial secondary school opportunity—including trade and technical schools—and university education has been greatly expanded. University admission in Egypt has been simplified and streamlined. The secondary-school-leaving examination is also the university entrance examination, and students are ranked according to their performance on it. All applications for admission are made to a central office, and the decisions of the office are final as to the institution and the program to which students are admitted. Unsuccessful applicants may not reapply.

High-ranking students are permitted their choice of programs, including medicine, engineering, or science. Lower-ranking students are admitted only to the theoretical faculties, such as law, economics, commerce, and letters. Pedagogy is recognized as a university subject and is among the theoretical faculties. When the quotas have been reached admission is closed, except that lower-ranking students may be admitted to the theoretical faculties as external students, on condition that they do not come to class or otherwise frequent the university. Their only privilege is that of taking the examinations. If they continue to pass, they eventually receive a degree. At Egyptian universities, unlike European ones, students are not permitted to remain in perpetual attendance without completing any work. They are expected to take examinations, and if they fail they are dropped.

About half the candidates in each year cannot be admitted, and, of course, cannot reapply. The government has now begun to establish a number of technical institutes which students who fail of university admission may enter; here they can prepare for teaching and work in advanced technology.

The program is coherent and better organized than in most countries, and for that reason highlights the problems of career choice. The scientific faculties, with their limited enrollments, are open only to the best students, who are not necessarily the students most interested in those fields. The professions that call for students with the highest ability and the highest motivation do not necessarily receive them, although they do get those who rank highest; these faculties probably have the highest completion rate of any in the university. However, considering the methods of admission and the length and difficulty of the program, it is hard to believe that the completion statistics, if revealed, would be much better than 50 percent. This means that the universities' most valuable facilities and their best students are being used ineffectively.

When the scientific faculties are filled, students, regardless of their interests and abilities, must go into the theoretical faculties, which carry very large enrollments. The professions for which those faculties prepare already suffer from mass unemployment and offer only a small chance of a professional career, so that government service becomes, de facto, the occupation for which most students are preparing.

The device of admitting "external students" is an ingenious one and lightens the pressure for expansion of the universities. But it cheapens the reputation of the theoretical faculties and crowds their facilities, since the external students do not, of course, abide by the requirement that they do not attend classes. Providing technical institutes as a refuge for those who fail of university admission is educationally desirable, but the manner in which they were provided and their entrance procedures stigmatize teacher training and technical training as inferior programs leading to inferior occupations.

The scale of values revealed by the Egyptian pattern is common to all countries that use the European system and also in countries that, like Japan and South Africa, have some of the characteristics of the American system. The conclusion that may be drawn is that all programs of higher education must be established with the same standards of full equality as to entrance requirements and terms of admission, if they are to draw students of equivalent quality and preparation and to enjoy comparable esteem in the public view. Programs not so established will, apparently inevitably, attract inferior students and will produce graduates who cannot command the respect, position, or incomes of university graduates.

A subsidiary problem with respect to career choices turns on the question of student guidance, about which it is only necessary to say that it is an almost meaningless phrase in most countries. It is officially a part of the French educational system in the form of two *cycles d'orientation* within the secondary schools, and it is recognized in England in the person of the "Careers Master," who is occasionally—and increasingly—found in the grammar schools. Otherwise, the concept and purpose of guidance appears to be unknown.

The American system

Having for most of this report discussed the European system of education, which is operative in most countries of the world, it is time to talk about what I have called the American form of organization, which is very similar to what the Soviets call the Soviet form of organization. This operates in only six or seven countries, but it touches more than half of the world's students in higher education.

Technically, one of the two important differences between the two systems lies in freedom of access to secondary education. This is unhindered in the American form and is related to the fact that all students, regardless of final objectives, follow general courses with certain standard features for at least part of the secondary school. The other important difference lies in the fact that the final secondary school examination does not establish an automatic qualification for university entrance as in the European system, but that decisions on a student's admission to higher education are made individually.

Aside from these two important points, which hold for all countries following this form of organization, there are major differences between the countries. Japan, Australia, New Zealand, and the Union of South Africa all introduce, during the last two years of secondary school, an examination which is, in effect though not in name, a preuniversity qualification. This reduces the university applications considerably. In the Soviet system, a major shift takes place at just the midpoint of secondary school, in which about half of the pupils withdraw to enter technical schools, or the so-called labor reserve schools, which offer a minimum on-the-job technical training program.

Another difference is in the form of higher education available. The Soviet Union and the United States stress diversity, breadth of choice, and the existence of programs suited to the individual's circumstances. None of the other countries following this pattern offer such diversity, and in most of them technical training and teacher training are dealt with as a form of higher secondary school work, perhaps overlapping higher education in a chronological sense, though not in an intellectual one. Much of the Soviet Union's diversity and a very substantial part of her huge enrollment in higher education—actually given by Soviet sources as 43 percent—come out of the practice of three parallel versions of the same program in the same institution, each with its own admissions standard. The day program has the highest standard of admissions and admits the smallest number of students. The evening programs, with a somewhat lower standard, come next; and last comes the correspondence program, the largest and with the lowest standard. The correspondence course represents the ultimate in freedom of opportunity: it is expected that 50 percent of those who enter will not complete, as against only 5 percent for the day course. The correspondence course, incidentally, brings students in for laboratory work and examinations during their vacation periods.

Entrance examinations constitute another major difference. The United States and to some extent Canada are the only ones making use of objective examinations, though both Australia and New Zealand are experimenting with them. The Soviet Union and Japan handle all entrance examinations on an institutional basis. In the Soviet Union this is carried to the extent of having the institution also operate a preparatory school specifically for the examinations it gives. In Japan entrance examinations are very profitable to the institutions and appear to be deliberately arranged so that students may expect to fail them the first time and have to go through a year's tutoring before reapplying.

Costs of higher education vary widely from one country to another. In the Soviet Union, at one extreme, all students are employees of the state and receive a salary, basically small, but graded according to accomplishment and seniority. At the other extreme, the United States expects, with a few exceptions, its students to contribute toward the cost of their education. Sometimes the contributions are high. Japan, Canada, and the Philippines have a mixture of tuition-charging and state-supported, virtually free institutions; Australia, New Zealand, and South Africa have state-supported institutions only. South Africa offers free education to the Bantus, but under heavy restrictions which make it a completely different system from the one that operates for the white students.

A final point of similarity. The countries that follow the American system differ widely in the formation of their economies and national modes of livelihood, but are similar in two respects: in none of the countries are the educational systems engaged in supporting an established elite, and in all of them superior training and ability command a premium in the employment market.

However, similarities and differences of form aside, the feature that differentiates the American and the European forms of education is the extraordinary sense of freedom and movement that pervades the American system, contrasted with the relative immobility and rather stern aspect that characterizes the European system. This, in a rather special way, is particularly true in Russia, where each educational achievement opens a door to another opportunity. This is not unique to Soviet education, except in the sense that it is fully administered by the state, but the complexity and number of these opportunities—*passarelles*, as they are called in French—is extraordinary. It is easy to accept and value the European concern with scholarship and continuity of system and method, easy to understand their approach to evaluation of any other system and their suspicion, even fear, of systems that appear to be moving inexorably toward universal higher education, a phrase that, within the European system, is a self-contradiction.

There are many other things I could say about the items turned up in the course of the study, but they can wait for the final report. I believe, however, that it is important to emphasize one conclusion—that most admissions problems have their root in failure to provide educational opportunity. In all fairness, it must be recognized that the demand for opportunity is recent, but it is clear that it is not being met as it should be and ironical that much of the failure to meet it is justified in the name of educational standards. There is no doubt, too, that much can be done technically and administratively to ease the admissions process. There are no serious problems involved in such actions, given willingness to undertake them.

Questions about American education

In a broad sense, the question that has recurred to me the most frequently is: "Why can't our secondary schools carry our pupils as far as European secondary schools carry their pupils?"

I know some of the answers. American schooling extends over 12 years; European over 13—except for Russian, which lasts for 11. American schooling is not based on the principle of elimination by competitive examination; European schooling is. American student bodies are not homogeneous, hence they are more difficult to move at a steady pace. The European student bodies are homogeneous.

These are all true statements, but none of them answers the question. One answer that I have heard is that European students go to school more hours, more weeks, more months. This is a myth. European school days begin at 8:30 a.m. and run to 5 p.m., but they include two hours for lunch. European schools are open on Saturday, but they are closed on Thursdays. The school year runs into July, but it opens in October. Pupils carry more subjects than American pupils, but for fewer hours a week, and for more years. There are no explanations in these differences.

Some differences do appear significant. American primary school teachers are better educated than European primary school teachers. They have been trained through higher education for the last 20 years. Movement in the same direction began some time ago in the Soviet Union and has recently been completed in England, but otherwise European primary school teachers are trained at the secondary level, with a possibility of further specialized training after some years of experience.

European secondary school teachers are better educated than American secondary school teachers. They have gone farther in their subject, know its relationships with other subjects, teach their subject as if the student were going to specialize in it. Secondary school teaching is on a continuum with university teaching in Europe; it follows the same methods, which are, in the main, different from ours.

But none of these points answers my question. I conclude that the answer is deceptively simple: more is expected of a European student than is expected of an American student. This is more a hypothesis than an answer, but it presents the following line of thought for exploration.

In the European form of organization, the secondary school preparing for the university has no other function than preparation, and, incidentally, the elimination of the unsuccessful. The American secondary school has a multiple function. Yet, in fact, the European school has not changed, while the American has, for the goal of the American school has, within the last 20 years, become preparation for higher education. Yet there is no general acknowledgment of this, and it does not show up in either the common program of studies in American secondary schools or in the expectation of accomplishment that is presented to the students. The end point of the line of thought is a proposition that can be put in the form of a question: "Is it not time for a new appraisal of the level of achievement that can reasonably be expected of American students?"

There are two elements in such an appraisal: first, what the schools can offer, and second, what the colleges can accommodate. Our own experience within the Board during the last 10 years has already raised this point. The Advanced Placement Program has shown that schools can teach, and pupils can learn, at a level beyond present normal expectations. It has also presented colleges with a difficult problem in accommodating the results of such teaching and learning. I think it is fair to say that no college has yet worked out a truly satisfactory method—satisfactory, that is, in an intellectual sense—of working with the Advanced Placement Program. The arrangements have, it is true, often been well handled, but they have been administrative arrangements for exceptional students. If we assume, and I think we can, that what we have learned from the Advanced Placement Program can be applied much more broadly, then we come squarely against the problem of what to do with a massive change in achievement and expectation. The problem can be dealt with piecemeal, or it can be examined as a whole. I suggest that this is the first matter to come out of this study that requires our attention.

A second matter is the shift in the economic balance. It does not take much examination of the operations of other educational systems to establish the conclusion that the ease of access to American higher education is based on a remarkably complicated financial operation. The complexity of this operation reflects the complexity of our financial operation as a nation, and its success depends on the continuing success of the national operation.

It does not require much observation to produce questions on the future of our financial operations as a nation. The success we now enjoy has been built on 60 years of industrial expansion and enjoyment of great freedom of distribution throughout the world. The question of whether this will continue is troublesome, particularly to anyone who has lived for two years within the embrace of the European Common Market. American goods on shelves are increasingly rare in Europe. The massive road building equipment on the European roads is painted yellow like ours and the new tractors on the farms are red like ours, but their nameplates are from unfamiliar European cities. In the developing countries one comes to a similar feeling—the only thing that appears to have come from America is money.

If these impressions prove in time to have some validity, there will be a change in the rate of the flow of money. In such case, there will be repercussions on our education. Specifically, the part of the present enrollment that is financially marginal—and no one knows how large it is—will either change its method of support or disappear. This leads to another proposition in the form of a question: "Is it not time to examine the relationships between enrollments and the various sources of income for our colleges, and to project the consequences of major shifts in income sources such as might arise if our nation is forced into a major readjustment to world markets?"

The problem is a complicated one, and I hesitated to present it. Nevertheless, I find it hard to accept the assumption that the major problems of educational finance have been solved and suggest that at least an inquiry should be made into some of the alternatives that may have to be faced.

What the Board can do

The two propositions that have been presented are both very broad, and it is not certain that either can be studied in the conventional sense of the word. Certainly, neither can be acted upon as a proposal without a good deal of preparation.

There are, however, three specific matters that the Board may wish to consider at some time in the future.

The first is the construction of a Spanish version of the Scholastic Aptitude Test. The uses of such a test for American admissions officers in judging the potentialities of applicants from Latin America have been obvious for some time, but it has also been obvious that such a market was not large enough to support a test. Several years ago, discussions with the University of Puerto Rico ended on a note of uncertainty, which shelved the matter pending further developments. During the last two years there have been signs of receptiveness for a Spanish SAT for use in connection with admission to several major Latin American universities, signs promising enough so that Adolfo Fortier, professor at the University of Puerto Rico, was asked to study the problem at first hand. His findings, which will be reported to the College Board trustees in December, are cautious, as indeed they should be, but indicate the feasibility of an experiment that, under favorable conditions, should become self-supporting within a reasonable time. I have put the matter in these generalities because I, too, have talked with many Latin American educators and am well aware of the gap between their enthusiasms, which are quick and exciting, and the actual results, which may well be disappointing. Nevertheless, it is now clear that such a test, if made, would be the basis of a series of validity studies that would involve approximately 10,000 candidates, and this indicates a promising outlook. The questions now turn on the cost and financing of an experiment, and these, we expect, can be reported to the Board during the coming year, with recommendations as to action.

The second specific matter is a direct product of the study on which I have been engaged, in that it comes through the initiative of Constantine Zurayk, of the American University of Beirut, who served with distinction as the chairman of the Commission of Experts for the study. Reduced to essentials, it is a request to adapt the Board's Advanced Placement Program for the purposes of establishing an academic credential which will be accepted as the equivalent of the *baccalaureat*, which is the standard university entrance credential in the Middle East. The problems in this case are not educational or financial, but are matters of Board policy. As we all know, the Board has never issued an equivalency credential, but has always insisted that the interpretation of Board reports was an institutional prerogative. This request, in effect, is that the Board, in supporting the major American institution in the Middle East, issue a credential with an interpretation attached, which is the practice followed by the University of London through its examining board, or by the French government with respect to the *baccalaureat*. There is no question that the possibilities are interesting, and I record my own hope that we will find a way to comply with the request.

The third matter is one that has been urged on me a number of times during the last two years by educators from several countries, who have suggested the need for a central clearinghouse to deal with foreign student applications to American institutions. It was with considerable surprise that I saw a strong hint along the same lines in the report of the Board's Special Committee on Foreign Students.

This is a most interesting idea, but also one that presents many difficulties, including that of resolving the interests of the many American agencies and institutions now concerned with fragments of this problem. At the moment, I can only urge that it be given careful thought, for there are many questions to be answered before any proposals can be considered.

This has been a long report, covering much territory, and, even so, there is much left unsaid. In closing it, I have only two summary points to make.

First, we are well satisfied, in the main, with our educational system and proud of the opportunities it offers. But, unless the achievements we demand are equal to the opportunities we offer, we are vulnerable within our pride. It is time we look to the proofs.

Second, we are committed, more than most of us have realized, to the world adventure of education. It is a costly commitment and endless, but it is the best of our hopes. What knowledge we have, what resources we have, must go into that commitment, for if it is not fulfilled we shall have no occasion to use them elsewhere.

This paper was an effort to present a dispassionate view of the problems of Southern education as seen from the outside. There is no need to expatiate on the point that the South has been dominated by educational feudalism; it is sufficiently covered in the paper. Yet it is worth emphasis because there are so few people who ever take time or indeed, have the opportunity, to view Southern education with any genuine detachment.

The real point of emphasis lies in the immense amount of work that will need to be done to bring the South's educational system up to the standard the South really needs. The years of sectarian control, of parsimony, of limited opportunity, and of maintenance of a strict duality have been terribly costly in terms of an educational system that is probably unprepared for the requirements of the last third of the twentieth century. There is a great deal to be done, and much of it comes within the particular competence of the College Board.

As far as I know, none of the actions suggested in the final paragraph of this paper was ever taken.

"Some Problems of Southern Education" Speech at Georgia Association of Colleges, Atlanta, Georgia, August 18, 1963.

I take it that your generosity in bringing a man from a distance, from another educational background, and from another branch of the profession means that you are interested in what we might call an outsider's view of inside problems. You would be too polite to use the word "outsider," but that is what I am, so let us accept it. I am, perhaps, more of an outsider for having spent about 28 of the last 36 months outside the United States, trying to identify, describe, and analyze problems of access to higher education. I accepted that assignment, three years ago, partly from a congenital taste for travel, and partly because I felt it necessary to get a detached view of American education in order to understand the functioning of my own peculiar organization—the College Entrance Examination Board. This experience of detachment, in a sense, terminated about three weeks ago in Paris, when I read the proofs on my report, and this is my first effort since my final reattachment to American education.

I want to direct this effort toward a discussion of the problems of American education and, particularly, education in the South, as viewed from where I have been sitting. Some of you heard me talk last spring in a rather Olympian way about some of these matters, with the stress laid on problems in other countries. I want to talk about our own country today, with perhaps a few illustrations drawn from other countries, and, above all, I want to avoid Olympianism. I hope my remarks will open out into a general discussion, and, as we know, it has always been difficult to discuss matters with the Olympians.

The central problem for all of education in the United States, as I see it, is how to respond to the large new wave of demand for access to higher education, which comes on top of our already monumental establishment. I do not think there is any doubt that such a wave has gotten into motion fairly recently. The percentage of the age group formally enrolling in college continues to rise. It is now at about 35 percent, which is, of course, very high and already above what some consider a reasonable level. But it shows signs of increasing, particularly in the area of terminal and occupational programs. Then, in addition, there is a whole peripheral area of education, having to do with television, radio, film, tape, and even such old-fashioned items as books, that is generating marked activity and is certainly a form of educational demand. We have discovered this at the College Board. Our Advanced Placement Program, which was originally begun to encourage high schools to go beyond the regular curriculum, has become the darling of educational orators all across the land just because it does go beyond regular programs and because it stands for the idea of an examination on which college credit can be given. A television program of Advanced Placement courses in American history and advanced mathematics has been such a success this summer in the New York area that it has been on the air 12 hours a day. Because of our experience with this idea of credit by examination, we have had requests three times during 10 months to embark on a complete program of examinations for the awarding of college credit on the basis of knowledge gained through some one of the new channels of mass communication, and it has been made clear that at least $1 million would be made available to start such a program.

I think these items are strong evidence that a demand for a new kind of higher education is in the making. I think it is a demand that is going to prove to be very important in a sociological sense, for I believe it represents the opening of effort, on the part of the lower class, or, if you like, the working class, to enter higher education. This may seem an odd statement to make in America, where we aren't supposed to have a lower class as such. But we do, and one of its distinguishing characteristics is that lower-class children drop out of school as early as possible. They receive poor schooling, but this is another issue and a speech or paper for another day. It has also always been an article of faith that lower-class children, if they existed, could enter higher education if they wished. So they could, and some did, but not many. Now I think there has been a change, and this group of children is commencing to enter higher education. In so doing, they are going to change the nature of our institutions and of our own jobs.

I believe, too, that here in the South you have received the first really heavy impact of this new wave.

I want to come back to this wave for further discussion, but, first, I want to digress to say that this demand for access to higher education is not just an American phenomenon. It is worldwide, and this fact, I think, is important enough to warrant a good look at it.

The United States has what I would call an open system of education. It is based on a single track for all pupils and, theoretically at least, a single standard. It has been open for a long time, and, despite some inequities and blocks, it has provided a great deal of educational opportunity. As a result, we have a very large enrollment in both secondary and higher education. Russia has an open system. Not quite so open, and not open for so long. Nevertheless, it provides a good deal of opportunity and is trying hard to expand. The socialist states in Eastern Europe have adopted a limited version of the Russian open system, but it has made only slow progress. Some of the Asian countries have gone to the concept of the open system and are having a difficult time because they have not opened it all the way to higher education. Communist China has gone farthest and apparently has created the same chaos in her education that the Russian Revolution created in Russia during the twenties. The Chinese have found that opening up a system before the populace as a whole is ready for it can also cause problems. Particularly, they have found that students were so eager to get employment, presumably because of meager living conditions, that they did not enter universities in sufficient numbers. Therefore, all high school graduates are now required to enter universities.

Everyone else has a closed system. It is what I call educational feudalism. Less dramatically, it is a dual-track and dual-standard system with one kind of education for the lower class and another for the upper class. I use the word "feudalism" because it denotes a way of life mainly in the past in which destiny was foretold by birth, and in which the entire resources of the society were concentrated to support a shining establishment at the top. The shining establishment might have been very bright, and sometimes was, in the past. In an educational sense, it sometimes is now. But it lived, and in some places still lives, for itself. Its luster is not reflected downward. Educational feudalism means educational placement in which the individual does not participate. This does not mean that the individual has no chance to rise. The chances are there, but they are controlled from above. A French attack on the French system of education written about 10 years ago described the dual track in essentially Marxist terms as offering classical education to the bourgeoisie, with the chance to go to the university, while limiting the lower class to a primary education with no chance to go to a university. This was not quite true, but near enough.

The difference between the two concepts in terms of the amount of education that is actually made available and used is, of course, tremendous. The open system enrolls 20 percent or more of the eligibles in higher education and 50 percent or more in secondary education. The closed system enrolls 5 percent, more or less, of the eligibles in higher education and 20 percent in secondary education.

It is obvious in a closed system that access to educational opportunity is one of the evident points of difference between the lower and the upper classes. From this it follows that when the possibility of social mobility arises, one of the very first points of attack on a social system, when it is mounted by the lower class, is on the educational part of the system.

However, it is never the first point. First, it is necessary to break down what I call the "working class syndrome." We all know what this syndrome is—the disgruntled post-office clerk, or filling station operator, or taxi driver, stuck for life in a dull occupation, who sees the world as a conspiracy in which he is the central object, doomed by the conspiracy never to rise. And he sees all like him doomed, so that it is never any use for him or his fellows to try to rise. Hence he sees no use in education, and his children drop out of school and grow up angry, as he is.

This was not an uncommon point of view in America during the 1920s and the 1930s, but we have not heard it vocalized for some years, although I suspect that it still is a basic philosophy for many. However, in Europe it has been strong for many years and has been the underlying reason for the existence of labor parties in every European country. Their theory, of course, was that the struggle for human rights and opportunities had to be fought out in the political arena, and, in general, that is where it was so fought in Europe. In other parts of the world it is still a strong philosophy, and, as an occasional observer, I must say I find it hard to disagree, in such countries as India, Brazil, and Venezeula, with those who hold it.

Theoretically, of course, the reason for the worker's syndrome has been banished long since, with national constitutions guaranteeing political and educational equality. Theoretically, yes, but in fact, no. It was not the political phrases that began to break down the syndrome but industrialization, which, by creating new work opportunities and new forms of consumption, brought change to the two most stagnant areas of the economy, which were also the two most stagnant areas of the social structure. These were the subsistence farmer and the unskilled industrial worker. Once the hopelessness of their outlook was broken, a whole sequence of changes could follow.

One of the very first steps in the breakdown was the rationalization of agriculture. This brought machinery and science to the farm and produced a tremendous increase in farm production. It freed a good deal of farm labor and retired a good deal of marginal land. Those who could leave the farm did so and went into industry, providing for many years a continuous augmentation to the labor force and the supply of cheap labor that could support industrial expansion. Often they left the old people behind them, and some areas became a kind of subsistence concentration camp for old farmers—noticeably true in some areas of Europe today. But the very separation of the old and young contributed to change for the young. At the same time, the increased plenty of food made life in the industrial concentrations easier.

The second and the more important step was the spread of industrialization to the point at which it changed the job and the job requirements of even the lowest-paid workers. With this change came rising wages, rising standards of living, and the time when the working class began to acquire some of the same living standards as the upper class. With these achievements came the realization that mobility has also an intellectual dimension and that this dimension can be measured out only during the years of youth.

Following the realization that education was one of the markers on the path to security and status, the increasing demand for education was accompanied by several imperatives of change. In those countries where educational feudalism held its power, the first necessity was to break its stronghold—which was in the dual system. But the dual system, under control of the upper classes, did not break easily. Schools expanded only slowly, and, as numbers of candidates rose, the numbers failing the selection examinations rose in proportion. Financial barriers such as books and fees in the classical secondary schools, which might have been nominal for the upper class, were real for the lower class. Attempts to open secondary education, so that the way to higher education could be cleared for all students who might show the ability to achieve it, moved slowly, and finally the struggle was shifted from the educational to the political arena. Here there has been more success. Fifteen years ago, England was the only European country that had recognized the need for even a limited version of universal secondary education, and, at the same time, made provision for aiding talented students to enter higher education, regardless of financial need. Today this recognition is actual, or is pending, in the legislation of every European country. Some countries are slower than others, but all are moving.

In England the movement under political impetus resulted in one of the most remarkable turnabouts of modern times. One week the government announced that there were *no* plans to establish new universities or to enlarge university enrollments, since there was no need to do so. The next week, after a huge political uproar, the government announced that seven new universities had been approved, and plans for their opening were launched immediately. It is true that two years later only one, the University of Sussex, had opened its doors and that it had only 50 students. Nevertheless, the political importance must be noted, and, of course, the other universities will open.

I have digressed to talk about educational change in other countries for two reasons. First, I wanted to establish the common causes of change and the parallelism of the actions. It is true that the time schedules are different. The changes that opened up secondary education in Europe within the last 10 years took place in the United States many years ago. We went through the democratization of our secondary schools during the 1930s and have already achieved what is now painfully under way in Europe. We have actually achieved substantial democratization of higher education before it has even been thought of in most countries. But it is of interest to note that here, as everywhere else where these things have happened, there has been political action at the base.

It was this opening up of American secondary education during the 1930s that, more than any other factor, produced the tremendous enrollment in higher education we have today. The results of it came 10 years later in the veterans' rush. Those who, like me, lived through the problems of that rush as administrative officers can still remember our continuing surprise at the intensity of the demand for higher education on the part of people who had obviously never thought about the matter before they entered military service. But these people could not even have gotten near their goals if they had not started toward them by attending high school.

Now the results of this rush of 20 years ago are, in their turn, producing a tremendous increase in demand for graduate and advanced professional education. However, that is still well in the future, and we are concerned with the present.

The second point I want to make is that it is the driving force of industrialization that underlies the change. This, I think, is as true in the United States as it is anywhere else, and this is of fundamental importance in viewing current problems in American education.

The current problems arise from the fact that a new order of demand appears to be coming upon American education. I am using the word "new" in a context in which I recognize three levels or types of demand for higher education. The first level is best seen in our higher education as it was about the time when I finished college in 1928. People went to college then to prepare for one of several things: practice law or medicine, become an engineer, become a preacher or a teacher, or age in a genteel fashion before going into business. With some modifications, these objectives held true for American colleges as late as the outbreak of the war.

The second level came into view in the early 1950s, when students began to search for, and institutions began to supply, additional education on both ends of the spectrum of higher education. At one end, a whole group of technological programs was developed to train technicians and specialists in a variety of fields, augmentations to what the planning jargon now calls the "third sector" of the economy, or the service force. This was a major augmentation and automatically doubled the scope and the size of our higher education.

At the other end of the scale, additional education began to be demanded in the research, higher professional, and scholarly areas. The whole of our scientific development today is so large that it could not possibly have been supported by the prewar system of graduate education. In fact, it is for the most part being supported today by the products of the postwar system, even though simple arithmetic reveals that very few of the postwar products can yet be 40 years old. This augmentation has been very costly and very extensive, and it has probably, in itself, contributed to doubling the cost of our higher education.

Augmentation in numbers has been considerable, but nothing like as large as the augmentation at the other end of the spectrum. In other words, to offer a sweeping oversimplification, during the 1950s we doubled the size of our higher education by adding new programs, and we doubled the cost by adding new depth to the programs we already had, particularly in science and research.

Now we are facing a third level in which the demand comes out of very complex factors that cannot be dealt with simply on the curriculum level. It comes in part from the fact that industrialization sets up job requirements for even the lowliest workers and that these requirements call for skills and maturity that are ordinarily beyond the achievement of a high school graduate. This means that students are virtually required to stay on in school and that higher education may therefore be, and in fact is, accepting students who would rather not be in school, who have nothing in particular that they would like to study, and who often are below the ability levels ordinarily expected of students in higher education.

But there is another part to the demand. This is the part in which education is to some extent a necessity and to some extent a symbol. This is the part in which the problems of race appear. This is the part in which the struggle has left the level of educational action to enter the political arena and in which political action is forcing changes that educational institutions have, for many reasons, been unable or unwilling to make on their own initiative.

The parallelism between what is happening in Europe today, in forcing open the institutions of higher education so that they can be entered by children from the working class, and the political actions that are forcing integration on Southern institutions is too clear to be ignored. In both cases, the action is essentially an attack on a dual school system and a dual standard. In both cases, the attack has tremendous political implications. In both cases, the motivating force is a drive for social mobility and equality of opportunity. And in both cases, the underlying and still largely concealed factor in the change is the base from which it started—a base of industrial and economic change working its way down through the levels of the labor force until at last every social stratum is moved and every established social value has been in some sense altered.

This problem of educational change for the South is a large one, and difficult. The South has three aspects of change with which it must deal, while most of the rest of the nation has only one.

I remarked a few paragraphs ago that the educational change taking place immediately after the war took the form of adding technological programs and graduate programs to the existing basic program of higher education. These additions took place in the South as in other parts of the country, but I believe that no one in this company would disagree with the statement that they have progressed more slowly in the South than in other parts of the country. I see no need to moralize on this; it is simply a fact. And it means that the South still has a good deal of work to be done in catching up to the changes in our national education that took place 15 years ago. The pace of this catching up has been remarkable during the last five years. There has been a very large expansion of technological opportunities at the undergraduate level. It has been slower on the graduate level, but, even so, the South's capacity in graduate education is far greater than it was a few years ago. So these changes are under way.

The enrollment increase taking place primarily at the junior college level, which has been so marked in the last few years, has certainly touched the South, but it has not yet affected its institutional structure. There has been a noticeable increase in the number of junior colleges, but it has not reached the levels of other parts of the country. I suspect this is because a great many of the four-year colleges are continuing to allow themselves to be used as junior colleges. That is to say, they are tolerating the entrance of a sizable number of students whose predicted college success indicates a certainty of a drop out of more than 50 percent. Such a rate of drop out automatically turns a four-year college into a junior college with a small, attached program for the upper years. Such institutions are far more expensive to operate than they appear to be, and, what is more to the point, they represent a loss of highly usable educational opportunity. The fact that many colleges still have enough room in their halls to permit their use in the very costly process of selection after admission means that a good part of the problem of Southern education lies in the area of preparation for college, plus guidance, counseling, and the provision of financial aid for needy students. These are difficulties that operate to close off access to higher education to children almost as surely as the formal closure of segregation—in fact, possibly even more firmly, because, as we have seen, segregation can be broken by formal action. Slow leaks in the educational system are more difficult to find and close. The lags in making changes in education 15 or 20 years ago are hurting now more than they were then.

These two national problems of educational changes are piled one on top of the other so far as the South is concerned. The deficit of increase in technological institutions to train for service occupations, plus the deficit in graduate, professional, and research institutions, is added to a developing demand for a kind of college work which will be essentially thirteenth- and fourteenth-grade continuation school. But these problems are not peculiar to the South. I submit that the one that is peculiar to the South is the elimination of the dual educational standard, and that this problem will continue to be a running sore until it is faced as an educational issue. I do not pretend to know how these problems are to be met, but, judging from what we learn through our own College Board channels, I offer the following suggestions.

First, a joint conference or commission of college and school representatives should do a careful study of the programs that are offered as preparation for college in Southern high schools, both white and Negro. This should be followed or accompanied by a study of what is actually taught in the freshman year in college. These studies should be followed by some joint school and college efforts to agree on the de facto requirements of preparation for college. This could easily pave the way for a continuing school–college conference on preparation. I am sure that I can offer you a forum through the College Entrance Examination Board if it would be of value.

Second, there should be a careful study, based on a selected sample of secondary schools of all types, of school dropouts and the reasons for them. All students should be tested according to a standard battery in all schools where such a study is made, in order to determine the loss of college-quality students before college entrance. A similar study should be done at colleges.

The purpose of these studies would be to get at the problem of use of human abilities, which is always a difficult problem in a system that does not stress advanced and specialized studies. I would suspect that the results of these studies would show that failure of preparation for college and failure of articulation between preparation and college work are together responsible for a considerable loss of students. I suspect that, beyond this, it would be discovered that there is a measurable loss of college-ability students dropping out of secondary school, and another loss after college entrance. I would also suspect that if all these students were retained in the system until college graduation, there would be an increase of at least 10 percent in secondary enrollments, and 25 percent in higher education enrollments.

In other words, I am oversimplifying the problems you face by saying that they fall into three categories, as follows.

1. You have a dual system with dual standards, which has finally developed as a source of serious friction. For the time being, much of the friction can be eliminated by working toward agreement on a standard which can be accepted by both systems. In time, the duality itself may be attacked, but the time is not yet.

2. You have a standard of preparation for higher education that is probably not high enough to support a large structure of higher education. This should be evaluated, and remedial action, which can be cooperative, undertaken.

3. The system of higher education has still to develop two forms of education: service education, and graduate education and research.

Thus, there is a reciprocal deficit problem in secondary and higher education, each contributing to the other, each remediable. They require joint recognition and joint action to be remedied.

I would like to emphasize that these problems I have mentioned do not appear to me as moral issues, and I am not presenting them in those terms. They seem to me to be problems on the utilization of abilities, proved and potential, on the elevation of the standard of living, and on the economical use of educational resources. I do not question that there are moral and social issues attached to these educational matters. There always are. But I should hope that we could hold our focus on them as educational concerns.

When this last report was delivered, my resignation had already been announced and was so well known that I did not even trouble to refer to it in the speech.

Most of the speech is reporting. One item was particularly important to me. The construction of a Spanish-language version of the SAT *had been on my mind since July and August 1961, when I had visited several South American countries. It had encountered substantial opposition from the trustees on the element of risk, and some objection from within Educational Testing Service, which was working with some Latin American test specialists. The fact that the program had been brought into being represented, therefore, a substantial victory. (Since then, I note, the program has developed into a base for a major College Board undertaking in Central and South America.)*

Aside from this item, my other interest in the report lay in the discussion of foreign student testing and admissions, which I had come to feel was not receiving the kind of handling it really required if we, as a nation, were to get reasonable return on the very large sums expended on importing and educating foreign students.

The penultimate sentence of the report was a reference to the fact that the Board had lost its meeting room at the Hotel Sherman, without notice, not many hours before we were due to start, and had found a new meeting place through great good fortune and notably fast movement on the part of the staff.

Address at annual meeting of the College Entrance Examination Board, Chicago, October 30, 1963. Published in *Fall Meeting Proceedings*, 1963, 63 pp., 1–9.

This is a two-part report on the activities of the Board during the past year. The first part deals with work accomplished, and is a very pleasant report. It is long without being exhausting, and it records a wide range of developments of real interest. The second part deals with problems, including a number that have only recently emerged into clear view. It is not unpleasant, but it is not light reading, and it offers a good many questions to carry away for homework.

The first part begins with some statistics.

Last year 1,106,000 candidates took admissions tests, an increase of 16 percent over the year before. This figure includes a 13 percent increase in the number of seniors and a 31 percent increase in the number of juniors. It is evident that the promised deluge of applicants for 1964 is arriving on schedule. Achievement Test takers increased by 18 percent, Scholastic Aptitude Test takers by 15 percent. A total of 2,277,439 score reports for all tests were sent to colleges and scholarship sponsors. This was an increase over the preceding year of only 8 percent, which was, of course, lower than the rate of increase in candidates.

These are substantial increases, but it is worth noting that they were below budget estimates.

The Preliminary Scholastic Aptitude Test was taken by 862,900 students, also a 16 percent increase over 1962.

The Advanced Placement Program showed the largest gain of any Board program, with 22,000 candidates for a 34 percent increase over 1962. It is comforting to note that per candidate costs dropped again and that we are actually within view, though not within reach, of the break-even point.

Our financial status reflects these candidate increases. Our estimated income for 1963–64 is nearing $14,000,000, as against $12,000,000 in 1962–63. For 1963–64, approximately $3,000,000 is budgeted to be spent directly for College Board activities, and $10,500,000 for the testing program and related activities.

Our membership, which has risen each year, will increase again after actions scheduled for this meeting. We will then have 543 member colleges, 204 secondary schools, and 43 associations. The College Scholarship Service, which uses its own membership criteria, has 516 members, many of which, of course, are Board members.

Another major ongoing activity was publication distribution. We sent out 7,400,000 free publications, an increase of 17 percent over 1961–62, and 207,000 paid publications, an increase of only 2.5 percent.

After statistics, I present a list of accomplished projects.

The College Admissions Colloquium series, opened in 1952, was closed with a tenth anniversary celebration, at which we discussed the relationship of the behavioral sciences to the admissions process. I should explain the use of the word "closed." There was no plan last fall to discontinue the colloquium series, but the staff decided not to organize one for 1963, for the immediate reason that we could not find any suitable accommodations. There was, however, another reason. We found that the meetings were increasingly attended by very junior admissions officers or other newly fledged administrators. We—the staff, that is—felt that this evident use of the colloquium for introduction and indoctrination had ironically removed from the group most of the experienced administrators—the very persons who could make this introduction and indoctrination effective. This, we felt, vitiated the original purpose of the series, which was that of year-to-year examination of the admissions process and its interaction with schools, colleges, and students.

Under the circumstances, we felt that a break with a 10-year tradition would do no harm, particularly since the program could be reinstituted at need. I do not know, of course, whether a new series will be established, but I can say, in tribute to the one just completed, that it probably did more to establish the concept of the admissions process and the admissions profession than any other activity of the Board or of any other organization. We can remember it with pride.

As this series ended, two others—its children—took form. The College Scholarship Service Colloquium on Student Financial Aid was reported as equaling in its second year the distinction achieved by its first year. To my regret, I was forced to miss it, but have hoped that I could be pardoned with an invitation for another year.

A Colloquium on Curriculum Change, under the aegis of the Advanced Placement Program, was concerned with the teaching of languages. It brought together a distinguished group of language teachers, who fell to with gusto on the importance of teaching language and the importance of language teachers. Suggestions for curriculum changes were mostly in the direction of increasing the resources for language teaching.

We had another session—one that might be characterized as an extended colloquium but that was, in fact, a summer institute on planning, one of the series of institutes operated by the Commission on English. This institute, in a sense, marked something very close to a final phase in the definition of the breadth and depth of the work of the Commission on English. With the publication of its remarkable book,[4] which actually does define the coverage and the basic standards of secondary school English, the Commission is now ready to move from definition to resolution and recommendations. I would hope that as part of that move the Board would continue to encourage, and perhaps even support on a small scale, more English institutes. The demand for them continues, and it is obvious that they are a powerful instrument in improving instruction in English.

I have long since lost count of the number of institutes, workshops, conferences, and study groups, all concerned with study of some body of fact or method connected with the admissions process, for which the Board was responsible last year. I know that they included training for new admissions officers, prediction seminars, financial aid workshops, guidance workshops, and advanced placement conferences. I suspect that any number from 20 to 50 could be defended. The only thing about which I am certain is that there were not enough. This type of activity is our true task, and I hope the Board will never fail in its recognition.

We joined last summer with television station WNDT-TV in New York City in the televising of Advanced Placement Program courses in American history and mathematics. They were both splendid teaching achievements, and both produced significant numbers of students who passed Advanced Placement Examinations with satisfactory grades. There was reluctance within the staff and the committees to embark on this undertaking. I hope, now that it has been established that no dangers to standards are involved in this approach, that the Board will be willing to examine other possibilities. I am particularly interested in seeing the results of an Advanced Placement course in English, which I think would go far to establish a general understanding of the college expectations of student performance at this level.

A film, "College Perspectives," dealing with reasons for going to college, was completed to our order and has been available for use for some time. It is a good job, well planned, well filmed, and fortunate in its ama-

---

4. *End-of-Year Examinations in English for College-Bound Students, Grades 9–12.* New York: College Entrance Examination Board, 1963, 193 pp.

teur and impromptu cast. I recommend it to the attention of those who have not seen it.

In mid-October we concluded an exercise in test construction that I feel represents a remarkable achievement. Last December the trustees authorized the construction of a Spanish form of the SAT. In February Adolfo Fortier and his colleague, Professor Jorge Dieppa, both on leave from the University of Puerto Rico, opened a College Board office in Río Piedras, Puerto Rico. In April a test construction committee under the chairmanship of Dean Agosto Bobonis, of the University of Puerto Rico, was assembled, including psychologists from Costa Rica, Colombia, and Chile, as well as from Puerto Rico and the United States. After pretest in Puerto Rico and the three Latin American countries, a second meeting of the committee, in New York two weeks ago, assembled a firm form of the test, which is ready for administration early next year to an estimated 11,000 high school graduates applying to the four institutions of higher education in Puerto Rico.

If I sound as though I am speaking with pride, it is because I am. I consider it a remarkable accomplishment (1) to construct and be ready to administer a professional-quality test within less than a year, even granting the existence of the SAT as a model, (2) to bring the institutions in Puerto Rico to immediate common use of the test, (3) to give American admissions officers a firm testing instrument for use in dealing with Spanish-speaking students, and (4) to accomplish this within a modest budget, without foundation aid, and with every prospect that the undertaking will be immediately self-supporting. Particular congratulations go to our two staff members in Puerto Rico for this achievement.

We have instituted a field trial of central prediction in Indiana with the cooperation of substantially all institutions in the state. This is essentially an inquiry into the possibility of central adjustment of school grades, or class ranks, or both, to be used in conjunction with test scores to predict college performance. This is a major field trial of a research proposal. If successful, it may bring important changes into both application and admission procedures.

As the final item in this report of projects accomplished, I record with pleasure the excellent program and fine attendance at the conference held on October 28 at Evanston Township High School and jointly sponsored by the National Association of Secondary-School Principals and the College Board. We value this association and look forward to continuing and enlarging it over the years ahead. We express, too, our particular thanks to Lloyd Michael and Evanston Township High School for their generous hospitality to the conference.

For the coming year, we have, obviously, enough to do in maintaining the program I have just described. But I do want to note one new activity, which we consider of particular importance. Thanks to the initiative and interest of Edward S. Noyes, who, having reported to you as acting president a year ago, now serves as vice president, a joint program has been worked out with the Institute of International Education for a series of regional workshops on problems of foreign student admission. We of the Board feel that this program fills a need long felt by admissions officers, and the IIE staff, we know, welcomes the opportunity to move closer to actual admissions operations. I hope these meetings can become a regular part of the Board's programs.

This listing of projects, programs, and undertakings has, by its nature, avoided discussion of problems that have appeared during the year. The problems, however, exist, and I have, for purposes of presentation, sorted out five of them. All these figure in today's agenda. There are some others, but I want to treat them under another heading.

The first is also the most recent, and the simplest. The Board's New York office is in process of outgrowing its present quarters and must move, if possible within three years. We have no present recommendations as to new quarters. This is merely a notice that a problem exists and that a move will be made.

The second is the problem of foreign student testing and admissions. No real study that I know of has ever been given to the essentials of an admissions process that would deal effectively with foreign students applying to American institutions. There are several facts that bear on this problem.

1. There is no settled testing program for foreign students, no nationally accepted test that has been used regularly in the admission of foreign students. The College Board, as I have reported, is about to administer a Spanish version of the SAT, and this test will include a section testing English competence. A test of competence in English as a second language is

being constructed at Educational Testing Service for an interagency committee with foundation support. These are useful undertakings, but they are not a program.

2. We do not know what other tests are needed, and at present there is no mechanism for study of that question.

3. Our colleges and universities handle the admission of foreign students in a manner very different from the handling of our home-grown candidates. The African Scholarship Program of American Universities has shown that our internal methods can be applied successfully outside the country. The officers have discussed with IIE the possibility of overseas admissions offices, which would serve groups of institutions, but we cannot seem to get from discussion to plans.

4. If our programs in Africa and South America develop as planned, we will have need of sound admissions methods, for foreign student enrollments will at least double, perhaps quadruple, within a decade.

Given these facts, it is clear that these problems touch the essence of the Board's commitment to its membership. If the Board should attempt to deal with them, either alone or with other agencies, substantial costs will be involved. These problems are now under consideration and will come before you again within the year in an organized presentation.

The third set of problems are the problems of membership, which are remarkably complicated. We are essentially facing the alternatives of accepting a large increase in membership or of limiting membership by application of criteria such as are now used. But if we enlarge our membership, we are certain to sacrifice cohesiveness as an organization.

There are a good many categories of institutions that have an interest in the Board's activities, and if we do not change our criteria to bring them into membership we will have to find some other way to work with them. The difficulties seem impossibilities, no matter where we look. Yet there may be an answer to these problems in the existence of our strong regional organization, offering the possibility of accommodating a larger membership in a series of regional meetings.

This problem comes before you in the form of a resolution which has the intent of requiring an early restudy both of membership criteria and of the effect of possible changes in them.

The fourth problem is the product of present difficulties in admissions policies and practices. The Committee on Entrance Procedures, working on the questions of institutional responsibilities and obligations in the admissions process, has produced a draft statement of policies and procedures. It covers points to which many of our member institutions do not subscribe. There are many who feel that it is the attitude or the practices of some member institutions, particularly with reference to the nonuse of the Candidates Reply Date, which produces the annual springtime admissions scramble. Certainly if all the member institutions could agree on the major principles of admissions, there is at least some reason to hope for abatement of the scramble. The member institutions will be asked to use the regional meetings for discussion of these problems next year.

Finally, there are the problems of organization and function. At the risk of oversimplifying, I note that they seem to me to be merely another group of problems such as we faced seven years ago, when we had to change from a town meeting to a representative form of government. They are a good deal more complicated this time, for they involve the balance between the committee structure, which has remained powerful in this organization, and the operation of staff, which has in many areas accepted a technical rather than an executive role. They are also complicated by the membership problem already noted.

These are problems that we hope will complete a final round of committee considerations during the coming year. If the hope is realized, recommendations as to staff reorganization and possibly changes in Board organization will be before you for action next year.

With this listing of problems that will come before you this year or next for consideration and action, I complete the listing of the Board's current business. Ordinarily I would end my report here. But this is a special occasion, and I take the liberty of adding some observations to this report.

First, the Board's major concern is its examination program. Our many activities as an organization and the concerns of the members tend to draw our attention from this central fact. I believe that this program is under pressure from two powerful forces, driving in opposed directions.

One of these forces has always been latent within the Board's structure. It derives from the graduate schools, the professional schools, and the research laboratories of the great universities, which dominate American education. Their strength has, within 20 years and almost without our noticing it, transformed a group of preferred undergraduate colleges, both part of and outside of universities, into single-purpose institutions preparing substantially all their graduates for continued study. These undergraduate institutions have benefited enormously from such programs as the Fulbright Scholarships, the Woodrow Wilson Fellowships, and the National Merit Scholarships. They now form a sizable and cohesive group enforcing very high standards at all levels from admission to graduation.

These institutions use the full range of the Board's program, but they are distinguished by their strong interest in advanced placement and in some form of test of ability in composition. In addition, they tend as a group to take personality factors into account in making selections. A look back over some years makes clear their increasing support of these forms of assessment.

I think it probable that the interest of these undergraduate institutions in selection will continue to stress these additional measures of ability to write and to do advanced work. They may go further and agree to try to solve their selection problems by raising their admissions requirements to the point where they can use the Advanced Placement Examinations for admissions purposes. In this case they would return to their old rapport with their major feeder schools in the selection of their students.

It is possible to ring several changes on this pattern. In one, a test of English literature and composition based on essay questions might be introduced into the Achievement Test series. This could be done now if there were agreement on the technical details. In another, the development of personality inventories might be pushed to the point of bringing them into use, although at present the Board's staff feels that such a development is some distance away.

But all these changes point in the same direction. This force is pushing the examination program to selective uses and inducing rising requirements as a by-product.

The second force is found in institutions relatively new to the Board. Their interest in the Board's program has been its adaptability to the problems of mass education. They require an honest, well-administered, inexpensive program, supported by a wide range of services, particularly in guidance, where the problems of mass education have been greatest. They do not have specific curricular concerns and are not in general pushing for higher requirements or for more precise selection instruments. They recognize the encouragement of the able and the nurture of the talented as part of their business, but they tend to rely on simple low-pressure selection methods to find these individuals and prepare them for graduate schools. Their selections are not based on precise expectations. Their demands will grow, for they are the great expansible section of American higher education.

I believe the ultimate solution for the Board in accommodating these two sets of admissions concepts lies in a two-phase testing program. The first phase would need to be broad and comprehensive, measuring a wide range of ability. The second phase would be directed, specific, demanding, pointed toward the support of highly selective admissions and a careful placement program. Such a planned program would be a logical development from our present activities and would have the added advantage of reducing the stresses that now urge our program in two different directions at once.

I don't suggest that this is the only possible solution for the Board's testing program. I do suggest that it is time to look at possibilities for development of new programs or adaptation of present programs.

As I close, I want to pay special tribute to my two predecessors in the post of executive officer of the College Board: John Stalnaker, who with Carl Brigham worked successfully to bring the Board into the twentieth century, and Henry Chauncey, who led it through the process of reorganization after the close of the war. We know of the achievement of both men since they left the Board, but our special acknowledgment must go to their services to the Board. A warm acknowledgment too goes to Helen Gise. It is not easy to credit that she and William Fels and I were the staff of the Board 15 years ago. When Mrs. Gise retires at the end of this year, the Board loses a loyal and able staff member. I cannot overstate the strength that has come with her quiet competence.

I had thought of adding some solemn words about obligation, but I think not. This is not a solemn organization, nor has work with it had any trace of the solemn. It has been a joyous experience to watch it grow, catch and hold interest, and move to meet new problems. I must say, in fact, that I have never before seen it move with the agility it has shown here in Chicago.

I am grateful for these years of experience and most of all for the friendships that have come with them.

7. Tribute to William C. Fels

In November of 1964 William Fels, then president of Bennington College, died of cancer. It was a loss so stunning that reason could not accept it. We knew it in our emotions rather than our minds.

William Fels took a tremendous role in the refounding of the Board, bringing a luminous rationality to what could easily have been an assemblage of pedestrian tasks. The problems of the Board fascinated him, and in some capacity he would have come back to them sooner or later, had he lived. It would have been an interesting return. The tendency of the Board as an organization in reality—as a power structure—is to subordinate the humane to the technical. He would have accepted this tendency as a challenge to battle and would have sought to reverse the outcome. Whether he could have succeeded is another matter, but he would have enjoyed trying.

The Board asked me to present a memorial minute at its meeting in the fall of 1965. It is fitting that it be the last paper in the book.

When I delivered my last presidential report to this Board two years ago, I did not anticipate that my next task would be the discharge of a final obligation to my friend and colleague, William Fels.

I was, even then, prepared to face the fact that this obligation might come soon, for I knew, as did many of his friends, that his cancerous condition was already well advanced. There was still a possibility that the condition might be arrested, but all who knew him were required to face, at least as cheerfully as he did, the probability that became a fact when he died in November of 1964, a month after his forty-eighth birthday.

This memoir is a very personal undertaking, to call back for our remembrance the qualities of this man who put so much of himself into the forming of this Board into its present purpose and structure. There is a need for such a recall, for he characteristically had little to say about himself and so far as is known left nothing autobiographical in writing outside of a few personal letters.

There is another need, an unusual one in our time, more objective—a need to satisfy a form of curiosity as to why the death of this man brought sorrow and regret of such intensity as to amount almost to a cosmic resentment, very like that which we all felt on the death of John Kennedy. It is a feeling that death in unfair, terribly unfair to some times and to some persons. But as Bill would probably have remarked, "Who ever said it was either fair or unfair?"

I think we had this feeling because of a personality created by the concomitance of several very different traits.

There was to begin with a great curiosity, which he assuaged with wide reading and with a continuous personal receptivity to all, regardless of age or degree in life, who had an intellectual offering to bring. He welcomed new information, new opportunities to observe, new problems, new minds. But he was also discriminating, and when repetition took the place of thought, he turned rapidly, but always courteously, to other sources, in search for other ideas.

There was another trait, well hidden but always working—the trait of introspection, which forced him to examine remorselessly each of his own actions and thoughts and to identify each fault that he found in himself. Unlike most introspections, it found outlet in establishing new goals for himself and for others.

There were also some vital facts of his life.

When Bill came to Columbia College in 1933 he was an orphan, without near relatives, with an insufficient income from an estate in trust. He was under the guidance of a remarkable Christian Scientist named Wallace Greene Arnold, who operated a camp named "The Toltecs" in the summers and ran after-school recreation programs in New York during the school year. Through Mr. Arnold he had employment after school, weekends, and summers. With these means and some scholarship funds, he made his way and learned to extract maximum value from each dollar spent.

More important, through Mr. Arnold he had a home and a parental figure to turn to. The influences that came from these, to judge from Bill's feelings as he occasionally expressed them, must have been rare and rich.

It is not surprising that this situation imposed a very personal rule of careful judgment upon him. What is perhaps surprising is that he was able to emerge from it with a basis for inner security and belief in human importance that permitted a continuously unfolding personality.

I have said enough to suggest that this was a many-faceted man, perhaps not enough to suggest how he worked.

He had many natural gifts and some traits that he acquired, which came to seem natural. He was instinctively a teacher, working from fact to interpretation to presentation. He was not afraid of decisions, but it took time for him to learn that decisions are best based on knowledge of details and also on careful forecast of consequences. But he did learn this and added to it the skill of effective delegation in preparation of decision. He early showed a remarkable skill in picking a central issue out of committee discussions and then offering a reasonable method of resolving it. But his abilities at self-criticism also revealed to him that he must withhold the use of this skill until he was certain of both his position and his timing, for there were occasions in early days when the solutions were more plausible than effective.

He had a quiet, very personal wit, which in his younger days was sometimes too sharp for an audience. His urge to explain, too, could on occasion carry him past the point of communication. But he understood these problems and how to deal with them, and spent dreary hours recording speeches on a primitive wire recorder and listening to them again, writing and rewriting, testing for clarity, unsparing in self-criticism. Out of the discipline he achieved a clear, sharp style and a genius for impeccable design of everything he said and wrote.

This was the man who gave so fully of himself to the College Board first as an officer from 1948 until 1956 and later as a member of the Board, as a committee worker and chairman, and as a trustee.

He contributed more to the Board than can be measured or even stated. The publications were his first love, and he stayed close to them until he saw a full program in operation. Then he turned to finding a rational formula for the fixing of examination dates and, in the process, hit upon the idea of the Candidates Reply Date to ease the pressures created by the old choice rule that had been inherited from prewar days. He gave essential support to my long campaign for the release of scores to candidates by helping to evolve the formula that finally made the idea acceptable. He was the real founder of the College Scholarship Service, and after taking half a year off to serve as a staff officer for the $500 million Ford Foundation higher education grants in 1955, he undertook his final act as a Board officer, to persuade me to accept the Advanced Placement Program.

This, I submit, is quite a record. If it leads some to wonder what my duties were as director during those years, I can only comment that I sometimes too wondered about that point. Looking back I think that they mainly consisted of trying to state and enlarge the concept and the scope of the Board to make effective the mechanisms that he developed. Certainly there was never any conflict of purpose. It was in fact a harmonious combination, and I do not remember that we ever failed to acknowledge our partnership or our respective roles.

The harmony endured, but I felt him lose interest as the problems began to yield to solutions and to our developing prosperity. When he resigned in 1956, I was quite prepared for it. It was already apparent that he had a destiny of his own, which he would work out in his own way. His intellectual restlessness could not be denied then or in the years to come. It was a part of him, and it would have continued however long he lived. He knew his worth, and in time he would have sought new fields in which to prove himself.

To those new fields he would have carried those qualities of clear intelligence, detachment, curiosity, human understanding, and above all, the abiding hunger of the spirit to reach beyond all horizons which he had forged into a unique strength.

These words we can record as our tribute to a man who has touched our lives. They are our statement of our gratitude for his works and our happiness in his remembrance.

Documents Quoted